Devolution And Development In Kenya

Selected Issues, Challenges and Remedies

Simon Thuranira and Ezekiel Mwenzwa
(Editors)

Nsemia

First Edition: July 2017

Published by Nsemia Inc. Publishers (www.nsemia.com)

Editor: Stella Riunga

Cover Design: Linda Kiboma

Layout Design: Linda Kiboma

Production Consultant: Matunda Nyanchama

Note for Librarians:

A cataloguing record for this book is available from Library and Archives Canada.

ISBN: 978-1-926906-61-4

DEDICATION

To all development students, scholars, practitioners, policy makers and other potential beneficiaries, who in one way or the other have toiled and strived to make the Earth a better human habitat.

TABLE OF CONTENTS

FOREWORD

It is widely acknowledged that scholarship is about constructive arguments and critiques. These afford everyone an opportunity to contribute positively in society, hear others and be heard. Devolution and Development: Selected Issues, Challenges and Remedies illuminates a number of challenges affecting development in Kenya, which the authors have ably pointed out as being the bottlenecks to the development of the nation. Although the individual authors deal with issues in their respective areas of specialization, there is a common denominator, that Kenya is far from achieving her true development potential especially with the introduction of devolution. Indeed, the book is an informative multidisciplinary exposition of what ails the country as far as devolution and development is concerned.

Individually and collectively, the authors have tackled the twin and topical issues of devolution and development in the country. They have made invaluable conclusions and recommendations that, if taken into account during development planning, would make a development mark in this country. I am convinced that the research and analysis that was invested in this book depicts a team that is patriotic and passionate about the future of this country. The degree of research that was undertaken by the writers is extensive, which enabled them to engage in original discussions of important topical issues that matter to development in Kenya. These issues include, among others, devolution as it relates to: natural resource management, agriculture, governance, education, youth and gender mainstreaming. The writers' interrogation of policies reveals glaring gaps and mismatches between policy and practice on devolution and development.

Such issues and their consequences are tackled by the contributors. These, as the contributors demonstrate, explain why Kenya, a resource-rich country, remains poor economically and a third-world nation about half a century after independence.

In addressing the foregoing bottlenecks, the writers re-engage some old and familiar debates such as the role of foreign ideas in a nation's agenda. At the same time, they frame new ones in a manner that enriches and defines development discourse in Kenya. While providing, and rooting, for homegrown solutions to the country's development, they appreciate the role of exotic ideas. They put emphasis on borrowing from the two divides, but only doing so as long as viability of the ideas has been tested and proven to work for

Kenya, based on her development needs and resource endowment.

In addition to the disconnect between planning and implementation of development initiatives, the authors identify other key bottlenecks to advancement of the country. These include negative ethnicity and mismanagement of public resources. They have hence suggested a paradigm shift in the way development is planned and implemented to ensure that corruption and negative ethnic do not water down the faith and patriotism among Kenyans. The foregoing notwithstanding, the optimism and hope in Kenya's advancement demonstrated by the authors is telling. It envisions a Kenya where everyone will be proudly in line with the ideals of Kenya Vision 2030.

They have suggested that, in order for the country to take her rightful development path, there should be a comprehensive transformation of the way development is implemented. This would be done with a view to engaging the public fully. In return, this would implant constructive civic engagement and moral decorum in the use of public resources. In particular and as far as development planning is concerned, the authors are of the view that devolution ought to be safeguarded and defended given its apparent grassroots benefits that hitherto were invisible before the inauguration of the Constitution of Kenya in 2010. For me, it would be an understatement to say that the book is a patriotic testament of the authors–it is the work of some of the most assiduous and visionary scholars of the 21st century.

On the whole, the work is yet another academic step for the authors, but most importantly an invaluable gift to students, scholars, policy makers and development practitioners. Specially, policy makers are likely to find the book very useful given its decisive evaluation of devolution and development, in addition to the incisive and constructive criticism it provides to the policies.

Dr. Kilemi Mwiria, (PhD)
Former Assistant Minister for Education (Kenya)
Senior Presidential Advisor on Education (Kenya)
February 2017

ACKNOWLEDGEMENTS

The editors would like to acknowledge and thank individual authors of the specific papers in this book, whose contribution is invaluable to the realization of this academic feat. The completion of this project could not have been realized without the support of the team of contributors that provided the perfect blend of knowledge and skills that went into the writing of this book. We thank each and every one of them for devoting their valuable time and efforts towards the realization of the book. We also acknowledge our two Universities-Karatina University and the University of Embu-from whose academicians we got the utmost encouragement and inspiration at our lowest levels in the compilation of the work. Thanks to Nsemia Publishers Inc. who played a crucial role in providing insights into the contents and the general organization and publishing of the book.

We could like to express our gratitude to Dr. Kilemi Mwiria, an astute scholar for his moral support while writing the book and for his humble acceptance to write the foreword. We cannot express enough thanks to our families who have been our inspiration and motivation in our pursuit of knowledge and academic advancement for their patience and understanding during the many times we had to be away from them to do this noble academic undertaking.

Ezekiel Mwenzwa and Simon Thuranira

(Editors)

CHAPTER ONE

Overview

Ezekiel Mwenzwa and Simon Thuranira Taaliu

In this chapter we discuss summaries of the chapters and recommendations of this book. Moses Kimnyango Beru and Elizabeth Murray Manoah in chapter two discuss mainstreaming indigenous knowledge systems in natural resource conservation in Nandi County in Kenya. Natural resources have always been scarce due to the high rates of population growth that surpass economic growth and development especially in the less developed countries. Thus there is need for the global society to put in place strategies that will ensure conservation of the scarce resources. Efforts have been made to come up with various environmental policies to ensure proper resource management and conservation.

In Kenya, the government came up with Environmental Management and Coordination Act (EMCA 1999), which established the National Environment Management Authority (NEMA), charged with, among others, the management and conservation of natural resources. However, indigenous knowledge is not yet fully utilized in the resource conservation and development processes. Conventional approaches imply that conservation and development processes always require technology transfers from locations that are perceived as more advanced. This has often led to overlooking the potential in local experiences and practices. **Chapter Two** assesses the integration of local people's indigenous knowledge into the management of natural resources in Nandi County in respect to EMCA (1999) and global development trends. Suggestions are made regarding best practices and strategic options to enhance proper integration of indigenous knowledge systems in natural resource conservation in the country.

In **Chapter Three**, Munene Mugambi and Ezekiel Mwenzwa deal with revitalizing urban solid waste management in Kenya. The major urban areas of Kenya that are cosmopolitan have been experiencing rapid population increase courtesy of among others, rural-urban influx driven by the need for alternative livelihood in the form of white collar economic engagements. Seemingly, the urban population expansion outmatches social service provision to the disadvantage of the majority urban poor. From unemployment to crime and shortage of housing to waste disposal, urban areas remain highly polluted, making some of their areas hardly suitable

1

for human habitation. In particular, solid waste litters these areas unabated exposing urban dwellers and the environment generally to great health risks. The foregoing is despite the existence of an elaborate institutional framework for waste management in the form of laws, regulations and policy directions. For example, Articles 42, 69 and 70 of the Constitution of Kenya, 2010, regard a healthy and secure environment as a human right and provide for remediation in case of violation. In addition, the Articles obligate both the government and the individual to safeguard the environment from pollution, although this remains largely wanting particularly in urban areas. Part of the problem has been weak enforcement of the regulatory framework, casual monitoring and irresolute public consciousness regarding waste management. This is a review paper that examines the challenges of urban solid waste management and suggests strategic options for its augmentation to minimize environmental hazards and assuage potential risks.

In **Chapter Four**, Joseph Muriithi devotes time on sustainable urban green development in Nairobi City County. Nairobi City County Government has consistently posted below-average ratings for most indicators of environmental performance in the Green City Index for Africa. This is contradictory, given that in the past when her population was manageable, the city was fondly referred to as "the green city in the sun". There is a dearth of green spaces and structures in Nairobi that makes the city susceptible to the perils of weak sustainability—a weakness that has already started threatening urban dwellers' wellbeing even in other parts of the world. Declining green developments are caused by encroachment into existing ones for dwelling and industrial spaces as well as failure to plan for new green areas as the city sprawls into neighboring agricultural areas and towns. With Nairobi's rapidly growing population expected to double in 2030, serious planning and policy rethinking is not optional if its leading position in terms of Gross Domestic Product (GDP) in East Africa is to be sustained. This chapter seeks to illustrate the great challenge to green development posed by the rapid urbanization that does not go along with strategic and up-to-date policies in the city. Here the authors bring out the effects of the foregoing on the quality of life of Nairobi residents. Finally, the chapter suggests policy direction as part of the solution to mitigate the current state of affairs.

Moses Beru, Mark Kiptui and Ezekiel Mwenzwa in **Chapter Five** look at Integrating Information, Communication and Technology in Agriculture to enhance Food Security in the Counties. Information, Communication and Technology (ICT) has become a very important ingredient in every sector of the economy in the world. Integrating

ICT in the economy is vital to gain competitive advantage. The agricultural sector in developing countries is the mainstay of the economy. In Kenya the sector is leading in the contribution of the country's Gross Domestic Product (GDP), food stability, provision of employment opportunities and livelihoods. In order to fight food insecurity and enhance livelihoods, sustainable agriculture is paramount. ICT becomes key in enhancing sustainable agriculture and integrating it enables the majority small scale farmers' access information. Information is power and a key ingredient for investment. ICT integration in agriculture is significant given the small number of extension officers and the fact that training and visit programmes are no longer popular among the small scale farmers for various reasons. Hence, this chapter looks at the opportunities and challenges of integrating ICT in agriculture to enhance information access and boost food security in the country. Suggestions will be made regarding best practices in integrating ICT in agriculture to revitalize national development.

In **Chapter Six** Michael Chesire examines livelihood diversification and sustainability in rural Kenya. Efforts to improve human quality of life the world over have been continuous. In the developing world, a significant proportion of the population derives their livelihood from agriculture related activities and the natural environment. In Kenya, about 80% of the population live in rural areas and are employed in the agricultural sector. Over the years since colonial times, efforts have been made to develop the rural areas and ensure citizens have meaningful and sustainable livelihoods. Kenya has developed and implemented a number of rural development strategies while bearing in mind that rural areas play a pivotal role in the overall development of the counties and the country. This chapter examines Kenya's rural development strategies from independence to date and explores some of the best practices which have had positive impacts in rural transformation. In addition, the chapter elucidates some of the strategies under implementation and the lessons learnt. It recommends diversification of rural livelihood without having to over rely on agriculture.

Moses Mutiso and Jamin Masinde in **Chapter Seven** deal with labor policies and gender inclusiveness in Kenya. From a gender perspective, labor participation in Kenya has always been skewed in favor of men and hence to the disadvantage of women. The foregoing state of affairs is against the existence and implementation of various labor laws and policies since independence. In particular, Article 27 of the Constitution of Kenya provides for gender mainstreaming in the public sector. Moreover, International Labor Organisation Gender Mainstreaming Guide of 2010 aims at enabling labor practitioners including employees, employers and trade unions to implement gender sensitive policies and practices. Based on the foregoing, this chapter traces the genesis and rationale of government-propelled labor policies since independence, while laying particular emphasis on their implementation and contribution in bridging the gender gap in the public sector. The effect of the various labor policies and their strengths and weaknesses are also discussed. Further the major challenges towards gender equity in labor participation are assessed with a view to draw lessons for the future. The chapter concludes by highlighting the importance of balanced labor participation and the way forward to augment it.

In **Chapter Eight**, Ezekiel Mwenzwa elucidates on transparency and accountability in Kenya. Ethics and integrity that presuppose honesty and openness are integral components of any undertaking to ensure efficiency in the utilization of resources and effectiveness in service delivery. This requires a minimum threshold of transparency and accountability in the conduct of public affairs. For this to occur, a measure of moral standing among individuals and institutions must exist to check on excesses. The preceding is expected to arrest such vices as corruption, enshrine appropriate work ethics and prevent other underhand deals that disadvantage the public with regard to service delivery. Corruption, which is deep-rooted in Kenya, has largely been blamed for scaling down domestic saving and investment and the misallocation of inventive talent. While in the last few decades transparency and accountability have been catchwords in the Public Service of Kenya, this is yet to completely tame corruption therein. In response to the foregoing, the government of the Republic of Kenya, while acknowledging that corruption is serious development bottleneck, has come up with several control mechanisms to fight it. The foregoing is the institutional framework that is expected to provide the necessary guidelines on the conduct of government business as well as check against individuals and institutions that act otherwise. This is a review paper which was presented during the 3rd Global Conference on Transparency Research held in HEC Paris, France between 24th and 26th October 2013. The gist was to appraise and analyze the existing institutional framework for transparency and accountability with particular emphasis on the Public Service of Kenya. It points out the challenges inherent in implementing the institutional framework and suggests the legal policy reforms as a panacea to augment transparency and accountability in public service.

In **Chapter Nine** Tom Wanyama and Hannah Kinyanjui tackle devolution and inclusive development in Kenya. They stipulate that from the much acclaimed Sessional Paper No. 10 of 1965 on African Socialism and its Application to planning in Kenya to the current development blueprint, the Kenya Vision 2030, policy makers in the country have never shied away from reminding everyone that inclusive development is not optional. While the sessional paper committed the government to engaging all development stakeholders, the Vision has, under the Social Pillar envisaged a just and cohesive society that enjoys equitable social development. Incidentally, despite such passionate policy stands, inclusive development has hitherto remained elusive, a mirage so to speak. In a drastic move the government promulgated a constitution in 2010 that fundamentally transformed the country's governance landscape. Driven by a desire to redress marginalization, the government made exclusive development unconstitutional. In addition, the Constitution of Kenya, 2010 introduced devolution as the remedy to exclusive development. Based on the foregoing, this chapter examines the institutional framework for devolution in Kenya, while explicating its prospects for inclusive development. In addition, the paper brings out the challenges bedeviling the new development model and finally provides the necessary policy directions towards revitalizing inclusive development.

In **Chapter Ten** Hannah Kinyanjui and Tom Wanyama take on performance management amid devolution in Kenya. They point out that through the IMF/World Bank-engineered Structural Adjustment Programmes (SAPs) of the 1980s to the Economic Recovery Strategy for Wealth and Employment Creation of 2003, the Public Service of the Republic of Kenya managed to institutionalize key performance management strategies, instruments and tools. These saw commendable performance improvement across many sectors in the public service. For example, performance contracting was rolled out in 2004, followed by Performance Appraisals in 2006 in addition to work planning and Rapid Results Initiative (RRI) to enhance service delivery. With the promulgation of the Constitution of Kenya in 2010, devolution and the attendant re-organization of government came into being. With the decongestion of the centre to the counties, service delivery effectiveness has been felt at the grassroots level. It is expected that the pre-devolution gains would not only be safeguarded, but also enhanced manifold. Flowing from the foregoing this chapter seeks to interrogate how these gains have been secured in the face of devolution. The key question will be: How effective is the institutional framework to facilitate continuity, improvement and sustainability of these gains? What performance management strategies have devolved units established? How has the National-County government intercourse affected performance management in the devolved units? Finally, radical proposals are suggested to sustain and improve performance management gains.

Mercy Thuranira and Simon Thuranira in **Chapter Eleven** have focused their attention on change of attitude for wealth creation in the counties. They argue that an attitude is a tendency to evaluate people, objects, event, activities, and ideas in a certain way. Such evaluations are often positive or negative, but they can also be uncertain at times. For example, you might have mixed feelings about a particular person or issue. Attitudes are acquired through experience and they are measurable and changeable as well as influencing the person's emotion and behavior. For wealth to be created in a county the residents must utilize every available opportunity, which is only possible if they embrace a positive attitude towards the resources in their disposal. Devolved government being a new undertaking in Kenya is understood differently by residents depending on their source of information. One of the objectives of devolution is to ensure equitable sharing of national and local resources throughout the country. However, a common occurrence in Kenya is where residents see it as an opportunity to enrich themselves with anything available since decisions can be made at a local level. Such an attitude will lead to consumption only rather than creation of wealth. Kenyans have acquired an individualized outlook of all situations in life (which is rather selfish) lacking the objectivity necessary for the success of the devolved government.

Negative attitudes towards the devolved government, job opportunities, natural resources, human resources, education and other factors surrounding the creation of wealth have to be eradicated and replaced with a view of recognizing opportunities in them. The paper explores the misconceptions held on the above mentioned issues and recommends the change on attitude that can enhance the creation of wealth in the devolved government.

In **Chapter Twelve** Paul Muthee Kanyi, P.K Kamau and C. Mireri examine effects of land use change on airport and flight safety at the Wilson Airport in Kenya. The aviation sector is one of the most important for any country especially its ability to promote international interconnectedness within and between countries. However, the sector faces many risks caused by various emergencies and accidents and much so in the precincts of airports. The impact of these accidents causes monumental social, economic and environmental consequences to victims. The exponential growth of the sector in the country calls for special attention by relevant stakeholders to devise strategies to address disaster preparedness issues, given that the country has already experienced a number of aviation disasters. Consequently, this study sought to assess the effects of land use changes on airport and flight safety at Wilson Airport. The qualitative design was applied in this study to analyze and describe the effects of land use changes on airport and flight safety in a rapidly growing aviation sector. The target population for the study comprised of 50 aviation regulators, 50 air operators, 100 service providers and communities living around the Airport. Primary data was collected by use of questionnaires and Focused Group Discussions and was supplemented by secondary. The study found that 74% of the respondents believed that land use changes have effect on flight safety. The land use changes included: setting up of shopping malls, airport proximity to Uhuru gardens, adjacent Nairobi National Park, Mitumba slums, upcoming high-rise buildings and existence of motor garages next to the airport. It was recommended that the government should do an urgent operation on land encroachment to avoid possible aviation disasters.

Josephine Wambua in **Chapter Thirteen** analyses social rehabilitation and transformation in Kenya. She argues that with the development challenges including political maladministration, negative ethnicity and corruption in Kenya, social rehabilitation and re-socialization of children is not optional in rejuvenating stability and confidence in Kenya's social institutions. In vicarious learning, when responses corresponding to a model's actions are positively reinforced and divergent responses are non-rewarded or punished, the behavior of others comes to function as cues for matching responses. Ills such as corruption in the country have often gone unpunished and the perpetrators seen as the victors. This trend is repeatedly modeled by the young in society when they come of age and find themselves in position of authority previously held by their models. Given that their models went unpunished, the vice is reinforced in the young. Indeed, after watching models perform certain behaviors, observers can later describe the entire pattern of behavior with considerable accuracy and given the appropriate conditions, they often reproduce the behavior with precision accuracy. The action of an individual serves as a social cue that influences how others will behave in the same circumstances because the behavior already exists. This is more so when the behavior is socially sanctioned through silent approval and failure to punish. Corruption, like any other behavior, can be learned and reproduced by subsequent generations. Hence, this chapter provides a paradigm shift from the conventional and proposes the application of Bandura and Rogerian psychology to explain the continuous political maladministration, corruption and negative ethnicity in Kenya. The chapter concludes by providing the necessary remedial measures to rid future generations of the foregoing social evils.

In **Chapter Fourteen** Moses Mutiso focuses on pitfalls and prospects of sheltering the urban poor in Nairobi, Kenya. He deeply delves on decent shelter as a human right envisaged in international, regional and national legal documents. However, this has been a tall order to realize particularly in low income countries like Kenya. Such countries have largely been grappling with unsuccessful attempts at meeting the basic needs of their populations since independence. Indeed, for the urban poor, decent housing is a luxury that they can ill-afford and are hence condemned to informal settlements that have several deficiencies. Consequently, this chapter examines the government policy framework regarding housing with particular emphasis on the urban poor in the City of Nairobi. It starts by situating the housing problems in the context of Kenya's general urbanization trends, tracing historical development of slums from the colonial period to the present and highlighting challenges and prospects for quality shelter for the urban poor. Given that urban housing policies have not succeeded more than half a century into political independence, a paradigm shift seems to be part of the answer to housing the urban poor with a view to engaging stakeholders in concerted planning and critical review of the past pitfalls.

A number of pertinent issues have been identified in the preceding chapters of this book that point at the same thing-that Kenya's devolution and development is held back by herself, her people, her policies and the intercourse between them. Although the issues are neither conclusive nor exhaustive, the pointers are clear-that there is a need for a paradigm shift to moderate the development malaise that has been experienced in the country more than half a century into internal self-rule. From corruption and other ethical issues to gender-based discrimination and below optimum use of resources, the country's development status can be explained by several issues that combine to reinforce one another and deny Kenyans the development they deserve as tax payers. It is therefore the argument in this chapter that the foregoing issues among others must be alleviated in a collaborative way as part of the efforts towards the development of the country. As such, the gist of this chapter is to look at the development history of the country and use it to predict its future development, while pointing out the milestones as well as the challenges that stand in the way of putting Kenya on the right development path. Finally, the chapter proposes some measures that may be taken going forward to make Kenya attain higher heights of development.

CHAPTER TWO

Mainstreaming Indigenous Knowledge Systems in Natural Resource Conservation in Nandi County, Kenya

Moses Kimnyango Beru and Elizabeth Murray Manoah

Introduction

The purpose of this chapter is to stimulate discussion on the wealth of indigenous knowledge in the African setting and Kenya in particular. The focus is on Nandi County inhabited by the Nandi ethnic group, a sub-tribe of the Kalenjin community in Kenya. This chapter provides an overview of the active role that rural communities in Africa and Kenya in particular have played in generating knowledge based on a sophisticated understanding of their environment, and devising mechanisms to conserve and sustain their natural resources. Indigenous knowledge is a precious county and national resource that can facilitate the process of natural resource conservation. In fact, Environmental Management and Coordination Act of 1999 at Section V 43 reads: 'The Minister may, by notice in the Gazette, declare the traditional interests of indigenous communities customarily resident within or around a lake shore, wetland, and coastal zone or river bank to be protected interests". The foregoing quotation shows how significant indigenous knowledge is to biodiversity conservation.

Nandi County is located in the Rift Valley region of Kenya and borders the following counties; Uasin Gishu to the North and East, Kericho to the South East, Kisumu to the South, Vihiga to the South West, and Kakamega to the West. It has an area of 2,884.2.2 Km2. Temperatures range from a mean annual minimum of 12°C to a mean maximum of 23°C, with rainfall amounts of between 1,200mm and 2,000mm per annum. The county has a population of 752,965 (Male – 50 %, Female – 50 %). Its headquarters is Kapsabet town. It has six constituencies namely Aldai, Emgwen, Nandi Hills, Chesumei, Mosop, and Tinderet. Among the Nandi ethnic group just like any other African community, environmental resources (land, water, animals and plants) are not just factors of production, but also have their place within the sanctity of nature. Certain areas have a special spiritual significance and are used for traditional rituals and other cultural activities. These areas are quite often patches of high biodiversity which are well conserved and protected by the community.

Conceptualization of Indigenous Knowledge

According to Waren (1991), indigenous knowledge (IK) is the local knowledge – knowledge that is unique to a given culture or society. It is key to the survival of the community and Waren (1991) further says IK is the basis for local-level decision making in agriculture, health care, food preparation, education, natural-resource management, and a host of other activities in rural communities. Flavier et al (1995) say Indigenous Knowledge is the information base for a society, which facilitates communication and decision-making. Indigenous information systems are dynamic, and are continually influenced by internal creativity and experimentation as well as by contact with external systems. It is the knowledge that people in a given community have, and continue to develop over time. It is based on experience, often tested over centuries of use, adapted to local culture, environment, dynamics and changes.

Indigenous knowledge also referred to as traditional or local knowledge refers to the large body of knowledge and skills that has been developed outside the formal educational system, it is embedded in culture and is unique to a given location or society. It is an important part of the lives of the poor and forms the basis for decision-making of communities in food security, human and animal health, education and natural resource management (Warren 1991). It is thus a significant aspect in the development process and the livelihoods of many local communities. The challenge that African countries normally face is how to reconcile indigenous knowledge and modern science without substituting one for the other, respecting the two sets of values, and building on their respective strengths. The following are the characteristics of indigenous knowledge worldwide according to Warren (1991):

- Locally bound: it means that it is indigenous to a specific area.
- Culture- and context-specific.
- Non-formal knowledge.
- Orally transmitted, and generally not documented.
- Dynamic and adaptive.
- Holistic in nature.
- Closely related to survival and subsistence for many people worldwide.

Globally, there is increased acknowledgement of the significance of indigenous knowledge as invaluable, its underutilization and as an asset in environmental conservation. Thus there is need to integrate this knowledge at policy level in the process of environmental conservation. In Kenya application and use of traditional knowledge in environmental conservation is still prevalent and harnessed among the local communities, although not to the optimum. One such community in Kenya is the Nandi community of Nandi County.

Indigenous Knowledge and Natural Resource Conservation

Natural resources worldwide are ever scarce and under constant threat such that if care is not taken they may become depleted, leading to the manifestation of the Tragedy of Commons hypothesis. Population increase, development of agriculture, urbanization and industrialization has placed a lot of pressure on natural resources the world over. On their part, communities have had cultural practices that helped to manage and conserve these scarce resources. These cultural practices are what are referred to as indigenous knowledge in various communities in the world. Kenya has various communities and each community has its own peculiar cultural beliefs and practices that make it distinct it from other communities. Among the Nandi community of Nandi County, the following cultural practices that form part of the community's indigenous knowledge are still prevalent. The members of the community still hold this knowledge and practices with utmost respect.

Traditional Beliefs and Practices

In Africa everything is believed to belong to Almighty, the creator, giver and overseer of all creations, visible and invisible ones, giver and taker of life. This Almighty in Nandi is given a lot of names including Asis, Chebonamuni, Chebongolo and Chepkelien sogol. Therefore, anything created by the Almighty was and is still revered by all members of the community. It is treated with utmost respect and not destroyed. This explains why during ceremonies animals to be slaughtered were identified by the elders whom the community presumed to have requested God for permission to slaughter the animals on behalf of the community. Before such an event, prayers were conducted asking for blessings from God. The livestock was slaughtered only after the prayers were offered to God. The beliefs were used to conserve resources in the community as people could not slaughter any livestock, as this amounted to destroying God's creation. Therefore, if well integrated into the modern resource management practices, it can assist in the management and conservation of natural resources including cutting of trees and utilization of other resources. Such may be done through making a policy that borrows from both in order to ensure hybrid policy.

Knowledge of Weather Patterns

Knowledge on weather patterns was quite elaborate and significant both as a livelihood booster and as a means to conserve natural resources. This knowledge was a preserve of the elders in the Nandi ethnic group, based on the fact that they had accumulated knowledge through experience and apprenticeship. Despite the fact that there were specialists in knowledge about weather patterns, many of the old people through experience could predict the kind of weather conditions expected by reading the signs within the natural environment. For instance, they could read storm routes, wind patterns and the color of the clouds and use them to predict the future weather conditions. Besides, change in birds cries (immense cries indicated the onset of a rainy season), onset of the birds' mating period (an indication of onset of rainy season) and change in the position of nests on riverside trees would be used to predict possible flooding. For example, if the nests were adjacent to the river bank as opposed to being on the topmost part of the trees, this indicated possibility of flooding.

The foregoing knowledge is not only important for preparation of a planting season among the Nandi ethnic group, but is also important for conservation of the natural resources and disaster management. For instance this knowledge enabled the local community to grow trees in order to serve as wind breakers during the stormy season and to come up with the type of shelter suitable for a particular season. Besides the use of birds to predict weather conditions, the Nandi ethnic community has for a long time learned from moths. An increased number of moths in the surroundings indicated the onset of a rainy season. Therefore the Nandi community treats the birds and the moths with utmost respect and destruction of such creatures was met with dire consequences from the elders. This helped in the conservation of such bird species in the environment because the community knew their significance in weather forecasting.

Totems

A totem is a spirit being, sacred object, or symbol that serves as an emblem of a group of people, such as a family, clan, lineage, or tribe. The totemic symbol may serve as a reminder of the kin group's ancestry or mythic past. The word totem comes from the Ojibway word dodaem and means "brother/sister kin" (Magelah P 2007, Chinoda PM, 2010). In Nandi it is referred to as Tiondo, the archetypal symbol, animal or plant of hereditary clan affiliations. People from the same clan have the same clan totem and are considered immediate family. It is taboo to marry someone from the same clan. The concept of using totems demonstrated the close relationship between humans, animals and the lived environment. In Africa, chiefs decorated their stools and other court items with their personal totems, or with those of the tribe or of the clans making up the larger community. It was a duty of each community member to protect and defend the totem.

This obligation ranged from not harming that animal or plant, to actively feeding, rescuing or caring for it as needed. African tales are told of how men became heroes for rescuing their totems (Magelah, 2007; Chinoda, 2010). This has continued in some African societies, where totems are treasured and preserved for the community's good. Totems have also been described as a traditional environmental conservation method besides being for kinship. Totemism can lead to environmental protection due to some tribes having multiple totems. This implies that the totems must be cared for and protected. In Nandi every clan has its own totem that they identify themselves with and therefore it is the responsibility of the clan members to take care of such totems. The Nandi peoples have totems or Oreet each identified by an 'animal' or tiondo, which no clan member could eat. The identification by Oreet helped prevent inbreeding since marriage within Oreet was largely not permitted. Clan symbols (tiondo) range from birds, wild animals, frogs and snakes to bees (Snell, 1954; Chesaina, 1991). For example:

Segemiat (bee)

Solopchoot (coackroach)

Kong'oony (Crested Crane)

Soeet (Buffalo)

Kergeng, Cheptirkiichet (Dik-dik)

Kogos, Chepkogosiot (Eagle)

Kergeng (Antelope)

Ng'etuny, Lion (Kuutwo, Talai Orkoi)

Moseet (Monkey)

Muriat (Rat)

Ndareet (Snake)

Tisiet (Baboon)

Ropta (Rain)

Birechik (Safari Ants)

Beliot, kiramkeel koe mooi (Elephant)

Kipleng'wet (Rabbit)

Mororochet (Frog)

Kimageetiet (Hyena)

Chereret (Vervet monkey)

Association and identification of clans with totems can be used to conserve these totems for future generations and hence the conservation of the natural environmental resources.

Taboos

The word taboo derives from the Tongan 'tabu' and is related to the more general Polynesian word, 'tapu, and the Hawaiian 'kapu'. Literally it means 'marked off', 'off-limits' (Holden, 2000). Taboos contain within them a certain quality of dire consequences or danger that will befall those who break them (Ahn, 2003). Webster (quoted in Magesa, 1997) describes taboos as a system of prohibitions with regard to certain persons, things, acts or situation. They have the power or force to sustain the existence and operation of the universe, ensuring a bountiful life for humanity (Scanlan, 2003). Taboos were not to be broken as their breaking was believed to endanger life and were therefore seen as sacred requirement. The punishment for breaking of a taboo could come from God, divinities, ancestors or spirits (Scanlan, 2003). This dangerous situation could be normalized or reconciled through a specific ritual (Andemariam, 2001).

They therefore provided a set of rules serving as a moral guidance or a law in the community. They ensured peace and harmony prevailed and served as a means of social advancement if one observed the taboos of the community. In addition, taboos ensured harmony between the invisible and visible world. They also play a significant role in the community by helping people realize that improper behaviour would always have negative consequences on individuals, community and nature. The most important thing about taboos is that individuals learn about them while still young (children) from parents and significant others, which makes it difficult for them to forget. The children are taught the consequences of breaking taboos — particularly punishment from the ancestors and the Supreme Being Himself. Some of the consequences attached to the taboos were dire, which caused fear, reverence and therefore instilled obedience in the community.

The foregoing implies that if well utilized, taboos can be used to deter individuals from degrading natural resources. Some examples of taboos related to resource conservation and management include:

1.   It was a taboo to eat meat and drink milk at the same time. Members of the community believed that it would lead to damaging the cow; the source of meat and milk. The rationale behind the taboo was that taking both would lead to waste of resources given that both are rich in proteins.

2.   It was also a taboo to kill and eat small birds and animals. These small birds and animals could not provide enough meat for an individual or members of a family. One would need to catch or kill a lot of them so as to provide enough meat for family members and this would lead to depletion of the species. This explains why birds generally (hens and ducks) and small animals (rabbits and antelopes) were not eaten in the Nandi community.

3.   It was a taboo to destroy places of traditional ceremonies like Menjo or Kaptarus (the place of seclusion during circumcision). These places were highly guarded and individuals were not allowed to destroy even vegetation around that place as it was sacred among the Nandi ethnic group. It was then the responsibility of all members of the community to protect such places and report anyone found destroying it to the elders for punishment.

4.   Places of worship (Kapkoros) were also highly regarded and protected by the community. It was a taboo for anyone to cause any form of harm to sacred places of worship and the consequences for such a crime were dire. Among the Nandi ethnic group, it was a taboo for anyone to treat nature in any way regarded to be destructive to the natural status quo.

Sacred objects

The concept of sacredness means revered due to association with holiness. Holiness, or sanctity, is in general the state of being holy (perceived by religious individuals as associated with divinity) or sacred (considered worthy of spiritual respect or devotion; or inspiring awe or reverence among believers). Objects are often considered holy or sacred if used for spiritual purposes, such as the worship or service of gods. The property is often ascribed to people ("a holy man", a "holy prophet" who is venerated by his followers), objects (a "sacred artifact" that is venerated and blessed), times ("holy days"), or places ("holy places", "sacred ground") (Jean-Pierre, 2013).

The word "sacred" descends from the Latin sacrum, which referred to the gods or anything in their power, and to sacerdos and sanctum, set apart. It was generally conceived spatially, as referring to the area around a temple. In most African communities land is seen as sacred and everything on the land is sacred. Among the Nandi ethnic group, ancestral spirits dwell on the land and therefore land was regarded as sacred. This explains why libations are poured on the ground before every meal is taken to appease the ancestors. African sacred objects may include among others; shrines to ancestors, feathers, skins, skulls, skeletons, carved figures or branches, spears, cutlasses or animal horns. Among the Nandi ethnic community, places of circumcision are seen as sacred and should be protected by all. There are also sacred objects like the leaves of a plant known as sinendet. This plant is special in many ways: it is medicinal, it is a sign of peace and therefore used in many Nandi community ceremonies. Due to its importance, it was supposed to be preserved and conserved, which is tantamount to environmental conservation in general.

Knowledge on medicinal plants

Herbalism or herbal medicine is the use of plants for medicinal purposes, and the study of such use. Plants have been the basis for medical treatments through much of human history, and such traditional medicine is still widely practiced today (Nunn, 2002). Modern medicine recognizes herbalism as a form of alternative medicine. The scope of herbal medicine is sometimes extended to include fungal and bee products, as well as minerals, shells and certain animal parts (Hong, 2004, Robson, Berry & Baek, 2009). Among the Nandi ethnic group, various plants are used for medicinal purposes to treat different ailments.

Medicinal plants were protected by both herbalists and community members because everyone knew their benefit to the community at large. As such, the indigenous knowledge is innovative, makes a difference in the living conditions, quality of life and environment, and provide a sustainable effect and hence has the potential to be a source of inspiration to others. Therefore, Indigenous Knowledge is important for all the stakeholders in environmental conservation and management. It is most important for the local community in which the bearers of such knowledge live and where it can automatically be passed to the next generation through socialization.

Development agents dealing with environmental management and conservation (CBOs, NGOs, governments, donors, local leaders, and private sector initiatives) need to recognize, value and appreciate the value of Indigenous Knowledge in their interaction with the local communities. Before incorporating it in their approaches, they need to understand and critically validate its usefulness for their intended objectives. Lastly, Indigenous Knowledge forms part of the global knowledge, in which context it has both value and relevance in itself as it can be preserved, transferred, adopted and adapted across time and space.

Planners and implementers of environmental management and conservation alike need to decide whether Indigenous Knowledge would contribute to solving existing environmental problems and achieving the intended environmental management and conservation objectives. There is a need for a careful amalgamation of indigenous and modern knowledge in conservation of natural resources. Indeed, traditional regimes for environmental conservation may need to be mainstreamed in law for this purpose. However, the rate and the degree of adoption and adaptation should be left to the clients to decide. Foreign knowledge does not necessarily mean modern technology as it also includes indigenous practices developed and applied under similar conditions. We therefore need to capture and validate Indigenous Knowledge in order to disseminate it for universal utilization.

Knowledge on food items

Members of the Nandi ethnic community also have a list of plants and animals to be used as food items. This knowledge and practice was passed to subsequent generations through traditional folklore (myths, legends, trickster narratives, proverbs and riddles). As already mentioned, some animal species (small animals) were not eaten by the community members. The community also identified species of plants and fruits to be eaten by community members.

The species of plants and animals earmarked as food items were cared for and protected by community members as a source of food for the people (for example livestock, millet and sorghum).

Challenges facing Indigenous Knowledge

One of the challenges facing indigenous knowledge is the fact that we are in the information age and yet we have not adequately documented such indigenous knowledge for future generations. The indigenous knowledge of most communities in Kenya has not been documented and thus risks being forgotten. Therefore there is need to recognise, reward and protect indigenous knowledge systems for future generations.

Due to technological innovation, the present generation tends to believe that it can access more information today than ever before. However, it should be noted that the present generation is actually losing more information than it is acquiring. Most shocking is the erosion of culturally based knowledge represented by thousands of disappearing cultural practices.

A final challenge emanates from migration of people from one place to another, leading to loss of farming communities, languages and indigenous cultures; all of which represent the erosion of human intellectual capital on a massive scale. In many communities, local language (a strong cultural vehicle for information dissemination) faces the danger of being interfered with by other languages, for instance, English, Kiswahili and the most dangerous of them all — sheng (a hybrid of English, Kiswahili and various local languages). Very few people can speak their local dialects fluently, let alone know the local names of vital plants and animals.

Way forward

It is evident that traditional knowledge on conservation and management of resources is important in the 21st century.

First, the past and present cultural practices, knowledge and socio- cultural institutions involved in conserving natural resources on one hand should be brought to light. On the other hand, the role and place of ethnicity, government policies and institutions in enhancing or inhibiting traditional institutions of natural resource management and conservation needs to be identified.

There is need for an explanation of the role and place of socio-cultural practices in conserving natural resources in a dynamic and changing world. This is expected to be the bridge between indigenous knowledge and modern technology and consequently their amalgamation to ensure hybrid resource management strategies.

The significance of indigenous knowledge and its impact on the welfare of the human population as far as natural resource conservation is concerned needs to be emphasized. This is one part that has been ignored particularly by the present generation and it is partly responsible for the wanton destruction of natural resources and the degradation of the environment.

There is need to visit and list historical conservation sites of various communities in Kenya and emphasize their significance in conservation and management of natural resources. This will make the communities realize their importance and help them shift their focus to conservation as opposed to environmental degradation.

There is need to record some case studies in various communities on indigenous knowledge and its role on natural resource management and conservation. Six, in addition to the foregoing, there is need for identification of communities' cultural norms and tools and recording their uses, relevant to conservation of nature. Seven, there is need to organize local indigenous knowledge workshops to enhance the role of indigenous knowledge on environmental management and conservation. Eight, there is a need to integrate cultural aspects into modern ways methods of natural resource management especially at policy level. Finally, successful strategies should be formulated and implemented to save our indigenous knowledge through environmental impact assessment awareness, research, documentation and publication.

References

Ahn, J. (2003). *Sexual taboos and morality among the Agikuyu people of Kenya.* In Katola, M (Ed). MIASMU *Research Integration Papers to Moral Teaching and Practices of African Religion.* Jan-Apr semester

Andemariam, M. (2001). *Place of taboos in Gikuyu morality.* In Magesa, L. (Ed). MIASMU *Research Integration Papers to Moral Teaching and Practices of African Religion.* August Session.

Bussmann, R.W., Gilbreath, G.G., Lutura, M., Lutuluo, R., Kunguru, K., Wood, N., Mathenge, S. (2006). *Plant use of the Maasai of Sekenani Valley,* Maasai Mara, Kenya. In Journal of *Ethnobiology and Ethnomedicine.*

Chesaina, C. (1991). *Oral Literature of the Kalenjin.* Nairobi: Heinemann Kenya Ltd.

Chinoda P.M. (2010.) *Moodie's Boy: Growing Up in Africa Xlibris Corporation*

Magelah P (2007), *Totem, The Encyclopaedia of Earth,* Retrieved from http://www.eoearth.org/view/article/156667/ on 2/2/2017

Republic of Kenya, (1999). *The Environmental Management and Co-ordination Act, No. 8 of 1999.* Nairobi: National Council for Law Reporting.

Flavier, J.M. (1995). *The regional program for the promotion of indigenous knowledge in Asia,* pp. 479-487 in Warren, D.M., L.J. Slikkerveer and D. Brokensha (eds) *The cultural dimension of development: Indigenous knowledge systems.* London: Intermediate Technology Publications.

Holden, L. (2000). *Encyclopedia of Taboos.* Oxford: ABC CLIO Ltd.

Hong, F. (2004). *History of Medicine in China.* McGill Journal of Medicine 8 (1): 7984.

Jeruto, P., Mutai, C., Ouma, G. and Catherine, L. (2011). *An inventory of medicinal plants that the people of Nandi use to treat malaria in Journal of Animal & Plant Sciences,* 2011. Vol. 9, Issue 3: 1192- 1200. Publication Retrieved from:, http://www.biosciences.elewa.org/JAPS; on 28/2/2016

Jean-Pierre, K.B. (2013). *The Contribution of the Sacred in Traditional African Societies to Environmental Ethics.*

Magelah, P. (2007). *Totem, The Encyclopaedia of Earth,*

Magesa, L. (1997). *African Religion: The Moral Traditions of Abundant Life*. Orbis Books. The University of Michigan.

Nunn, J. (2002). *Ancient Egyptian Medicine. University of Oklahoma Press*. p.151.

Robson, B. and Baek, O.K. (2009). *The Engines of Hippocrates: From the Dawn of Medicine to Medical and Pharmaceutical Informatics*. John Wiley & Sons. p.50.

Scanlan, R. (2003). *The concept of taboos in African society with reference to the Kikuyu of Kenya*. In Getui, M (Ed). MIASMU *Research Integration Papers to African Culture*: An overview. Jan-Apr semester.

Snell, G.S, (1954). *Nandi Customary Law*. Nairobi: Kenya Literature Bureau.

Warren, D. M. (1991). *The Role of Indigenous Knowledge in Facilitating the Agricultural Extension Process*. Paper presented at International Workshop on Agricultural Knowledge Systems and the Role of Extension. *Bad Boll, Germany,* May 21-24, 1991.

CHAPTER THREE

Revitalizing Urban Solid Waste Management in Kenya: Drawbacks and the Way Forward

Munene Mugambi and Ezekiel Mwenzwa

Introduction

Urbanization in Kenya is occurring at a rapid rate courtesy of rural-urban migration, as rural dwellers seek a better life in the major urban areas of the country. This has made social service provision such as water, housing, health and solid waste management difficult. The main victim of rapid urbanization is Solid Waste Management, which has been rather chaotic as opposed to becoming civil. If one looks at towns such as Nairobi, Nakuru and Mombasa, the nightmare of solid waste pollution is a visible reality. The challenges that are faced in the institutional framework have been the main cause of increased solid waste management problems. Policies that are formed to guide proper dumping and collection of solid waste are not updated or are overlooked, thus leading to improper dumping and collection. The private sector has thrived financially in solid waste management, primarily due to weak policies and regulations. Furthermore, private sector's insubordination toward local government policies on solid waste management continues due to the fact that they have political influence or are owned by powerful financiers.

The public sector on the other hand or rather the local government, is limited financially and is tainted with corruption. The local government has the mandate to control all solid waste management activities in its area but abuse of power occurs frequently. Most of the dumpsites in Kenya such as the infamous Dandora dumpsite suffer from heavy pollution due to mismanaged waste disposal. The toxicity continues to increase even though the dumpsite has already attained its capacity. In other major towns such and Nakuru and Mombasa, the same occurs. The national government is supposed to lend a guiding hand to the local government in matters of policy formulation and resource supplication. It is supposed to ensure that the local governments act out the policies properly and if there are any disruptions, to step in and correct the situation. The on-going chaos in the solid waste management sector in Kenya can be overhauled through a series of well-coordinated processes. The processes could first begin by identifying the problem and then defining roles of stakeholders. By doing so responsibilities will be spelled out and meaningful solutions to the problem(s) will be identified.

Nairobi is a true testimony to the foregoing statement and especially so given that it is the capital of Kenya where more people are tempted to migrate toward in search of greener pastures. It is therefore characterized by rapid population growth and hence increasing urbanization and its associated problems. Thus, Nairobi provides the best case example in understanding the solid waste management sector in Kenya.

Challenges of the Institutional Framework

The major challenges of urban solid waste management are faced in institutional framework implementation. The municipal councils or rather the local governments create policies, laws, and regulations to mandate activities that proceed in their jurisdiction such as solid waste management. However, the enforcing of the institutional frameworks is manipulated by acts of corruption and self-interest.

In current legislative and institutional framework on Urban Waste Management, the responsibility of solid waste management emanates from the Constitution of Kenya under Article 42, which provides for the right to a clean and healthy environment and spells out the need to protect the environment for benefits of current and future generations. This is further complemented by Articles 69 and 70 of the constitution which dictate the obligations of the government with respect to the environment and the enforcement of the environmental rights respectively.

In light of the above; statutory laws that regulate the management of waste in Kenya are among others, the Environmental Management and Coordination Act (EMCA), which stands out as the mother of all legal framework with regards to environmental matters. Enacted in 1999 prior to the repealed 2010 constitution, it aimed at establishment of a perpetual and self-running system of monitoring the environment and all hazards it is exposed to. This was achieved through the institutionalization of the National Environmental Management Authority (NEMA). The EMCA seeks to address the issue of solid waste management under the first schedule. The role of NEMA as understood by most Kenyans is that it is an environmental enforcing agency or an environmental auditing company.

NEMA's role is more of an advisory body to the government regarding the environment and activities going on in the environment and also helps in developing environmental policies. NEMA does research and carries out reports that help in addressing key environmental problems. The local government then is the enforcing agent of environmental laws. In the case of solid waste management, NEMA is to undertake the environmental audits and report to the local government for enforcement of environmental code.

There are several factors that can be blamed for the ineffectiveness of the Municipal Councils of the local governments. Some of the argued factors are that "Pollution problems are mainly due to lack of appropriate planning, inadequate political will and governance, poor technology, weak enforcement of existing legislation, as well as the absence of economic and fiscal incentives to promote good practice, and lack of analytical data concerning volumes and compositions of waste substances" (UNEP, 2005). These factors are all related and are the challenges facing solid waste management. The fact that all of the above mentioned errors in the local governments are continual despite efforts to suppress them shows that the national government is reluctant to step in or that the government does not recognize the challenges of the local government(s).

Acts such as The Public Health Act in Kenya state that the Department of Environment in councils is responsible for implementation of policy, collection and disposal of waste, regulation and monitoring of activities of waste companies and generators of solid waste, enforcement of all laws and by-laws relating to solid waste, and coordination of actors involved in solid waste management. The manufacturing industries in Nairobi operate with little or any regulation, monitoring or supervision by the Nairobi City County (NCC). Most of the companies violate many of the solid waste laws and by-laws, especially those on disposal (van Dijk and Oduro-Kwarteng, 2007). Policy enforcement by the local government is supposed to be adhered to because it is the supreme authority in dealing with solid waste management on a local level. The challenges facing the authority of local governments in solid waste management comes from the private sector's uncontrolled participation in solid waste collection, which is spontaneous, unplanned and open to competition without the regulation of local government.

Why is the institutional framework failing? A question like this can be answered by claiming corruption. But before citing corruption, we have to look at the educational capacity of the policy makers. According to an article by UNEP titled Kenya Waste Management Sector,

"Moreover, policymakers (Members of County Assembly-MCA) are generally poorly educated and lack any power to discipline NCC workers. The mayor, who was normally elected by the civic leaders, must facilitate their corrupt deals to keep the seat. Consequently, mismanagement, corruption, laziness, and general chaos have become the hallmarks of the NCC. NCC by-laws, prohibiting illegal disposal of waste, specifying storage and collection responsibilities for SW generators, and indicating the Council's right to collect SWM charges are not adequately implemented" (UNEP, 2005).

Insubordination and corruption, accompanied by lack of education have rendered policy making in most urban councils futile. The fact that the workers themselves are incompetent and fail to implement laws that they create proves that man himself is indeed his greatest enemy towards development. Workers prove to be ineffectual due to their ignorance—an indicator that financial resources, human resources and authority are entirely abused. The genesis of the cancer of proper solid waste management lies in the implementation of the legal framework by competent personnel.

Poor implementation of Institutional Framework is the failure of the central government in manning the Urban Municipal Councils in Kenya. Having conveyed the responsibility of solid waste management to urban municipal councils, the national government has neglected to also monitor their irregularities, thus failing to play its oversight role effectively. This dysfunctional local administrative system has led to decline in the efficiency of councils and their operations (UNEP, 2005). The challenges facing the solid waste management sector are brought about by inefficiency of the municipal council systems.

Another problem that is affecting proper solid waste management is the lack of public involvement and the attitude of the citizens toward policies and the environment. We as the Kenyan citizens are quick to grumble when the prices of maize flour rise but say nothing when solid waste is indiscriminately dumped in our surroundings. The ordinary Kenyan citizen is not bothered by waste because it does not affect them directly. In the words of Nobel Prize winner Professor Wangari Maathai, "If we destroy nature then mother nature will destroy us." A state of equilibrium must be sought between man and the environment for peaceful coexistence because this is a war that man, though he appears to be winning, t will ultimately lose.

In order to make public involvement more effective, policies cannot be formed using the top-down approach. Policies have to be formed by ensuring that all stakeholders are participative, beginning with the local communities who are the biggest stakeholders.

With devolution taking centre stage in Kenya, it is important to note that some of the functions that were previously conferred to the municipal council will be conferred to the county government as spelt out under Section 25 of the Transition to Developed Government Act, 2012. It is imperative to note that the Urban Areas and Cities Act stipulates that prior to the conferment of city status, one of the criteria to be met is that the urban centre must have the capacity for functional and effective waste disposal (Part II, section 5, sub-section 1(h)). Devolution will ensure that county governments become independent in terms of institutional framework development. Given that most county governments are still developing, it would be wise for them to use the solid waste management system to earn revenue to help in their development. County governments should develop policies according to the solid waste burdens in their respective counties. This will ensure that they do not create policies that do not benefit them or otherwise cause more harm than good. Solid waste management policies in County governments should cover the whole county rather than just the cosmopolitan towns.

Impacts of Poor Solid Waste Management

Poor solid waste management in Kenya has impacted urban areas by altering the scenic beauty of the natural environment. With Nairobi serving as a case example, solid waste collection is a competition between private garbage collectors and the County Council. These collectors dump the waste in any manner they desire at the designated dumpsites listed by the Nairobi County Council. According to UNEP's article Selection, Design and Implementation of Economic Instruments in the Solid Waste Management Sector in Kenya,

There is also widespread indiscriminate dumping in illegal dumpsites, the only official dumpsite at Dandora is full and the city council has no waste transfer facilities. Another problem includes poor technical knowhow and lack of analytical data. (UNEP, 2005).

After a dumpsite attains its full holding capacity, the local government should shut it down and rehabilitate it for the sake of the estate dwellers around. Such dumpsites are hazardous s to the residents in the surrounding areas, yet they continue being used even when they are no longer viable as dumping sites.

As garbage continues piling up in a dumpsite, all forms of pollution begin taking place such assoil pollution, air pollution, and even water pollution. As with the dumpsites here in Kenya, air pollution occurs due to the spontaneous reactions that occur on the wastes as well as the open burning usually carried out either by those who visit the dumpsite to collect food and other items which are later on sold to the residents who live around the dumpsite, or by the local authorities (Muniafu and Otiato, 2010). Some of the products of the reactions include methane concentration from the decomposing wastes and smoke produced from burning the waste. This not only pollutes the air around but also poses a health risk to those officials working at the dumpsite, passersby and scavengers.

Another major impact on the locals who live around dumpsites is that they find it difficult to carry out activities such as small garden farming. According to Muniafu and Otiato (2010), "Garden farming around the site is poor due to the soil pollution. The soil around the site is highly polluted and therefore not conducive for any type of crop. The garbage mounds attract flies, rats and scavenger birds (such as marabou storks), which are a nuisance to the residents who live adjacent to the site." Residents in these areas are prone to suffering economically because, being already poor, it is difficult for them to get food. The little farming that they may do to sustain their lives will fall victim to dumpsite hazards and pests. Thus they will be forced to endure tough circumstances to survive.

It will be safe to say that crime rates will go up because dwellers of the dumpsite areas will need to do what is necessary to survive. In past occurrences, "The dumpsite is used as a hide out for thugs, carjackers, muggers and many others of this kind. Weapons are allegedly hidden within the dumpsite to be used for performing different mischievous activities" (Muniafu and Otiato, 2010). Security of the residents around the site is poor. The unrestricted access to the dumpsite means that anybody can access the dumpsite at any time. Many unfortunate passersby have been killed or injured in and around the dumpsite. School- going children also fall victim to poor solid waste management as they scavenge for a meal in the dumpsites. There have been cases where school-going children skip school on certain days when they know that waste is coming from high-end hotels and upper class neighborhoods.

Rivers that flow near areas where high amounts of solid wastes are dumped tend to become part of the dumping site.

The rivers flowing in and around the dumpsite are contaminated with leachates that continue to percolate into the rivers and eventually get to the water table. These waters are commonly used by neighboring communities to water their plants and animals as well as for domestic use such as washing clothes and bathing (Muniafu and Otiato, 2010).

The urban poor mostly use the water from the contaminated river(s). These waters serve their everyday needs, from washing clothes, cooking and cleaning to drinking, considering the fact that water scarcity is an issue in urban settings. Since a good number of the urban poor are not well informed on proper hygiene and water treatment techniques, they are continuously exposed to water-borne illnesses. This means that majority of their low income will be spent in clinics or on water treatment solutions.

The overall appearance of the environment is tainted by solid wastes. Citizens on their daily routines can no longer enjoy the fresh air or bask in the sun without being disrupted by foul smells or lingering solid wastes. On the other hand, the value of a clean environment is highly dependent on people's levels of appreciation. A filthy environment may disturb some people while others are perfectly at ease with it. One cannot measure by economic status or educational achievements one's value of the environment. It is more or less the practice in Kenya that those with the previous qualities are notorious for polluting the environment even though they are supposed to set a precedent. In contrast, in middle and high class residences garbage collection is readily accessible and is done once a week, and cleanliness is maintained to some level as opposed to those residing in slums or poorer neighborhoods who have no such services.

Revitalizing Solid Waste Management

Revitalization of solid waste management has to be done through a series of policy changes that will define appropriate measures for handling and disposing of solid waste and authorizing or uniting the public and private collectors. The most important step in rehabilitating solid waste management in Kenya is by closing dumpsites that have attained their capacity. The Dandora dumpsite for example should be closed because it is an environmental hazard. On the other hand, proposed dumpsites should be well planned and include stakeholders from both the private and public sectors. Private-public collaboration will help in forming solid waste management policies that are strong and effective.

Policy implementation by the local government will require a team of code enforcers such as the "municipal askaris" to enforce code of ethics in public such as proper solid waste disposal. This code enforcing team, which will acquire its mandate as being part of the local government, will be authoritative enough to prosecute those who violate solid waste management policies. As part of having easy to understand waste management policies,

"Enforcement mechanisms have to be strengthened and capacity enhanced in order for waste generators and handlers to respect and adhere to existing laws and regulations. Stiff penalties should be instituted including for contract cancellation. The current penalties and fines are not deterrent enough, they need to conform to the polluter pays principal, cost of environmental restoration and rehabilitation, and long-term monitoring" (UNEP, 2005).

The environmental department in the local government should be made responsible for collecting data, assessing various areas in their jurisdiction and creating/reviewing policies to ensure that they are productive. If productive, easy- to- digest policies are created, then enforcing them will not be difficult. In addition, if policies initiated by the local government are to be effective, then every employee should undergo the necessary training before they are employed. Periodically there should be seminars to address changes and new strategies that can help improve solid waste management. The morale of workers will also be improved by the seminars because of the opportunity given to them to share their ideas. The current failures in solid waste management can also be attributed to lack of training of municipal workers.

The chief nightmare of solid waste management in Kenya lies in the usage of plastic bags. Taming plastic bag waste is one of the key tenets in rehabilitating solid waste management in Kenya. It is no secret that Kenyans, as well as citizens in a good number of developing countries, use plastic bags in a lot of their daily activities. These plastic bags find their way into dumpsites, streets, rivers and so on, thus contributing to pollution experienced in major towns. There are no adequate policies on plastic paper management and thus there are minimal efforts in recycling. According to UNEP,

"Nepal, Bangladesh, Taiwan, parts of India, Philippines, and South Africa have banned the manufacture and distribution of some types of plastic bags with mixed success. Distribution of free single-use thin plastic bags is the major focus of these bans. Plastic bags are reused as bin liners or waste bags, lunch bags, and general carry bags. In some countries, used bags are collected and exported for reprocessing while other countries have built local reprocessing capacities. Denmark and Italy have 'hidden' taxes on plastic shopping bags, which are absorbed into the overall cost of the products bought" (UNEP, 2005).

In an effort to ban or control plastics bags and other solid wastes, there are a lot of measures that need to be put in place by the solid waste management sector. Data collection, storage and sharing systems have to be improved in order to help the waste collectors know how much waste they have dumped, which areas produce the most waste, and also how many tons of recyclable wastes were collected. A waste classification system and standards to avoid mixing of hazardous and non-hazardous wastes have to be developed. Easy to digest policies, regulations and standards need to be reviewed and improved, so that anyone who works in solid waste management can comprehend the dos and don'ts. Appropriate disposal methods for the various wastes have to be defined in line with international conventions and the law.

The finger of blame should not only be pointed at the government, but also the citizens. Citizens have to learn how to cooperate with the government in reducing solid waste problems. The government can initiate campaigns that spread awareness to the citizens about proper disposal methods for solid wastes and appropriate areas for dumping. Roles in solid waste management need to be defined in order to avoid confusion and inefficient service delivery. The local government should create laws to govern its jurisdiction on environmental matters and provide solid waste management services to its residents, the national government should provide local governments with the necessary support such as resources and cementing policies. The citizens should be participants in policy formulation and adhere to drafted policies.

The role of the local government authorities is the provision of solid waste collection and disposal services, making them the legal owners of waste once it is collected or put out for collection. According to Schubeler's Conceptual Framework for Municipal Solid Waste Management in Low-Income Countries;

Responsibility for waste management is usually specified in bylaws and regulations and may be derived, more generally, from policy goals regarding environmental health and protection. Besides their legal obligations, political interests normally motivate local governments. The authority to enforce bylaws and regulations, and to mobilize the resources required for solid waste management is, in principle, conferred upon local governments by higher government authorities. Problems often arise when local governments' authority to raise revenues is not commensurate with their responsibility for service provision. To fulfill their solid waste management responsibilities, municipal governments normally establish special purpose technical agencies, and are also authorized to contract private enterprises to provide waste management services. In this case, local authorities remain responsible for regulating and controlling the activities and performance of these enterprises. (Schubeler, 1996).

The role of the national government is to cement the institutional and legal framework for municipal solid waste management and spell out local governments' necessary authority, powers and capacities to ensure effective solid waste management. "To assist local governments to execute their MSWM duties, national governments need to provide them with guidelines and/or capacity-building measures in the fields of administration, financial management, technical systems and environmental protection" (Schubeler, 1996). Apart from being a guiding hand for the local government, the national government should also be ready to step in and confront any altercations or impunity that might be occurring at the local government level, to ensure that solid waste management services are running smoothly.

The local and national government can use these tenets defined in their roles to regulate private sector parties that are involved in solid waste management and also protect the informal parties. Private waste management firms can be aggressive in bidding for garbage collection and supplying tenders, thus they tend to believe they can buy their way through the system. However, what might limit them is corruption both financial and policy wise. A lot of developing nations have the capacity to develop, at a slow pace, waste management facilities that can attain some form of international standards. The problem seems to come from stakeholders in waste management who happen to be politicians and influential business people. The local governments need to eliminate corrupt activities and ensure that private/public interaction is done appropriately. The informal sector parties are those who earn a living from the dumpsites by collecting wastes for recycling and selling. It is important for the local governments to ensure that those in the informal sector are registered and protected as they use the dumpsite. This will ensure that their work there is genuinely recognized. The informal parties are an important factor in the solid waste rehabilitation strategy.

Conclusion

Revitalizing solid waste management in Kenya is a task that needs cooperation from all the stakeholders involved, such as the governments (local and national), the private sector, the informal sector and citizens. As rapid urbanization continues to be on the rise, demand for solid waste management services is increasing. But with the crippled municipal councils, these services are not delivered equally or sufficiently. For example the Nairobi County Council has been cited for suffering from inefficiencies and irregularities arising from corruption, private sector domination and various political interests. Vices in the NCC and various other municipal councils in urban centres are the cause of internal problems in solid waste management.

Some of the dumpsites used for solid waste disposal have been so heavily overused that their capacity has already been attained. Take for example Nairobi city where about ___ many people live. Garbage collection is in high demand yet the dumping methods and facilities are primitive such as the Dandora dumpsite. The Dandora dumpsite is situated near slums where a lot of the slum dwellers either earn a living or get their food from the dumpsite, thus putting their health at risk. The dumpsite has become so hazardous that spontaneous fires occur. The soil and the local river are also tainted and their viability can be questioned.

The private sector has taken great advantage of the local governments' weak un-enforced policies, thus making huge profits from the waste collection business. Powerful individuals who have influence to overcome local governments can bypass the policies and regulations established for solid waste management. Another loophole in the local government is the outdated policies. Outdated policies are the unfortunate cause of all the misconduct in solid waste management. The National government's role should be that of guiding the local government in policy formation and review while financially lending a hand in development. Agencies like NEMA also need to be given increased authority in enforcing regulation and policies instead of being a mere watchdog group. "Municipal askaris" on the other hand should also be given the mandate to enforce codes in the municipal towns and ensure that the citizens are obeying rules and properly disposing their waste. Data and other information on waste management collection need to be stored for future consultations. Solid waste management has to develop a technical team that can handle the logistics in garbage collection and disposal. Defining roles of different stakeholders will ensure that there is no confusion in service delivery and that service becomes efficient.

Kenya can attain the status of developed countries in solid waste management if effort and resources are put into rehabilitating the solid waste management industry. Self-interest and other vices have to be shed for the betterment of the country and the development of urban areas. However, the main challenge is the growing urban centres that receive thousands of people every year. Strategies need to be put in place to handle the wastes that will be generated from the growing urban areas. As an environmental agency, NEMA needs to ensure that rivers or waters in urban areas are clean and should at all costs be safeguarded from contamination. All in all, the government has to put in resources and time in order to develop a proper solid waste management system.

References

Muniafu, M., & Otiato, E. (2010). *Solid Waste Management in* Nairobi, Kenya. A case for emerging economies. The Journal of *Language, Technology and Entreprenuership in Africa* , 342-350.

Republic of Kenya. (2010b). *The Constitution of Kenya.* Nairobi: Government Press.

Schubeler, P. (1996). *Conceptual Framework for Municipal Solid Waste Management in Low-Income Countries. Nairobi:* UNDP/ UNCHS/WORLD BANK-UMP.

UNEP. (2005). *Selection, Design and Implementation of Economic Instruments in Solid Waste Management Sector in Kenya:* The case of plastic bags. Nairobi: United Nations.

Van Dijk, P. M., & Oduro-Kwarteng, S. (2007). *Urban Management and Solid waste issues in Africa. ISWA World Congress,* (p.8). Amsterdam.

CHAPTER FOUR

Towards Sustainable Urban Green Development in Nairobi: Policy Implications and Options

Joseph Muriithi

Introduction

Since the founding of Nairobi in the early 20th century, the city has been experiencing phenomenal growth- from a population of 11,500 in 1900 to 3.2 million by 2009 (Makwaro and Mireri, 2011). Over the last decade, the city has also expanded to new areas in all directions in a manner as to converge with neighboring counties of Kiambu, Machakos and Kajiado. The rapid growth of the city has however not been matched with corresponding growth in infrastructure like appropriate transport system and liveable housing, to support the wellbeing of the residents (Makwaro and Mireri, 2011). In the area of transport for instance, the existing road networks have not been up to standard. They have been narrow contributing to traffic congestion and causing attendant consequences such as emissions of CO_2. Nairobi City has consistently posted low ratings indicators of environmental performance in the Green City Index for Africa. This is contradictory given that in the past when her population was manageable, the city was fondly referred to as "the green city in the sun". The reduction of green spaces in Nairobi makes it susceptible to sustainability weakness that has already started threatening the residents and the inhabitants of its environs.

Declining green developments are caused by encroachment into existing ones for dwelling and industrial spaces as well as poor planning for new green areas as the city spills over into neighboring areas. These examples show that this kind of growth raises serious sustainability questions for the city in terms of accommodating its increasing population without developing the corresponding infrastructure. This chapter explains the effects of the above developments on the quality of life of Nairobi residents and suggests policy direction as part of the solution.

Sustainable urban green development in context

Urbanization is rapidly taking place in many countries of the developing world. Many cities in these countries and especially in Africa are however unable to manage the process of urbanization in more sustainable ways. As a result, the development of cities in these regions is laden with a myriad of social, economic and environmental challenges. While social and economic challenges and how they affect sustainable growth and development of cities have seen more analytical focus over the years, environmental concerns have not. Environmental concerns have only recently emerged as important variables and urgent issues for consideration in urban development due to a new focus on green developments discourses in Africa that have been seen to affect living in cities. Already, environmental challenges have impacted on cities in profound ways even as they become major growth areas (Siemens AG, 2012, UN Habitat, 2014).

Africa is one of the global regions that have witnessed rapid urbanization rates with cities experiencing unprecedented growth. Studies project that by the year 2035 about 870 million people will be living in cities across Africa (Siemens AG, 2011). Most cities, including Nairobi, will have doubled their population by the year 2030. While the growth of cities has potential to present opportunities such as employment and prosperity for the residents, observations also indicate that urban growth presents numerous challenges such as poverty and environmental degradation (Freire, 2013). In most cities, rapid growth outstrips the governments' ability to provide services to urban residents. As Africa rapidly urbanizes, the cities are likely to encounter more challenges associated with failure to adopt sustainable urban planning initiatives in key sustainability areas such as: traffic congestion management, greenhouse gases emissions, informal settlements, urban sprawl, environmental pollution, and resource degradation. Many of these activities and practices in cities have obvious negative environmental consequences that affect cities' sustainable development. Concerns over such negative consequences of rapid urbanization have necessitated cities in many parts of the world to push for green growth and development in cities or adoption of eco-city models (Hammer et al., 2011).

The interest in practices and policies to mitigate against cities sliding into further unsustainable growth has led to emergence of such terminologies as "green cities", "greening of cities", "urban green development", "urban green spaces", "eco-cities", and so on. These ideas are conceptualized to capture aspects of nature in urban planning, management and development. There has also been an erroneous association of "green" with the common notion of urban green practices that entail tree planting. The concept of "Green" does not just mean planting trees and shrubs but captures the requirement of overall concepts that support the improvement of living conditions in cities. Urban greening is thus a broader concept that includes the notion of adopting practices and technologies which enhance living in cities (Mensah, 2014). The concept "green" has come to symbolize safety, stability and sustainability of the environment, of the planet, of humanity and even of our cities.

In all, from an urban development context these green concepts represent broad ideas of how new approaches to city planning, management practices and technologies are adopted to enhance liveability in cities (Dittmer, 2005). Going green or adopting green developments or practices for instance, concerns itself with removing the traffic gridlock in cities, reducing air and water pollution, adopting better waste disposal practices, reducing use of fossils fuels and adopting renewable energy in cities, recycling and reusing materials among many other things that make cities more habitable by residents. Going green can therefore been seen as a transformational process of a city coming from a situation where there is poverty, congestion, urban sprawl, among other negative things associated with a conventional city to a situation where city dwellers are given choices for urban lifestyles that are sustainable, convenient and enjoyable places to live in.

The concept of a green city is better captured when looked at from a comparative perspective using a set of indicators. The German Company, Siemens AG, supported studies that developed a "green city index". This index compares purposely selected cities from across various global regions using a set of some 30 indicators, among them energy use and CO_2 emissions, land use practices, transport systems, waste management practices, water and sanitation practices, air quality and environmental governance (Siemens AG, 2011; Siemens AG, 2012). The index has made it possible to compare which city from a particular region is doing better in a criterion. The main regions captured were Africa, Asia, Europe, and Latin America. From the Siemens AG studies, it is clear that there are wide variations in adoption of green practices in the various regions (Siemens AG, 2012).

The results of the studies show that in Europe, Nordic cities perform betters in the composite index, with Copenhagen city judged as the best overall green city (Siemens AG, 2009). The study also shows clear a divide between cities in Western Europe and those in the east, with the former performing far much better in the adoption of green development practices. The same scenario is reflected in the African region, with the South African cities of Cape Town, Johannesburg and Durban doing comparatively better in various indictors than their peers from the region. From a comparative perspective, the studies show that in Africa where the rate of urbanization is very rapid, there is a huge gap in the adoption of green development practices in many cities when compared with other regions of the world. This finding means that efforts in improving the living conditions of the residents in many African cities are severely constrained.

What are the benefits of adopting green development practices or going green for cities? Generally, green spaces have been associated with providing social, economic and environmental benefits to city residents (Mensah, 2014). Socially, green and open spaces provide opportunities for recreation, social cohesion and promotion of children's development (Cohen, Inagmi and Finch, 2008). Adoption of green practices and technologies also provides enormous economic benefits. Natural green spaces have been shown to improve property value (Mensah, 2014). A survey study of 760 home sales conducted by Quebec's Laval University found that landscaping attributes (trees, flowers, plants, hedges) can command a substantial market premium (Des Rosiers, et al., 2001). Other studies have shown that maintenance of urban green spaces boosts employment opportunities associated with the creation and long term maintenance of urban open space frequented by visitors in parks, gardens and other civic areas in urban settings (Virginia Cooperative Extension, 2015). There are also further potential economic benefits envisaged through various opportunities presented by green jobs in the areas of green infrastructure, green building construction, green energy and so on (Haq, 2011).

Urban green spaces further provide variable health benefits to urban populations. Specific health benefits include psychological and health wellbeing through provision of open space areas such as play fields for physical exercise and parks that help in releasing stress and improvement of the quality of life (Lee and Maheswaran, 2010). Greening of cities also provides critical environmental benefits to the urban dwellers. Urban green spaces provide essential ecosystems services ranging from regulation of urban climate, improvement of urban air quality, conservation of biodiversity and creating aesthetic beauty in cities (Haq, 2011). Tree cover absorbs air pollution, reduces energy consumption by providing shade, and can improve water conservation by limiting rainwater run-off (Nowak, et al., 2006; Baycan-Levent and Nijkamp, 2009). Urban green spaces also offer ideal setting for reproduction of species and conservation of plants, soil and water quality. In light of these environmental benefits, greening of cities has become part and parcel of the urban heritage in many countries of the world.

Many of the benefits highlighted above are experienced in many cities and are the hallmarks for successful green practices and developments. Several of the successes of green developments have been achieved not because the cities are necessarily rich, though wealth is an important factor in adopting green practices and technology, but , largely due to development of good policies and leadership (governance) that promote greening of cities (Siemens AG, 2012). Therefore, adoption of green practices and technologies or going green as the process as is also known should be a desire of all cities aspiring to improve the living conditions of their residents. Some studies have suggested that many cities in the developing world are not only constrained by technological, financial and institutional factors in adoption of green initiatives, but also by legislative and adequate or proper policies (Kithiia and Lyth, 2011).

Countries in Africa have been noted to be weak in formulating appropriate urban planning and development frameworks that would help their cities grow and develop substantially and sustainably (Burra, 2005). It is against this background that this chapter illustrates the great challenge to green development posed by the rapid urbanization that is unmatched with corresponding sustainability policies or even practices. The challenges and prospects that face a rapidly growing city like Nairobi are highlighted below. Suggestions on policy directions to mitigate the current state of affairs are suggested to help improve the overall indicators of Nairobi as a sustainable city thus enhancing the quality of life of its residents.

Green development in the context of Nairobi city: Challenges and prospects

It has been observed that more than 60 percent of Nairobi's population lives in unplanned and poorly serviced slums areas (FAO, 2012). As a result, the city faces major housing inadequacies and performs poorly on various indictors of habitable sustainable housing. Other challenges that the city grapples with include inadequate water supply, poor drainage and sanitation systems and poor road conditions. Therefore, the implementation of the green city concept in Nairobi is urgent but is faced with many problems. The current outlook of Nairobi city from a green city development perspective presents a picture of a city caught up in a fluid situation of a desire to move ahead but also held back by a host of historical, planning, management, resident's attitudes and most important of all, policy hindrances.

Literature on green development suggests that Nairobi has over the years clung to the notion of a green city from the conventional tree greening perspectives. Most of the analyses of green issues in Nairobi city have largely focused on various aspects of urban green spaces (Makworo and Mireri, 2011; Mugo, 2011). Other issues directly impacting on development of an eco-city are just emerging in recent studies. Concerns in other aspects that characterize an eco or green city have become more pronounced with publication of findings of the green cities index for Africa (Siemens AG, 2011), in which Nairobi performs dismally in most criteria when compared with other peer cities in Africa. But the idea of Nairobi being a green city has been there for some time where the city has fondly been referred at as the "green city in the sun" (Omwenga, 2010). This has been in reference to its landscape that is characterized by natural forests, labyrinthine riverine ecosystems, and wetlands (Tibaijuka, 2011). The desire for green credentials has however not been backed by good environmental planning and management practices and policies. The city thus experiences major challenges that have diluted its green description.

Challenges in achieving a green city status for Nairobi
Rapid population increase of Nairobi city

It is estimated that in the next 15 years, the population of Nairobi could double to about 6.1 million people (Siemens AG, 2011; UN Habitat, 2014; FAO, 2012). Already, the increasing population of the city has created a serious problem of informal settlements across the city from Mathare area, to Mukuru, and Kibera. It has been estimated that more than 60% of Nairobi's population lives in unplanned and poorly serviced informal settlement (FAO, 2012). The poor performance of Nairobi in green indicators has been attributed to the urban sprawl and informal settlements or slums as a result of increasing population.

The increased population has led to destruction and decline of urban green spaces and failure to help the city become dense. Studies have shown that urban sprawl as opposed to densification of cities leads to less clean cities that are more costly to serve in terms of provision of basic services (Glaeser, 2011). If the population trends in the city continue this way in the future as expected, the situation will trigger multiplication of other challenges that will be borne by city residents such as need for more reliable supplies of electricity and water and other services like waste management and sanitation.

Poor transport infrastructure

Traffic remains a huge challenge for Nairobi today. Increasing volumes of vehicles in Nairobi unaccompanied by a corresponding growth in transport infrastructure presents daily nightmares. It is estimated that the city loses about Ksh 50million (about USD 517, 000) in lost productivity, fuel consumption and pollution to traffic congestion (IBM East Africa, 2012; Muyale and Murunga, 2015). The existing infrastructure was meant for slow traffic and had no provision for pedestrian and cyclists. Therefore vehicles, pedestrians, cyclists and handcart pushers compete for the same road space creating serious traffic gridlock. The traffic congestion problem in Nairobi is made even worse by the fact that about 75% of all vehicles are private and carry a single person (Gachanja, 2015). This creates serious problems in trying to reduce the number of motorized vehicles on the roads. Though the government has been trying to improve the road infrastructure by building by-passes and new road arteries, the challenge of traffic jam persists.

Water and air pollution in Nairobi

Various factors have contributed to the increasing water pollution challenges in Nairobi. These include presence of high fluoride content in groundwater, anthropogenic factors such as poor wastewater treatment and environmental degradation both within the city and its surrounding districts (Tibaijuka, 2011). Industrial and municipal effluent has contributed significantly to declining water quality and pollution in the city. Sediments load generation and various pollutants in many riverine ecosystems found in Nairobi present a great water quality challenge (Kithiia, 2012a; Kithiia, 2012b). This challenge has been attributed to policy failure or weakness. The studies above recommend that the declining water quality in the Nairobi River basins requires much more attention from policy makers than is currently the case especially through legal protection of riparian areas of the rivers (Nairobi, Mathare and Ngong') that flow through the city and engaging city residents in clean-up activities. Urban air pollution is also recognized as major public health and environmental issue. Nairobi experiences air pollution from several quarters including industries, vehicles, emissions from various municipal sources such as burning of waste and the use of wood fuel.

Waste management challenge in Nairobi

The increasing population of Nairobi continues to cause generation of large volumes of solid and e-waste. Waste generation and lack of an effective way of managing it contributes to emission of greenhouse gas emissions from landfill sites. From a sustainable green city perspective, this is a big problem that needs to be corrected or better managed. Two thirds of waste generated in the city is domestic waste. Non domestic waste from industries, markets and roads, and other sources contributes the remaining third of all the waste generated in Nairobi. The increasing middle class in Kenya with majority of it being concentrated in Nairobi and surrounding areas has also led to increased generation of new forms of wastes, e-waste. With their disposable incomes, the middle class can afford electronic gadgets such as fridges, computers, printers, among other office and home appliances which further increases the amount of waste generated at the domestic level. For all types of waste however, there have been poor waste disposal practices in Nairobi which escalates the problem of waste management for the city and increases the chance of emissions of greenhouse gases.

Parks and green spaces

For a long time, there has been no clear framework for development of open and green public spaces in Nairobi. The 1948 Master Plan which has overseen development of Nairobi city had provided for setting aside land for development of open public spaces (Makworo and Mireri, 2011). But since the Master Plan was meant to be implemented up to around 1975, setting aside of such areas has been done on an ad hoc basis. Though Nairobi has had important green spaces within its borders, these spaces have been ridden with threats of encroachment or excision by both public officials and ordinary citizens.

Karura and Ngong' forests faced such threats in the 1990s when politicians and influential business people planned to excise the forest lands and develop private properties in the land. Other open and green spaces like Uhuru Park also faced the risk of being taken away from the public in the 1990s. It was subject of contestation between the government of the time and civil society organizations like the Green Belt movement. The government of the day had proposed to build a 60 storey complex in the park. The Jeevanjee Gardens, the other green space in the city had also been targeted for construction of an underground car park.

The foregoing cases illustrate the governance challenge and lack of green accountability of public spaces on the part of the leadership. Thus, there hasn't been a clear green development policy for the city. In spite of these challenges, Nairobi has managed to retain a fair number of its green spaces such the Nairobi National Park, Karura Forest, the Nairobi arboretum, Nairobi national park, the Ngong' Forest, and the Ololua Forest. These green spheres are important in maintaining biodiversity, filtering pollutants in the air and also as water catchment for the city. For the sustainable conservation of these green spaces, a clear policy needs to be formulated.

Prospects for a greener Nairobi city
Slum improvement initiatives

Informal settlements present sustainability challenges to many residents of Nairobi. Improving the condition in slums is important in ameliorating the liveability in the city. There are already efforts in place to improve the situation in informal settlements. Cronin and Guthrie (2010) identify two approaches used in upgrading Nairobi's in slums. These are the more bottom-up integrated livelihood approach driven by the NGOs and the top-down multi-agency partnership approach driven by the government and other agencies such the UN Habitat. The former kind of initiative has a closer environmental and social economic goal focus to the local areas. The approach focuses on direct aspects of the slums dwellers' welfare by promoting improvements in environmental health through better clean water supply, access to water and sanitation facilities in the slum village, and reducing the incidence of water-borne diseases which are major challenges for the slums areas. The latter approach addresses important urban sustainability issues such as water and sanitation infrastructure but focuses on more large-scale projects.

Through nation-wide collaborative programmes like Kenya Slum Upgrading Programme (KENSUP) that brought together various actors such as UN Habitat, national government, local government and other partners, it has been possible to provide basic infrastructure like water and sanitation in the slums which has been used as an entry point to overall slum upgrading (UN Habitat, 2008). More recently other efforts that have shown prospects for improving the situation in the slums include the government led initiative that focuses on reconstructing the slum access roads, street lighting, and improving on waste management systems. This is an initiative of the Ministry of Devolution. It started in Kibera area and is spreading to other slum areas through the involvement of the National Youth Service (NYS) as a bid to change the face of informal settlements. Through such initiatives in slum improvement, other sustainable options can be developed, especially by anchoring them within concrete policy frameworks.

Programme of expansion and improvement of transport infrastructure

Transporting people and goods within Nairobi has been a sustainability challenge for some time. There have been a few initiatives to improve the mobility arrangements in the city especially through road network expansion and improving and upgrading the existing ones. Improving mobility provides opportunities to reduce congestions through traffic jams as well as reducing emissions from motorised vehicles. In the road sector, the construction of bypasses and ring roads has helped reduce the volumes of vehicles in the inner parts of the city. The proposal to build a light rail transport system connecting various city estates also offers a prospective step towards reducing the transportation challenge and its attendant sustainability challenges, among them congestion and CO_2 emissions.

The proposed Nairobi Master Plan

The draft report on the Master Plan for Nairobi city captures the greatest prospects of a greener and cleaner Nairobi (JICA, 2013). The plan proposes major initiatives to turn Nairobi into a modern green and sustainable city with practical initiatives and policies to address key green challenges mentioned above like waste management, sustainable land use proposals, modern urban transport arrangements, water and sanitation proposals, solid waste management practices and storm water drainage and sewerage proposals among others. Most of these sustainability challenges have been attributed to poor city planning endeavors (Opiyo, 2009). For more than half a century, Nairobi had been planned and managed through a colonial Master Plan (FAO, 2012; Makwaro and Mireri, 2014) which no longer carries the aspirations and vision of a green city in the contemporary sense of these words. As a result of lack of a modern master plan, Nairobi has grown bereft of any green innovative plan with the various urban development sectors hardly taking cognizance of emerging concerns related to sustainability of cities. These challenges are well addressed in the proposed Master Plan.

Policy options for green development and sustainability agenda for Nairobi

The Siemens AG Green Cities Index underlines six key factors that can contribute to development of sustainable green cities: good governance, adoption of holistic approach to addressing urban environmental problems, involving residents in city issues, adoption of right technologies, developing right environmental policies and reducing informal settlements (Siemens, 2012). Most of these can be done even among the not so rich cities.

The question of governance and development of right policies conducive for improving the liveability of urban residents in a city like Nairobi, for example, are so basic and urgent that they don't require any delay due to lack of financial outlays. For a long time, urban planning in Nairobi has experienced serious institutional and policy gaps (Opiyo, 2009). What are the policies options or guidelines that can help Nairobi transit to a greener, cleaner city? Which sectors do the policies need to be prioritized on even though a holistic approach ought to be adopted to hasten the realization of green developments and practices? This section dwells on policy highlights and options that can enable Nairobi transit into a more sustainable green city.

Urban transport

As discussed earlier, Nairobi has huge gaps in public transport infrastructure. The city is solely dependent on the private sector-driven matatu minibuses. The city needs a good and efficient public transport system which should be developed alongside a concrete public transport policy especially one that promotes non-motorized transport. In this case, there should be promotion of walking and cycling within the city. For this to be a practical option in the future, city leaders need to build special walking and cycling lanes on the side of the mainstream roads used by public buses. In formulating this policy, there should also be a component on public education and awareness creation on the health (avoidance of lifestyle diseases), environmental (reduction of carbon emissions) and economic (saving of fuel costs) benefits of the use of non-motorized transport such as walking and cycling. Much of this public awareness component would be to change the dominant public perception that these transport practices (walking and cycling) are demeaning as they are perceived as signs of poverty.

Furthermore, the transport policy should clearly suggest ways of reducing congestion. One way to reduce congestion is to discourage entry of private vehicles into the city. This can be done by imposing a tax or charge a fee on those drivers who go beyond a specified city radius that defines the city centre. This can only happen if an efficient public transport is already put into place. It is suggested that a light tramway or railway connecting various estates of Nairobi should be done as a matter of priority. If such an efficient transport method is developed, people would see no need for driving into the city. This of course can lead to some resistance in the implementation of the policy proposal especially from the matatu industry due to expected loss of jobs offered by the sector. But it is a more sustainable option because it would enable transport of a large number of people within a short period of time that would otherwise be wasted in traffic snarl ups, thus reducing congestion and significantly reducing the chance of CO_2 emissions for the huge city traffic.

Waste management

Policies that exist in terms of waste generation, collection and disposal, and even on recycling and reuse for Nairobi are hardly implemented. In most areas and especially in informal settlements, waste management is the effort of residents. In formal residential areas like estates, waste management is the effort of neighborhood associations. There is therefore no initiative to mobilize proper waste management practice in the city and so there is need for a waste management policy for Nairobi. Such a policy should suggest how the city environment department facilitates the categorization of various types of waste and suggest ways of collecting, disposing and even reusing them. There should be different strategies for separating and disposing domestic waste and industrial or hazardous waste. Indeed, there should be a method of waste-disposal monitoring on the part of the city environment department.

Most waste generated in Nairobi is disposed at the Dandora and Ruai waste disposal sites or in landfills with little or no sorting. A waste management strategy and policy should encourage private sector participation in waste management where waste is made a profitable venture. This should be done by developing a waste processing plant, for instance one procured to a private waste management firm. Funding for this should not be much of a challenge because in many residential estates of Nairobi, residents already pay for waste collection.

It is suggested that through engaging the residents, a process of even sorting waste at source should be encouraged so that waste collection already enables sorting different types of waste before being taken to a processing plant. This kind of private-public partnership is able to generate more business opportunities and employment through the concept of recycling and reusing. Recycled waste such as rubber, plastic and metals can be packaged and sold to other companies interested in these waste by-products. This way, it would ease the subsequent process of recycling and reusing of waste generated in the city.

Water and sanitation

Nairobi is susceptible to water stress. The city gets its water from the Sasumuwa and the Ndaka-ini dams which are far outside the city boundaries. With the increasing population, there is need for a good water and sanitation policy that emphasizes water use efficiency, water quality and water pollution standards among other things. Such a policy should point out the need for a robust water efficiency initiative, such as public promotion of water conservation or encourage rainwater harvesting. The city can also consider investing in technologies that can increase water sufficiency including setting up wastewater purification facilities.

In collaboration with the Nairobi Water and Sanitation Company, this can be achieved as an alternative source of water. Though this might be an expensive undertaking, such water can be used targeting certain high-end domestic users especially when marketed as purified water or used for industrial uses. Such an example has been used successfully in cities like Singapore thus making greater use of water that would otherwise have gone down the drain as waste water. Furthermore, there is need to develop a code that covers sanitation standards and infrastructure. The city also needs to have wastewater treatment standards in place and conduct monitoring on how the standards are observed. Regular monitoring of on-site treatment facilities in homes or communal areas as a way of ensuring enforcement of the policy should also be enhanced.

Land use and management

In Nairobi, much of the green space promotion has focused on conserving, restoring and preserving existing green areas. City leaders have promoted tree-planting within the city and along the various roads. However, the city needs to develop a green spaces development policy that does not only dwell on increasing tree and forest cover but also promoting developing of green infrastructure like buildings. Measures to curb urban sprawl by strictly enforcing building regulation also need to be put in place. One of the greatest challenges facing Nairobi is the escalation of informal settlements. Informal settlements are indicators of social exclusion and do not augur well for sustainable city development.

While some initiatives have been started in slum upgrading in various informal settlements, this has not been anchored in a proper policy framework. It is actually contestable as to whether upgrading is the right approach to address slum housing problems. Suggestions have been made that actually doing away with the current slum structures and establishing new housing structures like high-rise buildings, using proper construction standards that are uncongested is the more sustainable option. These measures should be given serious consideration.

Air quality

Much of Nairobi's air pollution is caused by automotive and industrial emissions. The two air pollution causes are as a result of the predominant use of fossil fuel powered cars and machines.

Increased greenhouse gases emissions from vehicular sources can be attributed to the increasing volumes of cars on Nairobi roads. Some emissions are also generated from burning of waste and construction activities around the city. There is need for initiatives that focus on regular monitoring of a range of key air pollutants and also developing public awareness programmes informing city residents, drivers and industry owners on the dangers of air pollution, especially in contributing to respiratory diseases.

With the transport sector being the main source of greenhouse gases emissions in the city, it is important for the National Environmental Management Authority (NEMA) in collaboration with the county government or interested private companies to conduct regular assessments of various greenhouse gases emissions in the city. This would lead to development of a plan for an annual vehicle certification regime that would include CO_2 emissions rates by vehicles. The County Government of Nairobi also needs to plan how to develop a rapid bus transit system to help reduce air pollution caused by cars idling for hours and hours in traffic.

Green capacity building

Two proposals are suggested here. The first relates to development of human capacity especially through skills improvement of local labor force to facilitate adoption and use of green technologies for the city. There is need to train and equip people in the various emerging areas green technologies in all urban development sectors including construction of various city infrastructure. Capacity building should target all levels of training ranging from universities to the local level polytechnics and institutes. In most cases, there has been overemphasis on university training on these matters, t which has unfortunately been more academic oriented as opposed to practical oriented polytechnics training which produces artisans involved in applying these technologies on the ground.

The second area of green capacity building relates to creation of awareness on green issues amongst citizens. Public environmental awareness programmes are important in this regard. This is because citizen participation is important to ownership and better stewardship of the various green developments started in the city. There is need to establish a Nairobi green urban community, an associational body that can be used as a community organization and mobilization vehicle for city residents to rally around various city greening initiatives.

The foregoing would also improve the previous project planning, management and implementation arrangements that were exclusionist in nature where decisions were made at the top and expected to be implemented at the bottom. Civic engagement and stakeholder participation in policy making is important in establishing a greener and more sustainable Nairobi. Inclusiveness entails bringing on board various categories of actors from the highest to the lowest people in a more collaborative approach, thus making the city livable by most urban residents. Citizen engagement also goes a long way in improving the governance environment, which is crucial to development of a sustainable city.

Conclusion

Nairobi has been growing rapidly. The growth has been associated with many consequent problems that have affected liveability in the city. The fact that there has been no living Master Plan over the years to guide Nairobi's growth into a more sustainable city can be seen as a major hindrance to emergence of a green city when compared to its peer cities in the African regions. Being a leading business, technological and innovation hub in the region and the fact that the city is instrumental to hosting international offices, governmental, non-governmental, business and developmental stakeholders, Nairobi can rise as an important green and sustainable city if the right policies are designed and implemented. The policy proposals for a green city can easily be a reality if the recently developed draft Nairobi City Master Plan can be implemented strictly. Even after implementation, the policy proposals and initiatives need to be monitored, if only to ensure that sustainable green city policy targets are realized within a reasonably specified period of time. This would bring a range of benefits to residents of the city ranging from social economic, health as well as environmental benefits.

References

Baycan-Levent, T & Nijkamp, P. (2009). *Planning and Management of Urban Green Spaces in Europe*: Comparative analysis. Journal of Urban Planning and. Development, 135(1): 1-12

Burra, S. (2005). *Towards a Pro-poor Slum Upgrading Framework in Mumbai, India. Environment and Urbanization*, Vol. 17 (1), 67-88.

Cronin, V and Guthrie, P. (2010). *Alternative Approaches to Slum Upgrading in Kibera, Nairobi. Urban Design and Planning*, Vol. 164 Issue DP2.

Cohen, D. A., Inagami, S. & Finch, B. (2008) *The Built Environment and Collective Efficacy. Health & Place*, 14, 198–208.

Dittmer. (2005). *Green Cities, editorial in Sustain, Journal of Environmental and Sustainability Issues*, Issue 12, Spring/ Summer, 2005.

Des Rosiers, et al, (2001). *Landscaping and House Values: An Empirical Investigation.* Paper submitted for presentation at the 17th Annual ARES Conference Coeur D'Alene, Idaho April 18-21, 2001

FAO. (2012). *Growing greener cities in Africa.* First Status Report on Urban and Peri-Urban Horticulture in Africa. Rome: Food and Agriculture Organization of the United Nations.

Freire, M E (2013). *Urbanization and Green Growth in Africa,* Green Growth Series Report No. 1, May 2013.

Gachanja, J. (2015). *Mitigating Road Transport Congestion in the Nairobi Metropolitan Region,* Policy brief, No. 2/2015, Kenya Institute of Policy Analysis and Research (KIPRRA), Nairobi.

Glaeser, E. L. (2011). *The Triumph of the City.* London: The Penguin Press

Haq, S A. (2011). *Urban Green Spaces and an Integrative Approach to Sustainable Environment. Journal of Environmental Protection,* 2011, 2, 601-608

IBM East Africa. (2012). *A vision of a smarter city:* How Nairobi can lead the way into a prosperous and sustainable city.

JICA. (2013). *The Integrated Urban Development Master Plan for the City of Nairobi in the Republic of Kenya,* Interim draft Report, Nairobi

Kithiia, S. M., (2012 a). *Water Quality Degradation Trends in Kenya over the Last Decade*, Water Quality Monitoring and Assessment, Retrieved from:

http://www.intechopen.com/books/water-quality-monitoring-and-assessment/water-quality-degradation-trendsin-kenya-over-the-last-decade, on 13th April, 2015.

Kithiia, S. M. (2012 b). *Effects of Sediments Loads on Water Quality within the Nairobi River Basins, Kenya. International Journal of Environmental Protection,* IJEP Vol. 2 Issue 6, 2012 pp. 16-20.

Hammer, S. et al. (2011), *Cities and Green Growth: A Conceptual Framework,* OECD Regional Development Working Papers 2011/08, OECD Publishing. Retrieved from http://dx.doi.org/10.1787/5kg0tflmzx34-en, on 8th April, 2015.

Makwaro, M & Mireri, C. (2011). *Public Open Spaces in Nairobi city. Kenya under Threat,* Journal of Environmental Planning and Management, Vol. 54, No. 8, pp. 1107-1123.

Mugo, S M. (2011). *Meeting the Challenge Greenways Networks for a more Healthy and Sustainable City,* 47th ISOCARP Congress 2011.

Muyale, B O & Murunga, E S. (2015). *Green Transport Solutions for developing cities*: A case of Nairobi, In Implementing Campus Greening Initiatives. World Sustainability Series, Springer International Publishing, Switzerland, 2015.

Nowak, D. J., Crane, D. E. & Stevens, J. C. (2006). *Air Pollution Removal by Urban Trees and Shrubs in the United States. Urban Forestry & Urban Greening,* 4(3-4), pp.115-23.

Omwenga, M. (2010). *Nairobi-Emerging Metropolitan Region: Development Planning and Management Opportunities and Challenges,* Nairobi Metropolitan Region, 46th ISOCARP Congress 2010.

Opiyo, R. (2009). *Metropolitan Planning and Climate Change in Nairobi: How Much Room to Manoeuvre?* Paper presented at the Fifty Urban Research Symposium Nairobi, 2009.

Siemens AG. (2012). *The Green City Index: A summary of the Green City Index research series,* Munich, Germany, 2012.

_(2011). *The African Green City Index: Assessing the environmental performance of Africa's major cities,* Munich, Germany, 2011.

_(2009). *The European Green City Index: Assessing the environmental performance of Africa's major cities,* Munich, Germany, 2009.

Tibaijuka, A. (2011). *Nairobi and its Environment.* In: Barr, J., & Shisanya, C. (Eds.), *Nairobi city development strategy top priority for 21st Century future of the Kenyan capital. Nairobi*: United Nations Environment Programme.

UN Habitat. (2008). *The UN-Habitat and the Kenya Slum Upgrading Project*: Strategy Document, Gigiri-Nairobi, 2008.

Virginia Cooperative Extension: The Value of Landscaping; Retrieved from, http://www.ext.vt.edu/pubs/ envirohort/426-721/426-721.html#TOC, 14th April, 2015

CHAPTER FIVE

Integrating Information, Communication and Technology in Agriculture to Enhance Food Security: Challenges and Opportunities in Kenya

Moses Beru, Mark Kiptui and Ezekiel Mwenzwa

Introduction

In Kenya agriculture is the mainstay of the economy. According to the Agricultural Sector Development Strategy (ASDS), the agricultural sector contributes to 26 per cent of the country's Gross Domestic Product (GDP) and is the main source of livelihood for over 70 per cent of the Kenyan population. It accounts for 65 per cent of Kenya's total exports; provides 18 per cent formal employment and more than 70 per cent informal employment in rural areas. This is because 70 per cent of the population is engaged in agricultural activities in Kenya. Any effort geared towards improving livelihoods in Kenya needs to begin from the agricultural sector.

The agricultural sector is key in the fight against poverty in developing countries (Muyanga and Jayne, 2006, MOA, 2008). It is observed that agricultural products' yield and value have either remained constant or have declined (MOA, 2008). Though the sector is the backbone of Kenya's economy, it is faced with a lot of problems that impede its development. One of the problems is the farmers' inaccessibility to agricultural information at the time of need. The problem has been worsened by the fact that the Ministry of Agriculture does not have adequate Agricultural Extension Officers. This is due to the fact that some were retrenched as a result of Structural Adjustment Programmes (SAPs) prescribed by World Bank and International Monitory Funds (IMF) in the 1980s to less developed countries.

Currently, the ratio of Agricultural Extension Officers to farmers is 1: 1,200 (MOA, 2008). This presents a small number of Extension Officers in the country which is a great challenge to the provision of extension services to farmers (Rutarora and Matee, 2001, Isinika, 2005). Rono (2013) observed that the agricultural sector is faced with the problem of insufficient personnel and funding. Besides, in Kenya, Agriculture as a subject at secondary school level, (Form three and Form four) is optional. Thus sensitizing the young right from high school about the importance of agriculture becomes difficult because it is made optional. This has led to food insecurity and unreliable sources of livelihoods for many Kenyans. There is need to address the problem of inaccessibility to agricultural information by farmers in order to improve food security and livelihood sources among the Kenyan farmers. ICT provides a safe avenue for this. In future it can be projected that the demand for agricultural goods and services will double because of the expected population increase, urbanization and the need to reduce poverty and hunger in the society. Poverty can be reduced by increasing opportunities for poor farmers to enable them make better use of their scarce resources. ICT can be a sure way in achieving this goal.

Conceptualization of the term ICT

The term ICT is a widely accepted acronym for Information and Communication Technology. The integration of ICTs into everyday life, however, has not been universally defined. The UK has streamlined ICT learning modules into their national primary education curricula. The Government of Kenya has an ICT policy, established by its National ICT Board, for guiding the future direction of the country in terms of ICT.

The Kenyan government under the Jubilee administration established the Ministry of Information, Communication and Technology in March 2013 to nationalize the importance of ICTs in the country. The Government of Uganda has a fully-developed Ministry of ICT, established in January 2006, to nationalize the importance of ICTs. There is an entire area of development work called ICT4Dev, which currently yields almost 100,000 hits in a typical Google search. These examples illustrate the importance of having a term – or set of terms - that can capture the constantly evolving nature of the relationship between technology, communication and the people who use it. It also illustrates the significance of ICT in our societies today.

Efforts in research, education and extension in agricultural development have not been fruitful. This is attributed to weak linkages in agricultural research-education-extension nexus. ICT offers an excellent opportunity in bridging information gap, sharing information and creation of knowledge. This will go a long way in linking research, extension and education that has for a long time remained delinked (Everson, 2001). Lack of relevant knowledge in agriculture has led to poor strategies to support livelihood strategies of individual farmers and communities (Beintema and Pardey, 2003). For example, Uganda is highly ranked in banana production but at the same time rated low in the sales of the same bananas globally. This is attributed to lack of information on availability of markets for the bananas. ICT offers an excellent opportunity for improved coordination across the agricultural nexus, bridging the information gap, sharing information and creation of knowledge. ICT can increase the economic and social well-being of poor people, and empower individuals and communities.

Extension services involve transfer of knowledge and good practices to farmers. Traditional extension practices involved extension officers visiting farmers in their own farms or at farmers' training centers (Stringfellow et al., 1997). In most developing countries there are very few extension workers (Due, Magayane and Temu, 1997). This was made even worse by the introduction of Structural Adjustment programmes by World Bank and International Monitory Fund (IMF) to the developing countries in the early 1980s. This led to reduction of subsidies in the agricultural sector that resulted in retrenchment of extension officers and privatization of key services like Artificial Insemination (AI) and veterinary services. It is now very expensive for small scale farmers in third world countries and Kenya in particular, to access extension services. This is because the farmer has to bear the full cost of the service. Thus, there is need to boost the work of the few extension workers available in these developing countries (Lwoga, Stilwell and Ngulube, 2011). ICT provides a safe window for this (Gakuru, Winters and Stepman, 2009).

The use of ICT e.g. mobile phones as a platform to deliver services to underprivileged populations and rural communities has been experienced all over the Developing World, particularly in India and some countries of Africa. Many countries have demonstrated the ability for ICT-based applications to improve people's lives and increase their incomes with simple services (Jensen R., 2007). The underprivileged population and rural communities' sources of livelihoods are generally agricultural based. This emphasizes the fact that integration of ICT in agriculture as an extension service can do a great deal in improving people's livelihoods, ensuring food security and thus reducing poverty levels in the less developed countries especially in Africa. This chapter is aimed at shedding light on the role played by ICT in ensuring food security in Kenya.

ICT channels

ICT integration in agricultural extension services can be channeled through a number of platforms.

Mobile phones

Mobile phone technology has become of great significance in the world today. Mobile phones are presenting Africa's smallholder farmers with the opportunity to run their operations more productively and to improve their livelihoods and food security. Mobile phones can be used for their short message service (SMS) and Voice service application. Kenya's M-Farm, fo example, allows farmers to come together through their mobile phones to sell and buy products in bulk. For example, farmers connected through M-Farm can save on the cost of inputs such as fertilisers and pesticides by buying in bulk.

Mobile phones also play a significant role in enabling farmers' access agricultural insurance products. A product called Kilimo Salama, Swahili for 'safe agriculture', enables smallholder farmers in Kenya to insure their agricultural inputs against adverse weather conditions, for instance drought or too much rain. Developed by UAP Insurance, the Syngenta Foundation for Sustainable Agriculture and mobile operator Safaricom, Kilimo Salama allows smallholder farmers to insure as little as one kilogramme of maize, seed or fertiliser. To be covered under the scheme, farmers only need to pay an extra 5% for a bag of seed, fertiliser or other inputs.

Radio

Radio is said to be a significant tool for ICT. It is an important medium of mass communication (Chapman, 2003, FAO, 2011). It is seen that radio is a medium of mass communication, is portable, affordable, has large coverage in terms of network and makes use of varied languages, for example in Kenya there are a large number of vernacular FM stations (Kuponiyi, 2000, Ronoh, 2013). In Kenya, 95 per cent of Kenyans listen regularly to radio. Even with desktop or laptop computers, one can access radio programmes through the internet. Through podcasts (a technique where individuals put together recordings that resemble radio shows and then post online for anybody to listen to), radio stations can post agricultural programmes for individuals to download and listen to.

Television

Shamba Shape-Up is a new reality television (TV) programme in Kenya that visits shambas (Swahili for small farms) across the country and aims to give both farmers and the audience the tools they need to improve productivity and income on their farms. The programme, created and directed by David Campbell and hosted by African actor Tonny Njuguna and Naomi Kamau, focuses on increasing farmers' crop productivity by providing expert advice on livestock, crops, soil fertility and storage. Typically the film crew will spend four days with one household, allowing enough time to build any improvement structures and invite the experts in to offer advice. Experts include veterinarians, soil analysts and specific crop specialists from partnering companies in Kenya. The helpful tips don't just benefit the visited farmer however; throughout the programme viewers are encouraged to access all the information and advice via text message – an innovative method of educating smallholder farmers across Kenya.

Tele-centres

There is need to utilize the services of tele-centres or information resource centers to disseminate information to farmers in Africa especially on emerging new methods in agricultural practice, new input methods, crop prices and other extension services. Tele-centres are better-placed to inform farmers through audio-visual materials, workshops, trainings and even demonstrations in farms with the assistance of agricultural and livestock officers. Farmers can also visit the centres to read materials, watch videos, listen to taped radio cassettes, CDs or DVDs and browse the internet to gain more knowledge on areas of their interest. At the same time farmers can use tele-centres as meeting points among themselves to exchange ideas and get advice from professionals in agricultural topics/areas of their choice. The tele-centres can be mobile.

Videos

Video is an electronic medium for the recording, copying, playback, broadcasting, and display of moving visual and audio media. Rural community needs can be identified and extension workers trained in shooting and editing videos using local content. The tapes/broadcasts produced can serve large numbers of farmers, which facilitates the work of the extension services. Videos have the advantage that they can be used to illustrate a point in agricultural extension, they provide information in greater detail than text and graphic formats, they sustain the participants' attention for a long span of time and they can be used to show real life examples in the advocated-for agricultural practices. In addition, videos stimulate discussions, enhance problem based learning and appeal to the participants. In fact the adage goes — if a picture is worth a thousand words, what is a video worth?

Teleconferencing

The benefit teleconferencing has to offer is the ability to meet with people in remote locations without incurring travel expenses or other expenses associated with face- to- face communication. Business meetings, educational meetings, healthcare conferences and more can all be easily conducted courtesy of video conferencing technology. Individuals living in remote areas can also use teleconferencing to keep in touch, if you will, with the world at large. More people are easily accessed and contacted using video conferencing. Because of this technology information and knowledge are often disseminated at more rapid rates, and collaboration between people occurs more willingly and freely. Farmers can take advantage of video conferencing to take agricultural lessons to distant locations that would normally be unavailable. They can also take agricultural lessons that will accommodate busy schedules. Teleconferencing can stimulate better brainstorming, knowledge sharing and information gathering. However, it is a very expensive venture.

Web and internet

The Web can be used to provide information on practices in the field; research findings; technology transfer methods and support skills; training materials; statistics and other data; a discussion area; and access to other agricultural sites via a desktop or a laptop computer (Maru, A. 2005).

The Role of ICT in Agriculture

Computers were introduced in the 1980s; internet, email and mobile phones were introduced in the 1990s; while global navigation satellites, wireless communications and social media were introduced in the last decade. The application of ICT in agriculture at the moment is increasingly important. E-agriculture is an emerging field focusing on the enhancement of agricultural and rural development through improved information and communication processes. More specifically, e-agriculture involves the conceptualization, design, development, evaluation and application of innovative ways to use ICT in the rural areas, with a primary focus on smallholder farmers.

E-agriculture is one of the action lines identified in the declaration and plan of action of the World Summit on the Information Society (WSIS). The "Tunis Agenda for the Information Society," published on 18 November 2005, emphasizes the leading facilitating roles that UN agencies need to play in the implementation of the Geneva Plan of Action. The Food and Agriculture Organization of the United Nations (FAO) has been assigned the responsibility of organizing activities related to ICT Applications on E-Agriculture. This gives emphasis on the significance of ICT in the development of agricultural sector in the entire world and specifically the less developed countries in the world, Kenya included.

The agriculture industry include crop cultivation, livestock management, water management, fertilizer application, pest management, harvesting, and post-harvest handling, transport of food products, packaging, food preservation, and food processing/ value addition, quality management, food safety, food storage, and food marketing as the main phases. All stakeholders of the industry and most importantly the small-scale farmer, need information and knowledge about these phases to manage them efficiently. This information and knowledge for making decisions in any industry should be delivered in an accurate, complete concise and timely manner. The information provided must be in user-friendly form, easy to access, cost-effective and well protected from unauthorized accesses. This is the only way the information will be of much benefit to the recipient.

Small scale farmers require ICT to make agricultural production marketable and business-like. ICT integration in agriculture plays a key role. Some of the important roles played by integrated ICT in agriculture include:

1. Improving agricultural production. Agricultural production requires the technical knowhow. Agricultural knowledge can be disseminated through ICT. ICT leads to increased efficiency, productivity and sustainability of small-scale farms.

ICT enables the small-scale farmers to access information about pest and disease control, especially early warning systems, new varieties, new ways to optimize production and regulations for quality control. This in the long run will lead to improved agricultural production. Once agricultural production goes up, food security objective will be realized, peoples' livelihoods will be improved and their living standards will definitely improve.

2. Improving markets. Markets are very important for improved agricultural production. Markets are a motivation behind successful farming. Improved markets can be realized through small scale farmers getting to understand markets better, resulting in informed decisions about future crops to be planted, commodities in the market and best time and place to sell and buy agricultural goods. Up-to-date market information on prices for commodities, inputs and consumer trends is also realized (International Finance Corporation 2013). As a result, the small scale farmer is better able to market his or her products with ease. This will ensure a stable source of livelihood for many rural dwellers who rely heavily on agriculture. Poverty levels will be reduced and better living standards for rural people will be realized.

3. Capacity Building. Rothman, (2001) says if community members can learn to communicate across class, ethnic, and racial lines, and to set up organizations, systems, and policies to take advantage of their resources and address their problems, they can make life better for everyone. This is capacity building. ICT strengthen capacities of small scale farmers and better representation of their constituencies when negotiating input and output prices, land claims, resource rights and infrastructure projects. ICT reduces social isolation, widens the perspective of local communities in terms of national or global developments, opens up new business opportunities and allows easier contact with friends and relatives. It enables sharing of information among small-scale farmers, thus building their capacities.

Challenges

As already mentioned, ICT integration in agriculture is quite significant in the growth of the economy and improvement of peoples' standard of living, especially small-scale farmers in the rural areas. The benefits of ICT integration discussed can be hindered by the following challenges:

1. Just as roads are significant for rural development, digital connectivity is becoming essential for research, extension, and e-agriculture. Connectivity does not depend on national policy alone; it is affected even by the policies prevailing in an institution. Researchers may want to disseminate results through ICT more widely and increase their usefulness, for example, but they can be hindered by institutional information technology (IT) and intellectual property policies that limit opportunities to tap into the open access systems. If national research systems (like agricultural research institutions, universities and other private research institutions in Kenya) do not digitize their research results and create repositories for them, other organizations are limited in their ability to access and share findings in a wider network. Extension programs, other agricultural services, and producers (especially the small scale farmers) suffer the consequences. Thus there is need to come up with appropriate institutional policies and make everyone develop general e-readiness so as to build innovation cultures where ICTs thrive and are put to good use (Annor- Fremponge F., 2006).

2. Even if all farmers in poor countries have access to ICT (mobile phones, computers, radios, televisions, internet, CDs etc.), this connectivity will not ensure that extension agents and researchers will listen to what farmers have to say and adapt their programs accordingly. Nor will it guarantee that farmers can use any knowledge they may obtain; farmers learn best when the information is carefully targeted to their needs and when multiple stakeholders provide incentives for learning (for example, in the form of a mobile phone for learning any time and any place, and a bank loan to put their new knowledge to use). Investments in agricultural innovation systems should give particular attention to building the capacity to innovate (especially the capacity to share and use knowledge) and to the enabling environment that fosters innovation (Annor- Fremponge F., 2006).

3. For ICT to facilitate communication and engage many stakeholders, much stronger farmer representation and influence in the form of farmers' cooperations {for example Kenya Farmers Cooperation (KFA), Kenya Farmers Federation

of Agricultural Producers (KENFAP) among others} are also needed in the forums where research and program priorities are determined. Specific reforms and incentives are needed for service providers to become more accountable to clients (farmers), and ICTs can make a difference by strengthening feedback systems and accountability. ICTs can help people to learn the interactive skills (collaborating and negotiating, for example) that have proven critical in effective innovation systems, and they can help them to acquire agricultural and technical skills as well (Banjade, 2006).

4. Building research networks, data repositories, and expert query systems and engaging in large data collection efforts requires effective management and collaboration. In addition to committing resources, the right climate and culture must be created by the government for collaborative planning, knowledge sharing, communication, cross-functional teams to function, and critical review of current information and communication systems (Annor- Fremponge F., 2006) by all the stakeholders in the agricultural sector. For this case the government needs to encourage public-private partnership in order to ensure effective integration of ICT in agricultural sector. If this element is lacking, then ICT may not be effective in bringing the desired change in rural communities.

5. ICT is also significant in ensuring advisory services and capacity building fulfill their primary role in an agricultural innovation system, which is to serve as a central node for knowledge sharing and innovation brokering (including brokering new partnerships). The nature of farmer engagement, two-way communication, information requirements, and the complexity of extension networks all make the design of advisory service programs critical to their ultimate success (Kapange, 2004).

6. ICT in the third world countries is faced with the problem of network coverage and network overload and hence its slowness in connectivity. This affects mobile phone technologies, internet technologies and social network technologies that depend on internet services. In addition, there is the problem of inadequate access to appropriate equipment like computers and mobile phones. This problem is worsened by the fact that traditional methods are deeply ingrained in the local mind (Annor- Fremponge F., 2006).

Way forward

ICT integration in agricultural extension is paramount in order to enable smallholder farmers achieve their targets. For the integration process to succeed the following should be addressed:

The government should strengthen private-public partnership programmes to enable the private sector participate actively in service provision for the smallholder farmers. This is because the private sector plays a key role in provision of agricultural services to smallholder farmers especially in privatized services like artificial insemination and veterinary services.

1. There is need to have and maintain a farmers' database with their farming details, to enable an expert provide appropriate solutions to the concerned farmers. This data base should be region-specific.
2. There is need to interlink location-specific information from various service providers to cater to the specific needs of the farmers.
3. There is need for smallholder farmers to be enabled, through friendly and simple interfaces, to access information and advisory services in effective manner, if possible in their local language.
4. There is need for expert support system which has user-friendly interfaces and reference content (e.g. knowledge repository, farmer's details, etc.) for fast and proactive delivery of advices. The system should also facilitate an expert to be virtually available by giving him/her any time anywhere access. Such expert systems should be located at the county level as agriculture is devolved in Kenya.
5. There is need to develop tele-centres at every location in Kenya which can be combined with the Farmers Training Centres so as to enable ICT integration in agriculture.
6. There is need to establish Mobile Extension Services that are ICT enabled to enable farmers in remote areas access the agricultural services.

Conclusion

ICT can increase the efficiency, productivity and sustainability of the agriculture sector which is an important economic sector, since it provides income and food for a large segment of the population in Kenya. ICT can play a key role in providing the rural population with all information needed for their work including crop production, credits, input supply, pest and disease control, weather forecast, post-harvest techniques and improving market access. ICT can be used to strengthen the capacities of rural development workers, farmers, farmer organizations and rural communities as a whole. An example is the supply of fertilizer, which is being done electronically as the ministry in charge of agriculture has developed a programme to the same effect in collaboration with the National Cereals and Produce Board.

References

Annor-Frempong, F., Kwarteng, J., Agunga, R., & Zinnah, M. M. (2006). *Challenges and prospects of infusing information communication technologies (ICTS) in extension for agricultural and rural development in Ghana.* Proceedings of the Annual Conference of the International Association of Agricultural and Extension Education, 22, 36-46.

Banjade, A. (2006). *Voice to the Voiceless in Western Nepal: An Audience Survey of Community Radio Madanpokhara.* The Journal of Development Communication, 17(1): 72-91.

Beintema N. M. and Pardey P. G., 2003. *Recent developments in African agricultural research and developments.* Paper presented at the second Forum for Agricultural Research in Africa (FARA) plenary, Dakar, 19-20 May.

Chapman, R Blench, R Kranjac-Berisavljevic', G & Zakariah, ABT 2003, *Rural radio in agricultural extension: The example of vernacular radio programmes on soil and water conservation in N. Ghana.* Agricultural Research & Extension Network, Network paper No. 127.

Due, J.M., Magayane. F. and Temu, A.A. (1997). *Gender again— Views of female agricultural extension officers by smallholder farmers in Tanzania.* World Development, 25(5):713-725.

Everson R. E.,(2001). *Economic impacts of agricultural research and extension.* In: Gardner, B. L., and G. C., Rausser (Eds) *Handbook of agricultural economics.* Amsterdam North Holland: Elsevier.

FAO (Food and Agriculture Organization) (2011). *The State of Food and Agriculture 2010–2011*. Rome: FAO. Available at http://www.fao.org/docrep/013/i2050e/i2050e00.html.

Gakuru. M., Winters. K., Stepman, F. (2009). *Innovative farmers' advisory services using ICT*. Paper presented at W3C Workshop *Africa perspective on the role of mobile technologies in fostering social development*. Maputo, Mozambique. pp. 1-2

International Finance Corporation (2013). *Working with Smallholders: A Handbook for Firms Building Sustainable Supply Chains*. Retrieved from https://www.farms2firms.org on 7/3/2016.

Isinika, A.C., Ngetti, M., Kimbi, G.G. and Rwambali, E.G. (2005). *Contemporary challenges of agricultural advisory services delivery in Tanzania. In*: The 2nd National Agricultural Extension Symposium in Tanzania. 24 -25 February 2005, Sokoine University of Agriculture, Morogoro, Tanzania. pp. 1 -13.

Jensen, R. (2007) *The digital provide: information (technology), market performance, and welfare in the South Indian fisheries sector*. Quarterly Journal of Economics 121 (3): 879–924.

Kapange, B. (2004). *ICTs and national agricultural research systems –The case of Tanzania. Research and Development*, Ministry of Agriculture and Food Security. Retrieved from http://www.tzonline.org/pdf/icts and *national agricultural research systems*.pdf on 7/3/2016

Lwoga, E. T, Stilwell, C. and Ngulube, P. (2011). *Access and use of agricultural information and knowledge in Tanzania*. Library Review 60 (5): 3–3.

Maru, A. (2005). *Using Information and Communication Technology (ICT) for Agricultural Extension. Commonwealth of Learning*.

MOA. *Ministry of Agriculture Strategic Plan 2008 – 2012*. Nairobi, Kenya: Government Printer, 2008.

Muyanga, M., Jayne, T.S. (2006): *Agricultural Extension in Kenya: Practice and Policy Lessons*. Tegemeo Institute of Agricultural Policy and Development, Egerton University, Working Paper 26.

Ronoh M. K. (2013). *The Effects of Sponsors on Content in Vernacular Agricultural Radio Programmes*: The Case of Kass FM, Kenya. Unpublished Thesis.

Rothman, Jack (2001), *Approaches to community intervention.* In Rothman, J., Erlich, J.L., and Tropman, J.E., *Strategies of Community Intervention (6th edn.)*. Itasca, IL: F.E. Peacock, pp.27-64.

Rutarora, D. and Matee, A. (2001) *Major agricultural extension providers in Tanzania. African Study Monographs*, 22(4): 155-173, December 2001, p. 155.

Stringfellow, R., Coulter, J., Lucey, T., McKone, C. & Hussain, A. (1997). *Improving the access of smallholders to agricultural services in sub-Saharan Africa: Farmer cooperation and the role of the donor community. Natural Resource Perspectives 20.* Overseas Development Institute.

World Bank. (1999). *World Bank agricultural extension projects in Kenya.* Impact Evaluation Report No. 19523. Washington D. C: The World Bank.

CHAPTER SIX

Towards Livelihood Diversification and Sustainability in Rural Kenya: Strategies and Lessons

Michael A. Chesire

Introduction

The contribution of the rural sector in Kenya's national development remains crucial. It accommodates more than 60% of the total population, employs more than 70% of the total labor force, and provides the bulk of foreign exchange earnings, while accounting for close to 30% of the country's Gross Domestic Product (GDP) (Republic of Kenya, 2005). Upon attaining independence in 1963, Kenya identified agriculture as the mainstay of the economy providing food for the nation and employing a substantial proportion of the population. Subsequently, its first National Development Plan, 1964-1970 emphasized the need for rapid economic development and social progress for all citizens. In 1965, the Sessional Paper No. 10 on African Socialism and its Application to Planning in Kenya (Republic of Kenya 1965) identified agriculture and land tenure as some of the critical areas for development to enhance the wellbeing of her citizens.

The foregoing blueprint recognized the need to revolutionize agriculture through the development of idle and underutilized land. This would be done through provision of credit, extension services, training of farmers on new methods of production and proper marketing of farm produce. The ultimate outcome of such strategies included stimulation of commerce and industry, increased variety of agricultural products for consumption and provision of raw materials for industries.

The establishment of the Ministry of Agriculture after independence was in recognition of its contribution to development. This ministry had several departments, all of which addressed production, storage and marketing of agricultural produce. Priority areas identified for intervention included extension services in crop and livestock production with the aim of encouraging farmers to use high-yielding crop varieties and livestock breeds; use of modern technology in production processes including irrigation technology; development of the horticulture sector and cash crop farming. In addition, the fisheries sector was to be developed to contribute to domestic earnings and provide employment opportunities. The concept and practice of fish ponds would then be strengthened through extension services.

The realization of all these would be made possible with the participation of all stakeholders in this sector, notably, the government, private sector and the farmers. Notable challenges in the sector, which required immediate attention included pests and diseases, high cost of farm inputs and low prices for agricultural produce. These were to be addressed through establishment and strengthening of marketing cooperative societies, provision of extension education and marketing of farm produce (Republic of Kenya, 1964).

The Kenya Rural Development Strategy (Republic of Kenya, 2002), a sector-wide strategy for the development of rural areas was crafted with the intention of improving the well-being of rural inhabitants. This strategy identified a number of intervention areas to include provision of early warning systems with regard to climatic conditions especially to farmers; use of modern technology in production; timely marketing of produce; provision of extension services and water conservation and harvesting. Other areas of intervention included; exploration of ecotourism as an income-generating activity, infrastructure development, establishment of rural micro-industries, provision of rural finance, enhancing general security in rural areas, land reforms and establishment of Kenya Rural Development Strategy Trust Fund for the implementation of the strategy (Republic of Kenya, 2002).

The Economic Recovery Strategy for Wealth and Employment Creation (ERSWEC), 2003-2007 (Republic of Kenya, 2003) identified agriculture as one of the major productive sectors which required more resources for its revival in the face of liberalization. The focus on agriculture arose out of the realization that over the years, its growth had been slow. From around 1993, this sector experienced a decline in terms of production per unit area, thereby adversely impacting on food security, household income and employment creation alongside export earnings. A number of factors were attributed to this state of affairs. Key among these were poor governance of agricultural institutions, including cooperatives, rising cost of farm inputs, low credit uptake by farmers and below optimum adoption of modern technology (Republic of Kenya, 2003).

In an effort to revitalize agriculture as a key driver in transforming rural areas, the Government of Kenya came up with a number of strategies for the development of the agriculture sector. Among the strategies included legislative and institutional reforms, value addition, diversification, access to credit, irrigation and enhancement of research and extension. The overall aim of these strategies was to achieve maximum production and ultimately fulfill national food requirements and make agriculture an economic activity. In terms of institutional reforms, the government envisaged reviving the Agricultural Finance Corporation to offer affordable credit to farmers and streamline the operations of cooperatives so as to enjoy the benefits of procuring farm inputs at subsidized rates. In addition, it was also aimed at marketing farmers' produce at competitive prices (Republic of Kenya, 2003).

In 2007, the government came up with a development blue print, Kenya Vision 2030, which placed emphasis on the agriculture sector as a means to realizing economic growth especially in the rural areas. The Vision focused on value addition in agriculture, livestock and fisheries which would be achieved through processing of agricultural produce as a value-addition strategy. Other strategies included irrigating arid and semi-arid lands, developing arid lands for livestock production and improving market access to farmers. The fisheries sector would also be developed to contribute towards economic development (Republic of Kenya, 2007).

The numerous efforts made by the government of Kenya from independence to date to revive the agriculture sector faced several challenges. Key among these were poor infrastructure, high cost of farm inputs, declining land productivity, low level of awareness among farmers of new crop and animal production methods and pests and diseases. Other challenges included poorly developed markets for agricultural products, low prices of agricultural products, lack of capital to economically develop land and other resources. All these contributed to the low performance of the sector, thus deepening poverty. This state of affairs therefore led to a realization by the government and farmers that the continued reliance on agriculture was unsustainable, calling for livelihood diversification for enhanced human welfare.

Livelihood Diversification Strategies

Ellis (2000) defines diversification as the process by which households construct increasingly assorted livelihood portfolios, making use of increasingly varied combinations of resources and assets in order to survive and to improve their standard of living. Livelihood comprises the assets, the activities, and the access to these, mediated by institutions and social relations that together determine the living gained by the individual or household (Ellis, 1998). According to Niehof & Price (2001), the concept of livelihood needs to be conceptualized in terms of resources, assets and outputs from human activities.

Chambers & Conway (1992) define sustainability as the ability to cope with and recover from stress and shock, while maintaining or enhancing capabilities and assets. They note that households with vulnerable livelihood systems have neither enough assets, nor the capabilities to create or access them. Such households have problems in providing for their members' basic needs, are unable to create a surplus, cannot cope with a crisis, and are often chronically in debt. They are often burdened with liabilities, such as having unhealthy members or living in a degraded or hazardous environment, rather than having assets. Sustainable livelihood systems have a sufficiently robust and stable base of assets and resources. Even in a situation of crisis or stress, such households will be able to recover and bounce back. Many rural households do not have sustainable livelihood sources and therefore are mostly adversely affected by man-made and natural disasters. Niehof, (2004) notes that due to the lack of resources, the household chores carried out by women are time-consuming and hinder them from engaging in income-generating activities.

Diversification of areas of Production

Immediately after the introduction of Structural Adjustment Programmes (SAPs) and its attendant policies, the agricultural sector faced stiff competition from imported products. Tea and coffee were among the cash crops whose domestic and foreign earnings took a sharp decline. Kenya's staple food crops namely maize and wheat similarly experienced a decline in production occasioned by high production costs and cheap imports from the Common Market for East and Southern Africa (COMESA) region. In addition, the livestock production sector was not spared by liberalization as relatively cheap milk and meat imports from other countries flooded the local market.

These challenges led to the awakening of farmers to start diversification of livelihood sources and move away from traditional production systems. Key among the areas of diversification were fish farming and apiculture. In 2007, the government department in charge of public finance introduced the Economic Stimulus Programme which was implemented by the Ministry of Agriculture. In this programme, fish farming was recognized as one of the ways of agricultural diversification and therefore interested farmers in each constituency were funded to construct fish ponds and were provided with fingerlings. The programme aimed at creating more employment opportunities and improving farmer income.

From 2007, the Ministry of Water and Irrigation in collaboration with the Ministry of Agriculture began joint farmer extension programmes on modern crop production methods, particularly through irrigation. The focus of the programme was development of the horticultural sector since returns were high and there was a ready market. The Horticultural Crops Development Authority (HCDA) played a leading role in providing trainings to farmers, with emphasis on greenhouse farming given that disease and pest incidence under this method are minimal in addition to production of high quality crops.

In an effort to enhance food security and put idle land into productive use, the Government of Kenya undertook irrigation projects in arid and semi-arid areas. Irrigated crops included rice, maize, tomatoes, mangoes, oranges, onions and pineapples. The National Irrigation Board was given the mandate to irrigate rice in Mwea, Bura and Ahero irrigation schemes. Maize irrigation was done by regional development authorities such as Kerio Valley Development Authority, Lake Basin Development Authority and Tana and Athi River Development Authority. In 2013, the Jubilee Government tasked the National Irrigation Board to irrigate 1,000 acres of maize in Tana River County to boost food security and create rural employment opportunities.

The Kenya Agricultural and Livestock Research Organization (KALRO) has also been undertaking irrigation with the aim of identifying the high yielding crops. Non-governmental organizations such as World Vision and Action Aid whose operations are mainly in arid areas also undertake irrigation activities and urge residents of such areas to emulate modern production through irrigation. Mohammad et al (2014), in a study on rural diversification in Shangla district, Pakistan, note that farmers who had diversified by practicing crop and livestock farming had more incomes similar to those who had used high-yielding crop varieties. The adoption of latest seed technologies in maize and wheat farming had also increased productivity and hence income of rural households.

Adding to the foregoing, agro-forestry as a new land use practice has witnessed widespread adoption by many rural inhabitants in both high and low potential areas. The establishment of the Kenya Forest Service in 2005 saw a rejuvenation of extension services by the agency. The introduction of fast maturing tree species with a ready market saw rural people across Kenya planting the same. Equally, rural inhabitants have continued to do intercropping as a diversification strategy. Farmers have followed the Non-Residential Cultivation (NRC) commonly referred to as the 'Shamba System' introduced by the Kenya Forest Service. The Forest Act of 2005 also established the Forest Users Associations (FUAs) whose members access government forests and utilize forest resources through an organized structure. Communities adjacent to forests are able to graze and water their livestock in the forests, extract medicinal herbs, extract fuel wood and construction materials and at the same time practice bee-keeping in the forests (Republic of Kenya, 2005).

Value addition

A major setback to agricultural and industrial development in Kenya's rural areas lies in the fact that all the products from the two sectors are sold in raw form which fetch low returns. The resultant effect has always been a decline in production due to the high costs. Efforts to reverse this trend are numerous with varying levels of success. In the crop production sector, a number of processing industries established in the raw materials catchment areas include fruit processing in Thika, tea processing in Kiambu, Kericho and Nandi counties, coffee processing in Kiambu, cashew nut processing companies in Kilifi, maize and wheat milling plants in Eldoret, Nakuru, Nairobi, Mombasa and Kisumu counties.

In the livestock production sector, a meat processing plant is situated in Athi River- the Kenya Meat Commission- which cans meat for domestic and export purposes. Currently, many county governments in arid and semi-arid areas where pastoralism is the mainstay, have established a number of abattoirs to enable farmers to dispose of their livestock, thereby reducing transport costs. Fish processing is done in Thika town for domestic and export use. The New Kenya Cooperative Creameries (New KCC) processes raw milk into powder, yoghurt, cheese, ghee, fermented milk, long life milk and fresh milk to meet national milk demand. The New KCC has several milk cooling plants in rural areas where farmers collect their milk for onward transportation to the processing factories in major towns like Eldoret and Nairobi.

The contribution of decentralization of manufacturing industries to rural areas remains significant as they provide employment opportunities. The setting of Export Processing Zones (EPZs) in rural settings such as in Athi River for textiles and Salt Mining in some parts of Malindi opened up such areas for development. Apart from establishing these industries in rural areas, the government has also established aggressive marketing agencies in the productive ministries including agriculture, trade and industry as well as tourism. Marketing agencies include Kenya Tourism Board (KTB), Magical Kenya and the marketing department in the Ministry of Agriculture among others.

Service Sector

The service sector remains an important livelihood diversification alternative in rural areas as it does not entirely dependent on weather patterns. In 2003, the Government of Kenya identified the tourism sector as a major income source in rural areas due to its multiplier effect. The sector impacts positively on the growth of other sectors notably, entertainment, transport and trade. It generates employment opportunities and provides a ready market for agricultural raw materials and other products in rural areas thereby contributing to its development (Republic of Kenya, 2003). Barret et al (2001) affirm that non-farm enterprises are not dependent on weather conditions and therefore are likely to yield sustained income to rural people.

The Kenya Vision 2030 highlights the critical role played by SACCOs and the financial sector especially micro-finance institutions in rural development. The government embarked on major reforms in the banking sector which would attract borrowers to take up loan products at low interest rates. Many commercial banks rolled out their products in the rural areas through agency banking for instance Co-op kwa Jirani (Co-operative Bank of Kenya), KCB Mtaani (Kenya Commercial Bank) and Equity Agent (Equity Bank). Telecommunication companies in Kenya also introduced money transfer services which are spread across the country and are now a common form of money transfer in rural Kenya. Safaricom introduced M-Pesa; Telkom introduced Orange money while Airtel introduced Airtel money.

Small and Micro-Enterprises (SMEs)

Small and micro-enterprise development in Kenya started as an informal employment sector to cater for the semi and unskilled labor. This was a result of the diminishing growth of the formal sector denying a large number of human resources the much needed white collar jobs. Over the years, the Government of Kenya recognized the informal sector and especially the SMEs as being instrumental in bringing about development of rural areas. In 1999, the National Poverty Reduction Strategy Plan, 1999-2015 highlighted the role of the SMEs in poverty reduction and the government's commitment to fund the sector (Republic of Kenya, 1999). A number of funds were established to enable individuals and organized groups to access seed money to start up micro enterprises both in rural and urban areas, including the National Youth and Women Enterprise Development Funds.

Some of the most common SMEs in rural Kenya include carpentry, dressmaking and metal-work. Women engage in textile work while men do woodwork and metalwork. A lot of SMEs are operated in open-air workplaces or semi-permanent market stall while others are done from homesteads. Whereas many have employed rural inhabitants, they are still faced by many challenges including inadequate capital, electricity, water, sanitation facilities and changing work locations (Parker & Torres, 1994). The 1999 survey on SMEs found out that the most serious challenges facing them are imperfect markets, competition from imported products, access to affordable credit and insecurity (Republic of Kenya, 2003). In a recent study, Vincze (2012) notes that women engage in petty trading, processing of farm produce, livestock selling and fish mongering as livelihood diversification activities in many parts of the country.

Paid work/income from sale of infrastructural raw materials

Infrastructure remains the cornerstone of development across all sectors of the economy. For a long time, rural areas in Kenya have been neglected in infrastructure development. With the realization that stagnation in development results from under-investment in infrastructure, the Government of Kenya in 2003 began devolving funds to constituencies to facilitate development. The Constituencies Development Fund (CDF) and Road Maintenance Levy Fund (RMLF) were among the major funds disbursed to aid in development (Republic of Kenya, 2003).

The CDF was meant to fund development in several sectors such as water, health, education, energy, roads amongst others. Through the construction of schools, hospitals/dispensaries/health centres, polytechnics, roads and water projects, the rural inhabitants get temporary or permanent employment opportunities, supply raw materials for construction, gain experience in project management and acquire skills and knowledge for future initiatives. In counties such as Nakuru, Uasin Gishu and Elgeyo Marakwet which produce horticultural crops such as French peas, cold storage facilities were constructed to ensure their shelf life.

Later in 2005, the Government of Kenya established rural specific institutions to address rural infrastructure notably; Rural Electrification Authority (REA) and the Kenya Rural Roads Authority (KERRA). The REA is tasked with the responsibility of identifying and subsequently providing power connection to rural institutions such as schools, health centres, and market places to spur development. The expectation is that upon provision of power to rural market centres, several entrepreneurial activities would be implemented which create employment, diversify livelihood sources and improve rural income. On the other hand, the KERRA has the responsibility of constructing and maintaining rural roads across all the constituencies in Kenya. The ultimate goal of road construction in rural areas is to open up such areas for ease of movement of people and transportation of goods to the market. Other than the four factors of production, investors consider the mode of transport such as roads being crucial in facilitating their activities, making good road infrastructure a rural development incentive.

Success Stories, Lessons Learnt and Best Practices

Diversification and response to Markets in Embu County, Kenya

In a study conducted by Thorne and Tanner (2001), in Embu County, Kenya, it was found that poorer households could not meet their food needs because of their small land holdings. Instead, they tended to specialize in the production of high value commodities that they would then trade for staple foods produced elsewhere. A livelihoods study found that:

1. Wealthier farms are relatively specialized enterprises that focus on staple food crops (maize and beans) sold on to local markets. These farms can afford levels of technology (such as fertilizer) that maximize efficiency.

2. Most medium-sized farms pursue a traditional strategy of food production for home-consumption, with occasional surpluses sold into the market. These farms struggle to compete with the 'technology-rich' farms, and are increasingly dependent on off-farm sources of income.

3. Poorer farmers are unable to produce sufficient food for their own consumption. They are forced to take risks by diversifying into unconventional but high value agricultural products such as milk, flowers, French beans and snap peas. These goods are sold to middlemen who offer a better deal than the collapsing marketing parastatals. Most food needs are met through purchases from the local market, using cash obtained from the sale of high-value agricultural produce.

From this case study, it can be concluded that many rural households diversify production so as to meet their basic needs and mitigate the risk of total crop failure in the event of adverse climatic conditions. Farmers have succeeded through diversification strategies such as planting high value crops as is the case with farmers in Embu County.

Service Sector and alternative Livelihoods in Northern Kenya

Alternative livelihoods in Northern Kenya are based on a variety of strategies, including the marketing of livestock, dairy products, hide and skins, and cultivated crops; a variety of wage-earning occupations, ranging from professional to manual labor; and entrepreneurial activities including shop keeping, craft production and sales and transportation. With the exception of livestock, women play a key role in petty commodity trade activities, particularly the sale of horticultural products, tobacco, and miraa, (khat), and at lower rungs of the economic ladder, firewood or charcoal, beer brewing and prostitution. Alternative strategies for men include wage earning labor in construction, truck driving, security work, farm work, and shop employment, and entrepreneurial occupations including shop keeping, construction, and transportation. Education has played an important role, particularly in obtaining professional employment in hospitals and health clinics, government offices, military and police, and employment in Non-Government Organizations (Elliot et al, 2011).

Livelihood Diversification and Capacity Building at the Coast of Kenya

The Aga Khan Foundation through its rural development programme initiated the Coastal Rural Support Programme (CRSP) in Kenya which has been working in semi-arid, marginalized and rural areas of the Coast of Kenya since 1997. Over the last decade, the programme has grown from working with four village organizations comprising less than 300 community members to working with 195 village organizations comprising more than 30,000 members. The introduction of small farm reservoirs, which has provided the target population of 130,000 with critical access to water for both domestic and productive uses, has helped the majority of households to increase agricultural production and income, in spite of the increasing poverty in the Coastal region.

Many sub-counties in Kenya's coastal region are amongst the poorest in the country, where up to 70-80 percent of residents live below the poverty line. Often living beyond the reach of government services, rural families are left without clean drinking water, weak village infrastructure and limited access to basic education and healthcare. In addition, geographical and climatic characteristics leave them to cope with drought, dependant on degraded natural resources for survival. This has created living conditions that are particularly detrimental as the majority of residents are small scale farmers who depend on agriculture as their sole source of food and income.

When it was established, the CRSP was meant to complement an already existing project of the Aga Khan Development Network—

the Mombasa Primary Health Care Programme (MPHC). To support MPHC, CRSP implemented interventions that, by stimulating economic and social development, contributed to sustainable and equitable improvements in the livelihoods of poor households at the Coast of Kenya. As a result of the support that CRSP offers, it is referred to by its beneficiaries as sombeza (Mijikenda for "to push up or give a helping hand to those who are already doing something to improve their situation"). This is because communities see CRSP as providing a hand up, not a handout, in the process of improving their livelihoods.

The programme's enterprise activities include four main components: bee-keeping, poultry production, goat rearing and vocational training. Each component engages poor households in small-scale enterprises intended to generate income and improve livelihoods. The process begins when communities identify what resources they feel that they posses, the start-up investment that would be required for a small enterprise and the hours of labor that would be required to run the enterprise. They then determine which, if any, enterprise they would want to engage in.

To diversify enterprise activities and increase employment opportunities, CRSP supports vocational training for youth. Youth have been trained in areas such as shoe making, automobile mechanics, barber, carpentry, dress making, electronics, food production, hair dressing, mobile phone repair, patient care and first aid, screen printing and tailoring. CRSP encourages youth who have received training to start up their own enterprises and links them with microfinance institutions and mentors for support.

CRSP has set up four notice boards or Community Resource Centers to disseminate information among the community. To further aggregate this information, CRSP is currently implementing a Community Knowledge Centre in Mariakani. The centre would have 15 computers to be used by farmers to access market prices and devolved funding, by youth for computer skills training and by community members to access CRSP documentation. The Coastal Rural Support Programme has achieved all the above by working with communities through Village Development Organizations as well as other development agencies including the government of Kenya. (Aga Khan Foundation, 2007).

Conclusions

Several efforts have been made both by the government and development partners through a number of strategies to improve rural areas; such strategies are both farm and non-farm. Government efforts are seen in the establishment of institutions to address rural issues as well as funds meant for financing rural initiatives— for instance the youth fund and the women fund.

Many of the rural livelihood diversification strategies are being adopted by rural inhabitants. These strategies are mainly multi-sectoral, although many are still agriculture related. In areas where such strategies have been adopted there has been significant positive change in the lives of the adopters.

Despite the many challenges faced in the rural areas, the urge to change and subsequently improve rural areas is evident from the several attempts made by the government of Kenya and development partners especially in Kenya's arid and semi-arid areas. This is evidenced by the Coastal Rural Support Programme and the Marsabit project in north eastern region.

Capacity building through trainings and extension service are the key drivers to the adoption and implementation of rural development strategies. Government ministries and departments as well as non-governmental organizations are instrumental in providing the same to facilitate faster uptake of innovations by intended beneficiaries.

Recommendations

Whereas a number of strategies undertaken both by the government and development partners, have registered significant contributions to rural development, not much has been done to ensure their sustainability to yield continued results. For this to be realized, capacity building of beneficiaries through trainings and provision of extension services need strengthening. In addition, income generating activities are key to meet recurrent expenditures and ensure operations and maintenance costs of rural development projects are within the ability of the beneficiaries.

Deliberate investments by national and county governments in productive sectors in the rural areas is an incentive to attract investors. Such investments could be jointly funded by governments and the private sector through public-private partnerships. These could include establishment of processing/packaging industries, commercial banks where the government is a major shareholder, construction of water dams for power generation, irrigation and industrial purposes. Processing factories such as Kenya Meat Commission need to be established in all the pastoralist areas in Kenya to enable pastoralists sell their livestock at higher prices and use the proceeds to improve their lives.

Capacity building of rural inhabitants by government and development partners on essential skills areas such as production as well as marketing of goods and services is required. Such could be done through organized community meetings, workshops and seminars to include all categories of rural people. Topical issues such as project feasibility studies, project appraisal, project management and diversification options should be included in the training sessions. Other skills areas include; time management, contract management especially with regard to supply of goods to businesses enterprises or organizations, risk management and resource management.

The role played by agricultural extension services cannot be over-emphasized. The government needs to strengthen the provision of these services by deploying staff both in crop and animal production sectors to the lowest levels to enhance quick service delivery to the farmers. Additionally, provision of the necessary equipment and drugs should be guaranteed. The ultimate goal in this should be enhancement of production using modern techniques, high yielding crop varieties and animal breeds.

Development of infrastructure is key to diversification efforts in rural areas; consequently, the government should invest more in the same. Roads, energy and water remain the key infrastructure required to facilitate transportation of inputs, products to the market, processing of produce, and storage of products, spur the development of small and medium enterprises and enable the growth of agriculture especially through irrigation.

One of the impediments to rural development is limited capital. To overcome this challenge, the government and development partners in rural areas like non-governmental organizations need to introduce or expand existing credit products to rural people to facilitate the acquisition of capital to either invest in agriculture or other ventures to improve their wellbeing. The loan products should be advanced to rural people at affordable interest rates. An example is World Vision, which currently advances loans to organized groups to start businesses through its subsidiary – Kadet. Other organizations could use a similar model to advance loans to rural people.

Cooperatives over decades have acted as vehicles of development in rural as well as urban areas. Agricultural, marketing, credit, arts and crafts, housing, wholesale/retail co-operatives have existed to benefit both members and consumers of their services/products in rural and urban areas. These cooperatives contribute directly to the development of rural areas by providing markets for their produce, directly and indirectly providing employment to the rural people as well as contributing to the development of rural infrastructure. The government should therefore create awareness in the rural areas on the relevance of cooperatives in rural development and encourage rural inhabitants to form cooperatives. The government should also provide incentives to cooperatives in areas such as subsidizing the price of their inputs.

References

Aga Khan Foundation (2007) Rural Development in Kenya: Coastal Rural Support Programme. Aga Khan Development Network. Nairobi.

Barrett, C. B., Reardon, T. and Webb, P. (2001) *Non-farm income diversification and household livelihood strategies in rural Africa*: Concepts, dynamics, and policy implications. Food Policy, 26(4), pp.315-331.

Chambers, R., and Conway, G., (1992). *Sustainable rural livelihoods*: practical concepts for the 21st Century. Discussion Paper 296. IDS, Sussex.

Elliot F.,Martha N. and Eric A. R. (2011) *Seeking Alternative Livelihoods in Northern Kenya:*

Costs and Benefits in Health and Nutrition. Paper presented at the International conference on the Future of Pastoralism. University of Sussex, 21-23 March 2011.

Ellis, F (1998) *Household livelihood strategies and rural livelihood diversification.* Journal of Development Studies, 35 (1) (1998), pp. 1–38.

Ellis, F (2000) *Rural Livelihoods and Diversity in Developing Countries.* Oxford University Press: Oxford (2000).

Kenya, Republic of (1964) *National Development Plan.* Nairobi: Government Printer.

Kenya, Republic of. (1965) *African Socialism and its Application to Planning in Kenya.* Nairobi: Government Printer.

Kenya, Republic of. (1999) *Poverty Reduction Strategy Plan (1999-2015)*. Nairobi: Government Printer.

Kenya, Republic of. (2002) *Kenya Rural Development Strategy. Nairobi*: Government Printer. Kenya, Republic of. (2003) *Constituencies Development Fund.* Nairobi: Government Printer.

Kenya, Republic of. (2003) *Economic recovery Strategy for Wealth and Employment Creation 2003-2007.* Nairobi: Government Printer.

Kenya, Republic of. (2005) *The Forest Act, 2005.* Nairobi: Government Printer.

Kenya, Republic of. (2005) *Economic Survey.* Nairobi: Government Printer.

Kenya, Republic of. (2007) *Kenya Vision 2030.* Nairobi: Government Printer. Muhammad I, Humayun K, Dawood J, and Nafees A (2014), *Livelihood Diversification: A Strategy for Rural Income Enhancement.* Journal of Finance and Economics, 2(5), pp. 194-198.

Niehof, A. (2004) *The significance of diversification for rural livelihood systems.* Food Policy 29, pp. 321-38.

Niehof, A., and Price, L.L., (2001). *Rural livelihood systems*: a conceptual framework.

Wageningen-UPWARD *Series on Rural Livelihoods no. 1.* WU-UPWARD, Wageningen, The Netherlands.

Nyoro, J. (2002). *Agriculture and Rural Growth in Kenya.* Tegemeo Institute. Nairobi.

Parker, J. C and Torres, T. R (1994) *Micro and Small Scale Enterprise in Kenya.* Results of the 1993 National baseline Survey. GEMINI Technical Report No. 75. Bethesda, Md. Development Alternatives, Inc.

Scoones, I. (1998) *Sustainable Rural Livelihoods*, a Framework for Analysis. IDS Working Paper 72.

Thorne, P. and J. Tanner (2001). *Analysis of Resource Use in Mixed Farming Systems.* System-wide Livestock Programme. Nairobi: ILRI.

Vincze, D (2012) *Understanding how intra-household and extra household gender relations influence women's choice of off-farm activities in Western Kenya*: An activity diversification in Rural Kenya. Unpublished M.A Thesis.

CHAPTER SEVEN

Labor Policies and Gender Inclusiveness in Kenya: Challenges and Remedies

Moses Mutiso and Jamin Masinde

Introduction

The principle of gender mainstreaming was initially developed by feminist development practitioners in the 1970s (Moser, 1993). It was then launched at the UN Fourth World Conference on Women in Beijing in 1995 (UN, 1995). Its origins lie especially in the context of feminist work within development, where different ways of including gender equity in the development processes had long been explored (Moser, 1993; Jahan, 1995; Kabeer, 2003). Gender equality is a development objective in its own right (World Bank, 2012). It is also instrumental for poverty reduction and achievement of development goals. A significant volume of research has established that gender inequality is adverse to human development and leads to economically inefficient outcomes (FEMNET, 2008; Economic Commission for Africa, 2009).

Globally, gender mainstreaming has been and is still championed by the United Nations. UN agencies including the UN Women, UNFPA and UNDP have invested in assisting UN member states reform their public planning and budgeting processes. For instance, UN Women have made significant contribution towards this by building political support, developing technical resources and capacity, generating good practice and increasing accountability, to gender equality (UN Women, 2010).

Within South Asia, most countries have made efforts to achieve gender equality by improving the socio-economic status of women through formulation of action-based policies (United Nations Economic and Social Commission for Asia and the Pacific, 2003). In India, feminist economists were utilized to engender the 2007-2012 India development plans. Consequently, gender equality goals are mainstreamed in all sectors (Planning Commission Government of India, 2010). In Nepal, for instance, the National Planning Commission examined structural obstacles to women's participation in the development process. Corrective measures were then taken in policy, legal and institutional frameworks (Guha, 2003). As a result gender issues have been integrated into the formal education and reproductive health system (UNFPA, 2007).

In Africa, states have committed to several instruments that promote gender equality. Consequently, African governments have established diverse mechanisms; including, policies, laws and institutions for gender mainstreaming (United Nations Economic Commission for Africa, 2009; Owulu, 2011). However, while there are so many instruments expressing the formal commitments of African governments to gender equality and mainstreaming, translating these theoretical promises into concrete action remains a formidable challenge (Owulu, 2011). For example, at the fifteen years review of Africa's implementation of Beijing Platform for Action in 2009, the outcome was a gloomy depiction of African countries' failure to meet their commitments on gender equality. In particular, many African countries had been unable to address gender issues in poverty reduction papers, public service appointments and in peace building processes among others (United Nations Economic Commission for Africa 2009). Generally, implementation of gender policies is still rather slow and uneven (Economic Commission for Africa, 2010).

However, successes can be observed in countries such as South Africa, Mozambique, Tanzania and Rwanda (United Nations Economic Commission for Africa 2010). In Tanzania, for instance, the Ministries of Planning and Finance have provided guidelines to all sector Ministries on mainstreaming gender into their budgets. Gender mainstreaming is also considered within the framework of the Public Expenditure Review processes at both central and decentralized levels (United Nations Economic Commission for Africa, 2009).

Gender Equality and Mainstreaming in Kenya

Gender mainstreaming is a pre-requisite for poverty reduction and sustainable development. The United Nations Economic and Social Council (ECOSOC July 1997) defined the concept of gender mainstreaming as: "...the process of assessing the implications for women and men of any planned action, including legislation, policies or programmes, in any area and at all levels. It is a strategy for making the concerns and experiences of women as well as of men an integral part of the design, implementation, monitoring and evaluation of policies and programmes in all political, economic and societal spheres, so that women and men benefit equally, and inequality is not perpetuated. The ultimate goal of mainstreaming is to achieve gender equality..."

Gender equality was officially recognized as a global goal for economic growth and poverty reduction by the world community (in the Charter of United Nations) in 1945. It was adopted on 7th November 1967 by the UN General Assembly of the Declaration on Convention of the Elimination of All forms of Discrimination against Women (CEDAW) and entered to force as an international treaty on the 10th Anniversary in 1989. The spirit of the CEDAW is rooted in the goals of the United Nations: "to reaffirm faith in fundamental human rights, in the dignity and worth of the human person, in the equal rights of men and women". This has been confirmed by subsequent international and regional treaties, conventions and agreements/instruments that promote gender equality and gender equity of which Kenya is a signatory.

Kenya has also adopted and ratified several international instruments on gender equity. These include the Convention on the Elimination of All Forms of Discrimination against Women, the Beijing Platform for Action and the Millennium Development Goals among others (ADB, 2007). Several initiatives in line with the international instruments on gender have been taken. Prominent is the adoption of a National Policy on Gender and Development in the year 2000. The goal of the policy is to facilitate the mainstreaming of the needs and concerns of men and women in the development process (GOK, 2000). The five year medium term plan (2008-2012), which implements Vision 2030, commits to the introduction of gender mainstreaming into all government policies plans and programmes (NCGD, 2009).

Kenya signed and ratified CEDAW in 1984; the BPFA in 1995; is committed to MDGs (2000) which are consistent with the 12 critical areas of concern in the BPA; the resolution of the African Union Summit (September 2004) on employment creation and poverty alleviation; Convention of the Rights of Children (CRC), 1989; United Nations Declaration on Violence Against Women (1993); International Conference on Population and Development(ICPD),1994; Nairobi Forward Looking Strategies for the Advancement of Women (NFLS), 1985; and NEPAD-Peer review mechanisms, African Union(AU) and the East African Community(EAC) Partnership Treaty; among others. In addition, Kenya has ratified two core labor standards of the ILO: Convention No.100 on equal pay for work of equal value and Convention No.111 on Discrimination (Employment Occupation Convention, 1968). The commitment of the Government of Kenya to mainstream gender in national development for equitable growth and poverty reduction is evidenced by the establishment of different national machineries with different but complementary roles.

These machineries include establishment of:

1. Special units to address women's issues in home economics, maternal and child health services in 1963.

2. Women's Bureau to integrate women issues into national development in 1976.

3. NGO Coordination Board in 1992 to regulate and harmonize the activities of the NGOs most of which addressed women advancement and the formation of the National Council of the NGOs charged with the coordination of Civil Society Organizations (CSO).

4. Women/ gender desks in all the government ministries under 1994-1996 national development plan.

5. Elevation of Women's Bureau to a department in the Ministry of Gender, Sports, Culture and Social Services (MGSCSS), with its own budgetary allocation.

6. National Commission for Gender and Development established by an Act of Parliament to provide policy guidance and act as the oversight body in terms of appraising performance of government institutions in mainstreaming gender concerns, thereby strengthening the national machineries for gender integration in development in 2004.

7. National anti-FGM Coordinating Committee in 2007.

8. Gender and HIV/AIDS Sub-Committee of the National AIDS Control Council (NACC) in November 2002. It is charged with developing strategies for gender mainstreaming into the Kenya National HIV/AIDS Strategic Plan.

9. Besides these government structures, the women's movement, civil society organizations, private sector, faith-based organizations and other non-state actors continue to provide structures for advancement of women issues and the gender equality discourse.

On the basis of the foregoing background, this paper seeks to discuss strategies for gender mainstreaming policies with regard to the labor force in Kenya.

Policies imperative to Gender Inclusive Labor Force in Kenya

The need to integrate gender issues into national development has been recognized in many government policy pronouncements and commitments reflected by signing and ratifying various instruments, treaties and international conventions. The existing national policies and legislations relevant to gender equality and women empowerment in Kenya are analyzed below:

National Policy on Gender and Development, 2000

The overall objective is to ensure women's empowerment and mainstreaming the needs of women, men, girls and boys in all sectors of development in the country so that they can participate and benefit equally from development initiatives. The policy framework underlines the need to focus on empowerment strategies that demonstrate understanding of essential linkages within sectors. In addition it recognizes that gender is central and cross-cutting, and therefore programme strategies should incorporate gender equality as a goal. To achieve these, mechanisms aimed at achieving gender balanced development through the removal of disparities between men and women should be put in place. It also underscores social, cultural, legal, and political factors that perpetuate inequalities.

This policy was succeeded by the National Gender and Equality Commission which was established under Act No. 15 of 2011. The Commission shall be a successor in title to the Kenya National Human Rights and Equality Commission established by Article 59 of the Constitution, pursuant to clauses (4) and (5) of that Article. The functions of the Commission shall be to:

1. Promote gender equality and freedom from discrimination in accordance with Article 27 of the Constitution;

2. Monitor, facilitate and advise on the integration of the principles of equality and freedom from discrimination in all national and county policies, laws, and administrative regulations in all public and private institutions;

3. Act as the principal organ of the State in ensuring compliance with all treaties and conventions ratified by Kenya relating to issues of equality and freedom from discrimination and relating to special interest groups including minorities and marginalized persons, women, persons with disabilities, and children;

4. Co-ordinate and facilitate mainstreaming of issues of gender, persons with disability and other marginalized groups in national development and to advise the Government on all aspects thereof;

5. Monitor, facilitate and advise on the development of affirmative action implementation policies as contemplated in the Constitution;

6. Investigate on its own initiative or on the basis of complaints, any matter in respect of any violations of the principle of equality and freedom from discrimination and make recommendations for the improvement of the functioning of the institutions concerned;

7. Work with other relevant institutions in the development of standards for the implementation of policies for the progressive realization of the economic and social rights specified in Article 43 of the Constitution and other written laws;

8. Co-ordinate and advise on public education programmes for the creation of a culture of respect for the principles of equality and freedom from discrimination;

9. Conduct and co-ordinate research activities on matters relating to equality and freedom from discrimination as contemplated under Article 27 of the Constitution;

10. Receive and evaluate annual reports on progress made by public institutions and other sectors on compliance with constitutional and statutory requirements on the implementation of the principles of equality and freedom from discrimination.

Sessional Paper No. 2 of May 2006 on Gender Equality and Development

The Sessional Paper provides a framework for gender mainstreaming and recognizes that socio-cultural attitudes held by men and women, and the socialization process are of great significance in determining the unequal status between men and women. It also recognizes that development initiatives impact differently on men and women and in turn women and men impact differently on development process.

National Poverty Eradication Plan (NPEP, 1999-2015) and Strategy Paper 2001-2004

One of the objectives of the plan is to "strengthen the capacities of the poor and vulnerable groups to earn income, narrow gender and geographical disparities and engender a healthy, better educated and a more productive population". On its part, the paper reaffirms the commitment of the government to address gender issues by providing an engendered poverty diagnosis.

Millennium Development Goals

The key elements of the framework of the Global Agenda in the context of goals, targets and indicators provides a road map for the implementation of the Millennium Declaration signed by UN member states in the year 2000 demonstrating the commitment of the international community to sharply reduce extreme poverty around the world. MDG 3 commits Kenya to promote gender equality and women empowerment as an effective way to combat poverty, hunger and disease and to stimulate development that is truly sustainable.

Economic Recovery Strategy for Wealth and Employment Creation, 2003-2007

It adopts the approach of revamping growth, raising productivity, facilitating private investments and alleviating unemployment while simultaneously addressing the socio-economic agenda and equity concerns. The ERS recognizes that women and men have differential needs, constraints, options, incentives and expectations regarding the outcomes and impacts on macro-economic management. The Investment Programme for ERS (IP-ERS) which facilitates implementation, monitoring and evaluation of ERS provides an opportunity for engendering the outcome indicators of the same.

Medium-Term Expenditure Framework (MTEF)

It recognizes the need to introduce gender indicators in the macro framework and encourages a paradigm shift in resource allocation mechanisms.

Annual Budget Strategy Paper (BSP)

It is formulated to provide estimates of available resources and set firm ministerial ceilings through providing guidance to government ministries and departments on aligning public spending patterns with stated national priorities. This enhances efficiency in public spending, provides an opportunity for gender responsive programming and gender focused implementation.

Kenya Joint Assistance Strategy (KJAS)

This is a statement of 17 development partners, on how to carry forward the Rome and Paris declaration on development aid effectives (March, 2007) by working with the government and the people of Kenya to consolidate and scale up the gains that have been made by ERS with the overarching tangible result of achieving MDGs targets while anchoring on the 3 pillars of Vision 2030, and improving the development impacts of available aid resources.

Vision 2030

It identifies the best options for fulfilling Kenya's enormous potential to realize the goal of becoming a middle income, prosperous country, providing a high quality of life for all our people. This will be achieved by building on the competitive advantages in the key sectors of the economy to substantially expand Kenya's share of the global market. The Vision 2030 singles out three pillars on which to realize our goal. The first pillar seeks to ensure achievement and sustainability of an average economic growth of over 10 percent per annum over the next twenty-five years. The second pillar seeks to build a just and cohesive society, with equitable social development, and a clean and secure environment. The third pillar aims at producing a democratic political system that nurtures issue-based politics, the rule of law, and protects all the rights and freedoms of every individual and society.

Gender and Labor Force Participation in Kenya

The level of gender participation in various sectors of the national economy varies considerably although most of the data is neither complete, accurate, up-to-date nor disaggregated by gender. Data from the 1995-1999 Economic Surveys indicate that men are more heavily involved than women in almost all the key sectoral activities. These data also show that between 1996 and 1998 there was insignificant change in the participation of women in the labor force. The level of female wage employment in most sectors remained at around 25% except in the domestic and education sectors where women constitute about 40% of the total labor force. These two are among the sectors which are traditionally considered as female domains. Women's heavy involvement in domestic work and other forms of non-market production often limits their participation in wage sector employment.

The foregoing is primarily due to the incompatibility between female reproduction roles and modern wage employment. Female labor force participation increased marginally from 28.7% in 1997 to 29.3% in 1998 due largely to the ongoing economic reforms and slight improvements in female access to education (Republic of Kenya 1999b; 1997). Despite this modest increase, the proportion of female employees in the traditionally male dominated industries has remained disproportionately lower than that of men. For example, the proportion of women employed in the building and construction industry declined from 8% in 1996 to 6.3% in 1998 while male participation in this sector increased from 92% to 93.7% over the same period. These are traditionally male dominated sectors where female entry has been fairly restricted.

Female labor force participation in the modern sector has remained below 30% over the last several years. For example, the proportion of female employees in the modern sector increased marginally from 26.2% in 1995 to 29.3% in 2000 while men have continued to hold a disproportionately large share of the modern sector jobs. It is, however, important to note that male participation in modern sector wage employment also decreased from 78.1% in 1990 to 70.7% in 1998 due mainly to the ongoing public sector reforms (Republic of Kenya, 2000).

The agricultural sector can provide a strong base for economic growth, employment creation and poverty reduction in Kenya if proper investment strategies are designed and implemented. About 80% of the women in Kenya live and work in the rural areas. Although farming is the major economic activity and the main source of income for the Kenyan rural population, women contribute about 71% of the agricultural labor, especially in small scale subsistence production.

The proportion of female wage employees in the agricultural sector only rose from 23.3% in 1994 to 24.8% in 1998 (Olum 1999). The low female participation rate in agriculture indicates that most women are confined to the growing of subsistence crops while cash crop production remains predominantly a male responsibility. During the same period (1995-1998), Kenyan women accounted for less than 25% of all wage employees in the agricultural sector despite the fact that the bulk of the rural Kenyan population is female. This low wage employment rate in agriculture points to the fact that much of the female labor contribution in agriculture is unpaid and not reflected in the national statistics.

The total number of people employed in all sectors of the Kenyan economy increased marginally from 4.7 million in 1997 to 5.1 in 1998. Most of the jobs were in the expanding informal sector. Employment in the informal sector expanded from about 2.2 million people in 1995 to 3.4 million in 1998. This expansion points to the significant role that the informal sector has continued to play in job creation, particularly at a time when formal sector employment is steadily decelerating due mainly to the ongoing public sector reforms. One of the problems with data on the informal sector employment is that they are not disaggregated by gender. However, about 52% of the workers in the informal sector were self-employed female entrepreneurs who had set up their own business enterprises in the rural and urban areas. A further 66.5% of the women in the sector were engaged as unpaid family workers compared to 33.5% of their male counterparts.

Although Kenyan women are gradually joining the civil service and making significant strides to develop careers in the previously male-dominated professions, they are still grossly under- represented in senior management and public decision-making positions. In 1995, for example, women held less than 6% of the senior positions in Job Group P and above compared to 24.3% of those in Job Groups A-G. Available data also show that male representation in top management and policy-making positions in the civil service is disproportionately higher than that of females in almost all the ranks. This trend has changed little over the years and the pattern that has emerged is one in which the higher one looks at the civil service hierarchy, the fewer women he/she sees. In 1998, for example, Kenya had only four women permanent secretaries out of a total of thirty, representing only 13.3% of the total establishment. In the same year, there were 38 women Assistant Secretaries Grade III compared to 60 of their male counterparts. Overall, women comprise less than 25% of the Senior Civil Servants in Kenya. This under-representation underlines their minority status in policy-making management positions.

The National Gender and Equality Commission (NGEC) has been closely monitoring appointments and nominations at national and county levels. Of interest is compliance with the constitution provision in accordance with article 81 (b) that says not more than two-thirds of members of elective public bodies shall be of the same gender. Table 1 and Table 2 show a summary of the distribution of men and women by selected public positions. The results indicate a significant gender gap.

Table 1: Appointment at National Level

Position	Total	Male	Female
Cabinet Secretaries	18	12 (67%)	6 (33%)
Principal Secretary	26	19 (73%)	7 (27%)
Chair-Independent Offices	8	7 (87.5%)	1 (12.5%)
Chair-Constitutional Commission	12	7 (58%)	5 (42%)
Head of Parastatals	36	34 (94%)	2 (6%)
Magistrates (Within Nairobi)	96	39 (43%)	57 (57%)

Data Source: NGEC data base, 2013

Table 2: Appointments at County Level for Selected Positions

Position	Total	Male	Female
County Secretaries	46	40 (87%)	6 (13%)
County Assembly Clerks	47	37 (79%)	10 (21%)

Data Source: NGEC data base, 2013

Challenges in Implementing Gender Sensitive Labor Policies in Kenya

Despite the existence of the policies, legislative reforms, plans and programmes, gender disparities still exists in legal, social, economic and political levels of participation in decision making, access to and control of resources, opportunities and benefits. Overall, the implementation of policies and laws has been slow; a situation attributed to gaps in the laws, delayed enactment of gender related legislations and lack of comprehensiveness in content for the same laws e.g. Sexual Offences Act and the Children's Act. Other challenges include:

1. Weak Coordination, harmonization and networking among actors at all levels.

2. Inadequate resources (human and financial).

3. Limited technical capacity and capacity consistency due to deployment / transfers.

4. Lack of Monitoring and Evaluation (M&E) framework.

5. Socio-cultural issues.

6. Misinterpretation of the concept of gender as women rather than women, men, boys and girls.

7. Lack of gender sensitivity at core sector indicators development and targets setting.

8. Lack of budgetary allocation targeting gender activities at sector levels and national budget.

9. Lack of structural linkages at different levels (community to parliament) to facilitate translation of commitment to actions with a sustained momentum.

The biggest challenge facing Kenya today is how to create an enabling environment for gender equality and translating commitments into action with concrete strategies to eliminate persistent gender inequality and recognize the roles of women and men in the development of the country.

Conclusion

Gender disparities in employment opportunities and economic investment patterns in Kenya have continued to widen across all sectors of the economy and at various levels of development intervention. This trend has led to increased unemployment, under-employment, poverty and powerlessness among many Kenyan women. Part of the reason for the persistent inequity is the slow process of mainstreaming gender into employment creation and poverty eradication policies, programmes and strategies in a coordinated, multi-sectoral and crosscutting way. The other reason relates to the existence of social, cultural and structural barriers to effective female participation in the labor force. These and other factors have jointly contributed to the low pay and productivity of women's labor and to their continued under-representation in senior management positions within the public and private sectors.

Although Kenyan women have joined the labor force in large and increasing numbers over the last two decades due to increased access to education, the majority of them are still concentrated in traditional "female occupations" and the informal sector. The urban labor force participation rate for women in Kenya has increased from 30% in the early eighties to 56% in 1995. Despite their growing participation in the workforce, there are still very few women in the top echelons of public decision and policy making positions in Kenya.

Most women in Kenya are concentrated in low paying, low status occupations with poor fringe benefits carried out under poor working conditions and therefore hold very little prospect for poverty reduction and upward mobility. On the other hand, the majority of the women in the rural areas spend a great deal of time on low productivity work which has created major income disparities between men and women. The reasons for gender disparities in employment opportunities include segregation in the labor market, social attitudes towards women, inadequate capacity on the part of women in terms of their knowledge and skills and lack of gender responsive policies and programmes.

Although a large number of women have entered the labor force over the last two decades they are mainly concentrated in low-status, low paying occupations such as teaching, nursing, secretarial work and domestic services. Some of the jobs held by women are viewed as extensions of their traditional roles. These perceptions about the suitability of men and women for particular types of jobs restrict or exclude most women from entering higher-status, more lucrative fields of employment as well as senior political and management positions.

The prevalence of gender segregation in the labor market has created a major barrier to the expansion of women's employment opportunities leading to a skewed employment pattern in which women are under-represented in the modern wage sector with decreasing incomes. Gender stereotyping of jobs is another major barrier to the expansion of women's employment opportunities leading to gender segmentation of the labor market (Suda 1991; Anker and Knowles 1986).

Although the informal sector has a tremendous potential for employment creation and has some businesses which have been developed into sustainable private enterprises, most female workers in the sector continue to experience several challenges. Among the major constraints facing women in the informal sector are limited access to credit facilities, inadequate education and skills training, registration and licensing, inability to pay rent and operate in authorized premises, lack of proper organizational structure, and inadequate access to markets for their products. In view of these constraints coupled with other social and cultural barriers to women's empowerment, many of the activities in the informal sector do not generate enough income to reduce female poverty.

The limited participation of women in the public sector employment at top management levels is linked to a range of social, cultural, political and economic factors. These include women's limited opportunities such as illiteracy and low educational levels, their concentration in unpaid household work, the public's perception of women's management abilities, lack of the necessary skills required by the modern labor market and cultural ideologies which prescribe appropriate gender roles. The other factors associated with the prevailing gender bias in the formal sector employment are women's limited control over productive resources and limited participation in political and economic institutions (Beneria and Bisnath 1996). These limitations have led to growing gender inequalities in access to and distribution of employment opportunities, income and power. These cultural and institutional biases have, in fact, contributed to the prevalence of structural poverty among women.

There is need for an Affirmative Action to eliminate gender imbalance in the Kenyan Civil Service, particularly at the upper echelons of power and privilege. This gender disparity is pervasive in all the other sectors within the civil service, including the Judiciary. Women judges are a distinct minority in Kenya.

A number of employment promotion policies and poverty reduction programmes which have been designed and implemented to assist the poor in Kenya have tended to by-pass women essentially because they have not paid sufficient attention to gender division of labor, systems of resource allocation and gendered dimensions of poverty. The absence of gender desegregated data by public and private sector institutions is one of the major constraints to the design and implementation of gender-responsive poverty eradication programmes.

Way Forward

Given the fact that women are the majority of the rural population and the poor in Kenya and are still mainly concentrated in agriculture and the informal sector, it is important that ongoing poverty reducing employment strategies target women to promote rural and agricultural development as well as non-farm employment.

Economic growth and other anti-poverty policies and programmes are necessary but not sufficient conditions for poverty eradication and employment creation. The Government should formulate policies and enact legislation to explicitly outlaw gender discrimination in employment.

In order to accelerate entry into the informal sector and generate jobs that can reduce poverty, the government, in collaboration with other development partners, should put in place a legal framework and regulatory mechanisms to promote the role of the informal sector in employment creation as articulated in a number of government policy documents such as the Sessional Paper No. 1 of 1986, and the report of the Presidential Committee on Employment of 1991. In addition to these kinds of policy review, increased access to credit facilities to women entrepreneurs and proper targeting of the types of informal sector activities operated by women is one of the strategies to reduce poverty.

National Commission on Gender and Development (NCGD)

It is an oversight body in terms of appraising performance of government institutions in regard to mainstreaming gender concerns. It is observed that according to the TOR of commissioners in the National policy on Gender and Development, the terms of service are not defined, thus the slow pace of service delivery. To re-energize NCGD for optimum impact, it is recommended that the commissioners serve on a full time basis with a security of tenure and performance contracts. It is noted that, there is an overlap and conflict in the interpretation of structure, mandate, power and functions of NCGD as set out in the Act and the roles of the Department of Gender Social Services. There is need for a comprehensive review of the Act.

In addition to the TOR in Sessional Paper No.2 of 2006, it is recommended that the NCGD scans the environment for gender issues and opportunities external to the mainstream sectors to ensure due process and follow-up for consequent implementation.

Department of Gender and Social Services

It is assigned the responsibility of improving the efficiency and effective integration of gender dimensions in future policy formulation, planning and implementation. It is therefore responsible for providing technical advice on gender mainstreaming through the national sectoral approach and implementation of the recommendations of international conventions. It also recommended that the Department of Gender and Social Services serves as the technical arm of the NCGD to provide harmony and direction on gender issues from other ministries, parastatals and institutions of higher learning.

Profiling gender through effective media strategy

This will be done through partnership with the media to sustain gender mainstreaming momentum and highlight gender issues at all levels and in all sectors.

Research and information dissemination

Continuous gender research will be carried out in collaboration with the Kenya National Bureau of Statistics to produce sex disaggregate data to inform policy development. Existing data will be analyzed, disseminated and utilized among staff of all ministries. In addition, creation of partnerships with Civil Society Organizations will be emphasized to facilitate information dissemination to the grassroots and continuous follow-up.

Monitoring and Evaluation Mechanism

There is need to develop and operationalize M & E framework to track progress, document experiences, challenges, lessons learned and establish impact and review the achievements in attaining gender equality.

Resource Mobilization

This will be realized through adequate resource allocation to the Ministry, Department of Gender and Social Services, and the National Commission on Gender and Development. In addition, budgeting process need to be engendered with adequate allocations at the sector ministry and the Commission. The mobilization of non-budget support from the community, development partners and other sources will expedite achievement of mainstreaming gender into national development. On the other hand, the timely preparation and sharing of itemized budget by the MoGSCSS with potential partners will suffice in improving the resource base.

References

Abagi, O. (1999). *Gender Responsive Policy Analysis for Poverty Reducing Employment Strategies for Africa*: From Theory to Practice. Nairobi: Kenya.

Anker, R., & Knowles, J. C. (1986). *Sex Inequalities in Urban Employment in the Third World*. London: Macmillan Press.

Beneria, L., & Bisnath, S. (1996). *Gender and Poverty: An Analysis for Action*. Gender in Development Monograph Series No. 2, UNDP.

Brettell, C. B., & Sargent, C. F. (1993). *Gender in cross-cultural Perspective*. Englewood Cliffs; New Jersey: Prentice Hall.

Commonwealth Plan of Action (1995). The 1995 Commonwealth Plan of Action on Gender and Development. A commonwealth Vision for Women towards the Year 2000. Common Wealth Secretariat.

Jacobs, J. (1994). *Gender Inequality at Work*. Philadelphia: University of Pennsylvania.

Jahan, Rounaq (1995). *The Elusive Agenda*: Mainstreaming Women in Development. London: Zed Books.

Kabeer, Naila (2003). *Gender Mainstreaming in Poverty Eradication and the Millennium Development Goals*. London: Commonwealth Secretariat.

Minas, A. (1993). *Gender Basics: Feminists Perspectives on Women and Men. Belmont*, California: Wadsworth Publishing Company.

Miller, C., & Razavi, S. (1998). *Gender Analysis Alternative Paradigms*. Gender in Development Monograph Series No. 6, UNDP.

Moser, Caroline (1993) *Gender Planning and Development: Theory, Practice and Training*. London: Routledge.

Olum, G. H. (1999). *Mainstreaming of Gender and Employment Concerns*. Paper presented at Strategic Planning Workshop.

Okumu, M. (1999). *Status of Women's Participation in the Labour Market in Kenya*. November, 11th 1999. Nairobi.

Republic of Kenya (1996a). *Kenya Population Census 1989: Labour Force.* Analytical Report Volume IX. CBS, Ministry of Planning and National Development, Nairobi, Kenya.

_1996b. *Welfare Monitoring Survey II 1994.* Basic Report. CBS – Ministry of Planning and National Development. Nairobi: Kenya.

_1997. *National Development Plan 1997–2001.* Nairobi: Government Printer.

_1999a. *Kenya National Human Development Report.* UON. Ministry of Planning and National Development. Nairobi: Kenya.

_1999b. *Economic Survey.* CBS. Ministry of Planning and National Development. Nairobi: Kenya.

_1999c. *Kenya Population and Housing Census,* Vol 1. Nairobi: Central Bureau of Statistics.

_2000 *Economic Survey.* Nairobi: Central Bureau of Statistics.

Stolen, K. A. (1991). *Introduction: Women, Gender and Social Change.* In: Gender and Change in Developing Countries, Kristi Anne Vaa (ed.), pp. 1-10. Norwegian University Press.

Suda, C. (1991). *Social Cultural and Demographic Factors in Female Labour Force Participation in Kenya. In: Population and Human Resources Development Planning in Kenya,* pp. 354-273. Ministry of Manpower Development and Employment, Nairobi: Kenya.

United Nations (1996). *Platform for Action and the Beijing Declaration. Fourth World Conference on Women.* Department of Public Information, New York.

United Nations Development Programme (1997). Guidance Note on gender Mainstreaming.

Vaa, K. A. (1991). *Gender and Change in Developing Countries.* Norwegian University Press.

Women's Bureau (1999). Kenya: *The Role of Women in Economic Development.* Nairobi: Government Printers.

CHAPTER EIGHT

Transparency and Accountability in Kenya: A Review of the Institutional Framework for Public Service Delivery

Ezekiel Mwenzwa

Introduction

The struggle for independence before the 1960s in Kenya and the eventual self-rule in 1963 was geared towards democratic transition from colonialism and into internal self-rule. It was expected to entrench democracy, accountability in governance, respect for human rights and other positive values of governance in the country. Indeed, it was expected that the newly created institutions of the presidency, premiership, judiciary, legislature and other public sector bureaucracies deemed as the pillars of western democracies would ensure maximum accountability and transparency in public service (Wanyande, Omosa and Ludeki, 2007). This never came to be as expected though, given that the independent government inherited colonial structures intact and manipulated them to their advantage (Kanyinga and Njoka, 2002; Mwenzwa and Bunei, 2012). To legalize the malpractices, the independence constitution was mutilated through politically expedient amendments that consolidated more and more powers on the presidency to the disadvantage of other governance institutions. The foregoing apparently sowed the seeds of discord and resistance mounted largely by citizens, organizations and the civil society.

Consequential from the foregoing, there emerged court poets and political support hawkers, which in effect threw to irrelevance the idea of transparency and accountability in Kenya. The result was a system of governance whose accountability was wanting as democratic institutions were dwarfed by informal networks that emerged and seemingly became the governance archetype. Wanyande, Omosa and Ludeki (2007) have summarized the accountability and transparency challenges that faced the independent government thus, Governmental representation and accountability, respect for rules and ethics, just distribution of resources for prosperity and moderation of social and political relations including conflict   resolution. (Ibid, 2007, 2)

Indeed, corruption in the public service during the post-colonial era became so endemic that it attracted a lot of academic theorizing and, most importantly, strained relations between the government and the donor community to the deterioration of public service (Wanyande, Omosa and Ludeki, 2007; Kibwana, Wanjala and Owiti, 1996; Kidombo, 2006; Mwenzwa, 2013). It became a serious bottleneck to development and with the World Bank/International Monetary Fund (IMF) engineered Structural Adjustment Programmes (SAPs) of the early 1980s; public service delivery nose-dived. Part of the problem was the Big Man Syndrome in the name of the president, whose word including roadside declarations became law on the spot. It is this unilateral decision-making that worked to blur the work of democratic institutions of governance such as the Judiciary and the National Assembly that would have checked the excesses of the executive arm of the government.

The foregoing dictatorship on the part of the ruling elite substantially squeezed the governance playground to its limits, almost rendering irrelevant the idea of participatory democracy. At the same time, transparency and accountability as governance archetypes were reduced to political rhetoric and mere paperwork as assertiveness and whistle blowing was met with dire consequences including detention without trial. It would seem that Kenya was actually getting to a situation, although not like Amin Dada's Uganda in the 1970s, reminiscent of George Orwell's Animal Farm (Orwell, 1945; Sembuya, 2009). The greed for accumulation of property by the political elite necessitated the making of many politically expedient decisions in their favor, in effect making transparency and accountability lose meaning.

The Animal Farm that Kenya became was justified and entrenched by the executive through appointment of regional political friends to core government departments like the Judiciary, Central Bank of Kenya, Kenya Revenue Authority, the military and the police. A clique of powerful individuals became Kenya's Board of Governors, and manipulated power to the exclusion of the majority, while extending undeserved favors to themselves and close friends. It was a real bourgeoisie exploiting the proletariat, with the latter protesting the excesses of the former in a Marxian conflict framework (Abrahams, 1982). Subsequent civic engagement including the clamor for multi-party democracy made change imminent even as the political elite mounted concerted resistance.

Public procurement, which is a major avenue for corruption and deterioration of public service, was shrouded in secrecy in which case officials could tender for services in their respective departments and eventually award themselves the tenders through their proxies (Cooksey, Mullei and Mwabu, 2000). The foregoing radicalized the marginalized majority and the clamor for legislative reforms eventually led to the introduction of multi-party democracy in the early 1990s. This paved the way for piecemeal citizen participation although mega corruption and related malpractices remained, but mutated. On their part, transparency and accountability remained largely peripheral as governance ideals during which infamous corruption scandals like Goldenberg and Anglo-Leasing were executed by the ruling politico-economic elite. One way of sustaining the malpractices was through a scheme that saw the Circulation of Elites in Vilfredo Pareto's framework of analysis. For example, regional political kingpins were easily replaced by their sons in subsequent elections or in important public corporate bodies in case of retirement.

However, the foregoing issues still persist and continue to affect the social fabric leading to undesirable civic engagement including negative ethnicity and violence (Barasa, 2013). The climax was perhaps the 2007/2008 post-election violence that saw more than one thousand people dead and many more displaced and dispossessed of their property (Mwenzwa, 2013). It is this violence that is the basis on which three prominent Kenyans have been arraigned at the International Criminal Court under the Rome Statute. Caveat is placed to the effect that the allusion to the three Kenyans in this paper does not in any way presume their guilt or innocence. Nonetheless, it is clear that corruption and its aftermaths are so convoluted and the casualty is normally public service delivery.

It is to be noted that transparency and accountability are matters of ethics that require a minimum threshold of behavioral transformation among individuals, institutions and organizations in terms of how they run their affairs. The foregoing transformation, if it has to take root sustainably must be enforced through legislation and monitored periodically to gauge conformity in line with set ethical principles whether in the public or private sector. In Kenya, the foregoing is anchored and echoed in every public service administration document including development plans, policies, regulations and legislation alike. It is perhaps the Kenya Vision 2030 (Republic of Kenya, 2007) that captures the foregoing most vividly. In this case, the Kenyan vision for public service is to have a citizen-focused and result-oriented public service (Republic of Kenya, 2007, 24). It is on the basis of this vision that several initiatives in Kenya have been put in place to revitalize public service delivery particularly through legislation and policy directions.

Prerequisites to Transparency and Accountability

Kenya recognizes that an effective public service is a prerequisite to socio-economic development of the country as envisaged in the Kenya Vision 2030 (Republic of Kenya, 2007; 2008). As a result of this realization many measures have been instituted to revamp the public service and ensure effective and efficient public service delivery that is accountable to the public. One way of ensuring the foregoing is to mainstream the public need and satisfaction in the development of policies and guidelines through incorporating them in governance structures to ensure their active participation. Active involvement in development planning and related decision-making therefore acts as an important ingredient to transparency and accountability as it also inculcates ownership among the citizenry. Mainstreaming public needs, interests and satisfaction though ought to be based on a sound and participatory assessment of the same.

Information dissemination, its accessibility and understanding also acts as an important avenue to reinforce transparency and accountability. It is on the basis of appropriate information that people make informed decisions to advance human welfare. This information should be provided to the public service human resource as well as the members of the public in order to ensure that actions from either side are based on grounded ethical standards and information. However, the top-down mentality among some government technocrats has largely worked to deny the citizenry the chance to interrogate and internalize government plans and their implementation, which has been a serious setback against transparency and accountability. However, with the enactment of the Constitution of Kenya, 2010 and several enabling legislation, it is expected that transparency and accountability will be improved substantially. Nevertheless, legislation on its own may not necessarily ensure transparency and accountability in the absence of related functional structures and firm political drive.

It is a prerequisite of effective service delivery to continually improve the skills of the public service human resource through performance-focused training and re-training in order to orient it to quality service delivery. Continuous training aimed at skills improvement must be seen as a precursor to improved and sustainable performance which in turn is expected to institutionalize ethics in public service delivery. This is expected to act as a key pillar of transparency and accountability. Indeed, skills-based training should be institutionalized in public service and such training carried out by competent authorities with strict requirements regarding implementation, monitoring and evaluation of the skills imparted. Short of such training, public service delivery is expected to nose-dive and by extension transparency and accountability ideals. These in turn make quality service delivery by public institutions difficult.

Leadership, the process of social influence in which one person is able to enlist the aid and support of others in the accomplishment of a common task remains a key pillar for transparency and accountability in public service. As the ultimate way to enlist people's support, it contributes to openness that is necessary for the masses to spotlight public service and ensure active involvement of all stakeholders. A democratic leadership ensures the development of ideals that work to ensure transparency and accountability and by extension the provision of quality public service in line with set standards. For this reason therefore, sound, transparent and impartial leadership becomes an important prerequisite to the institutionalization of transparency and accountability, not only in the public sector, but also across the board. In the absence of such leadership, the resultant environment breeds impunity and related unprofessional conduct that work to impede the institutionalization of transparent and accountable institutions. In such a case, public service deteriorates with human welfare moving from worse to worst.

Another key prerequisite of revitalizing transparency and accountability in public service and related to leadership is adherence to the rule of law. The Kenya Vision 2030 in this regard aims at adherence to the rule of law applicable to modern, market-based economy in a human rights-respecting state (Republic of Kenya, 2007, 132). Within the rule of law, state officials and agents as well as individuals and private entities are accountable to clearly defined and evenly applied laws. In addition, the process by which the laws are enacted, administered and enforced provides equity to all while at the same time justice is delivered by a competent and representative authority. It is the rule of law and its adherence that can ensure transparency and accountability especially when its letter and spirit are implemented backed by a firm political will.

Peace building and conflict management remain key indicators of development the world over, given their ability to make the environment conducive for constructive civic engagement and nation building. It is through engagement that democratic institutions of governance emerge to invigorate transparency and accountability. Indeed, the absence of peace is a recipe for civil strife and negative civic engagement, which overshadows transparent and accountable institutions of governance.

Related to the foregoing is the institutional framework, yet another important precondition for enhancing transparency and accountability, given its role in enforcing public service delivery regulations. Although the institutional framework when left alone remains a bulldog, its deterrence and guiding role in public service delivery cannot be overstated.

Institutional Framework for Transparency and Accountability in Kenya

The institutional framework for transparency and accountability in the Public Service of Kenya consists of the Constitution of Kenya, 2010, laws, policies and attendant guidelines with regard to the conduct of public business. Altogether, they aim to cushion the public against malpractices by public officials in cahoots with individuals and institutions in the private sector. Such malpractices especially corruption have the potential to divert resources meant for the public good into use that is generally sectarian in nature. Chapter Six of the Constitution of Kenya on Leadership and Integrity obligates public officers to make objective and impartial decisions with unqualified integrity and honesty in order to bring honor and pride in the offices held. In a nutshell, the Constitution of Kenya, 2010, creates many institutions for enforcing transparency and accountability in the Public Service of Kenya as discussed in the succeeding paragraphs. In general, the Public Service Commission of Kenya remains the engine on which public service revolves with regard to human resource management.

The Constitution of Kenya, 2010 creates the Public Service Commission to see to it that the institutional framework is implemented within the rank and file of the public service. This is a constitutional entity established by Article 233(1) of the Constitution of Kenya, 2010 with the responsibility of among others, ensuring high standards of professional ethics, efficient, effective and economic use of resources and accountability for administrative acts. Other responsibilities include transparency in the provision of timely and accurate information to the public, good governance, integrity, transparency and accountability. Nonetheless, the commission has also delegated this role to other public institutions and departments including university councils and parastatal boards.

In order to ensure adherence to the public service regulations and requirements, the Parliament of Kenya enacted the Public Officer Ethics Act of 2003, Anti-Corruption and Economic Crimes Act of 2003, the Public Procurement and Disposal Act of 2005 and the Leadership and Integrity Act of 2012 among other laws. The most important regulation with regard to public service management is the Civil Service Code of Regulations of 2006 (Republic of Kenya, 2006). This Code of Regulations provides the behavioral standards for all public servants during and after their exit from the service while safeguarding them from unfair labor practices. In particular, it expressly forbids public servants from engaging in businesses that may bring disrepute to the offices that they hold and the government in general. For example, in its preamble, the Code of Regulations avers that,

Public servants will be guided and inspired by a shared vision that the Public Service will be an efficiently performing institution; committed to serving the Public with integrity and utmost courtesy and giving value to the tax payers' money. (Republic of Kenya, 2006, preamble)

In Section G, on Rules of Conduct, the Code of Regulations points out the regulations governing the behavior of public servants that is to be found in the Public Service Commission and the Public Officer Ethics Acts. In particular, it clearly states that,

Each civil servant occupies a special position within the Civil Service and ought to be proud of that position and ensure that his conduct both in public and in private life does not bring the Service into disrepute (Republic of Kenya, 2006, p64).

On its part, the Public Officer Ethics Act (Cap. 183 of the Laws of Kenya) of 2003 (Rev. 2009) while defining a public officer provides for the general code of conduct and ethics for public officers. Under Section 2, the Act defines a public officer as any one employee or member including of the government or its department, in service or undertaking any activities within a public institution set up for the administration of public finances. In particular, the Act requires that the members of the public and fellow officers alike are treated professionally and within the law. In the service to the public and in matters to do with human rights of people, the Act makes reference to Chapter Five of the Constitution of Kenya on the Bill of Rights as the standard on which adherence to human rights should be based. Such adherence to the rule of law is expected to facilitate the development of high moral ideals with regard to transparency and accountability in public service.

The Anti-Corruption and Economic Crimes Act (Cap. 65) of 2003 (Rev. 2009) establishes the Ethics and Anti-Corruption Commission which among others is assigned the role of investigating any matter that constitutes economic crimes or any conduct liable to allow or encourage commission of economic crimes. Other functions include assisting law enforcement agencies to investigate economic crimes and providing advice to parties that may be involved in the prevention of economic crimes. The Commission can also institute civil proceedings against any person for the recovery of property or for compensation and to recover public property that has been determined to have been acquired corruptly. The deterrence measures provided for by this Act are expected to dissuade public servants and the public in general from engaging in practices that constitute economic crimes and hence uphold high moral values. Nevertheless, such elaborate provisions have yet to tame corruption in public service and it would seem that the birds of corruption have resorted to flying without perching since its hunters became sharp shooters, to quote Chinua Achebe's, Things Fall Apart.

To reinforce the foregoing Act among others, the National Assembly enacted the Public Procurement and Disposal Act of 2005 (Cap. 412c) (Rev. 2010) to guide the process of procuring and disposing of public goods in order to minimize underhand deals between public officials and parties within the private sector. The purpose of this Act was to establish procedures for procurement and the disposal of unserviceable, obsolete or surplus stores and equipment by public entities to achieve a number of objectives.

These objectives include maximization of economy and efficiency, promotion of competition and fairness to each competitor and the integrity and fairness of procurement procedures. Other objectives are increasing public confidence in the procurement procedures and facilitating the promotion of local industry and economic development. Most important as far as this work is concerned, the Act aims to revitalize transparency and accountability in public procurement procedures. The foregoing is expected to be achieved through, among others, open and therefore competitive tendering of public goods, stores and services.

The foregoing acts of parliament are amalgamated into the Leadership and Integrity Act of 2012, which aims to put into force and hence actualize Chapter Six of the Constitution of Kenya on Leadership and Integrity. The Act is meant to ensure that public officers respect the values, principles and requirement of the Constitution as set out in various legislative provisions. Section 13 of the Act spells out the ethical and moral requirement for public officers as they dispense public services. Public officers are required to demonstrate honesty of public affairs subjects to the Public Officer Ethics Act, 2003.

In particular, public officers are required not to engage in activities that amount to abuse of office, not to misuse public funds or falsify documents in order to defeat justice. Other requirements include respect for the Bill of Rights as envisaged in Chapter 5 of the Constitution and to desist from committing criminal acts as defined by the Penal Code or any other legislation. In summary, public officers are expected by the Act to internalize and practice the principles governing the conduct of state officers under Article 75 of the Constitution of Kenya, 2010. The foregoing notwithstanding, acting otherwise among public servants is rampant and corruption and related practices are not uncommon.

Although these have not effectively dealt with malpractices that negatively affect sound public service provision, their critical role in scaling them down cannot be gainsaid. Hence, despite the elaborate institutional framework, ethics and integrity are issues of great concern in the Public Service of Kenya as corruption and related malpractices still persist. For example, the Kenya Anti-Corruption Commission (2010) reports that corruption has substantially compromised public service delivery in the health sector as health care fraud, conflicts of interest and other practices take root. On its part, the police service is believed to be the most corrupt in

Kenya, followed by Members of Parliament and local government in that order (Afrobarometer, 2005). In its 2012 Corruption Perception Index Report, Transparency International ranks Kenya among the ten most corrupt out of the 176 countries scored (Transparency International, 2012).

The political-economic elite are the drivers of the fights against corruption and are hence looked upon to ensure transparency and accountability in matters of public interest. However, an assessment of the major scandals involving public resources, particularly land and finances, reveals that the political-economic elite are the engines behind them. The foregoing contradiction brings to question their actual commitment to transparent and accountable governance in the utilization of public resources. This bring us to the conclusion that the institutional framework for transparency and accountability in Kenya and elsewhere is an enormous conspiracy among the elite to hoodwink the masses. Flowing from the foregoing therefore it is safe to see the laws, regulations, policies and institutions put in place to fight corruption and related malpractices simply as elite organized hypocrisy. The foregoing notwithstanding, there are structures that should be in place for sound transparency and accountability to take root, which we now turn to.

Best Practices for Transparency and Accountability

That transparency and accountability are of paramount importance in the running of both public and private affairs is obvious. Its impact is widely felt in society and is best captured by Breuning (2005) thus,

Corruption is a leading cause of human suffering. Funds destined for famine relief and water purification disappear into secret bank accounts. Bribes provoke lapses in the regulation of hazardous materials, airport security, food safety, and road safety. Corruption makes it impossible to sustain the infrastructure required by a modern economy. In the end, it raises prices and lowers service for everyone. (Ibid, 2005, 3)

To counter corruption in Kenya and ensure quality services to the public, Kidombo (2006) proposes that we require a minimum threshold of determination, honesty, high degrees of conviction and courage that it can be done away with. This is what we turn to as we highlight some of the best practices to enhance transparency and accountability and minimize unethical practices in the delivery of public service.

According to Breuning (2005, 2) ignoring corruption means ignoring the damage it does such as wastage of inventive talent, lost investment opportunities, compromised ethical conduct among officers and most important as far as this paper is concerned, less than optimal provision of public services. The foregoing can neither be better said nor can its implications be gainsaid. That actions and inactions by government officers and private individuals have negatively affected public service delivery is not subject for debate. Indeed, the laws, regulations and policies in operation in the country for transparency and accountability are corruptly circumvented leading to wastage and loss of public resources. What is the panacea for this impunity?

It is crystal clear from the foregoing exposé that the institutional framework for transparency and accountability in Kenya is elaborate enough to inculcate the necessary ethical behavior in the private and public sector. This is expected to substantially tame the seemingly runaway corruption and related malpractices. Nonetheless, there is apparently wobbly political will to the same effect given that many of the malpractices that negatively affect public service delivery are perpetrated by public officers. Indeed, it is very difficult to tame corruption given the Circulation of Elites nature in the constitution of one government after the other since independence in 1963. As such, even as Kenya held Jubilee Celebrations in 2013, transparency and accountability within the rank and file of its public service is yet to be institutionalized, at least in deed.

To tame corruption and ensure transparency and accountability in the public service therefore, political commitment and will are not optional. These are expected to inject the necessary ethical conduct among public officers particularly at the top level management and then cascade this to the lowest hierarchy of the public service. The foregoing is also expected to be replicated in the private sector.

Related to the foregoing is the institutionalization of democratic ideals within the Kenya population. This is more so given that dictatorial regimes are known to be highly corrupt, in which transparency and accountability are thrown out of the window. In such cases, human rights abuses and related malpractices become the norm and public service delivery becomes the overall casualty. It is therefore important to strengthen and materially and morally support institutions that ensure accountability and transparency including the judiciary, parliament, county assemblies and investigative organs of the government. This though as argued elsewhere requires political will and commitment in deed. Short of the foregoing, gains towards transparency and accountability in public service becomes effectively cancelled out with service delivery getting a major beating.

Many countries in the world have been seen to tame corruption and related malpractices to levels where their impacts can be said to be substantially inconsequential to public service delivery. How can Kenya learn from such countries? What lessons does Kenya have to learn from such countries? What anti-corruption strategies are in place in these countries? The starting point in this case would be to carry out benchmarking for best practices in developed and rapidly developing economies on the measures they have instituted to tame corruption and institutionalize transparency and accountability in public service delivery. It is through such data that strategies can be implemented to enhance transparency and accountability in public service delivery.

Some recently introduced practices in the public service are yet to be institutionalized in Kenya including performance contracting. Although this has been seen to work well where officers have set targets to achieve within agreed upon timelines, it is yet to be cascaded to the lowest levels of public service. For example, in many public universities performance contracting is yet to be implemented among heads of academic department even though education is an important service by the Government of the Republic of Kenya. Indeed, it is surprising that even though department in universities have work plans, these are yet to translated into performance contract targets. Even where faculties have performance contracts, evaluation is rarely done, which in essence affects public service delivery in the education sector. It is expected that cascading the idea to the lowest cadre of the public service will substantially improve public service delivery and in the process institutionalize transparency and accountability ideals.

Many government activities, programmes and projects are still planned and implemented using the discredited top-down approach. As such, although the institutional framework is clear on participation of all stakeholders, this has been more rhetoric than actual, leading to implementation of activities that do not go along with the needs of the intended beneficiaries. This alienates many would-be beneficiaries who henceforth become passive leading to less than optimum participation and by extension benefits. As a counter measure, it is important that where participation of the would-be beneficiaries is implied, monitoring to this effect should be carried out and bottlenecks to it done away with. In particular, strategies should be put in place such that the voices and opinions of the poor, marginalized, disadvantaged and the vulnerable are not peripheral. This is expected to ensure transparency and accountability in public service delivery given the expected scrutiny that is likely to be subjected to public officers by the masses.

In conclusion, corruption and unethical conduct with regard to public service delivery are so deeply embedded in the Kenyan society that continuous research is highly recommended. Indeed, bearing in mind its consequences, it is important that a training and research institute is set up to study and continuously research on the menace. Such should be a compulsory training for public servants as an induction into the public service. Related to the foregoing is training on patriotism right from early childhood and into working life. This is intended to instill the necessary ethical behavior for public service delivery, not just for those in public service but also in the ranks of the private sector.

References

Abraham, F. M (1982). *Modern Sociological Theory: An Introduction.* New Delhi: Oxford University Press.

Afrobarometer. (2006). *Corruption in Kenya*: Is NARC Fulfilling its Campaign Promise? Afrobarometer Briefing Paper No. 26, January, 2006.

Barasa, F. O. (2013). *Ethnicity: Reflecting on the Challenges and Opportunities in Kenya.* In: International Journal of Professional Practice, 4(1&2): 26-38.

Bennaars, G. A. (1993). *Ethics, Education and Development*: An *Introductory Text for Students in Colleges and Universities.* Nairobi: East African Educational Publishers.

Breuning, L. G. (2005). *Greaseless: How to Thrive without Bribes in Developing Countries.* Oakland: Systems Integrity Press.

Cooksey, B, A. Mullei, and G. Mwabu. (2000). *Forms and Causes of Corruption.* In: Mullei, A. (Ed). *The Link between Corruption and Poverty*: *Lessons from Kenya Case Studies.* Nairobi: African Center for Economic Growth.

Kanyinga, K, and Njoka, J. M. (2002). *The Role of the Youth in Politics: The Social Praxis of Party Politics among the Urban Lumpen in Kenya.* In: African Journal of Sociology, 5(1): 89-111.

Kenya Anti-Corruption Commission. (2010). *Sectoral Perspectives on Corruption in Kenya: The Case of Public Health Care Delivery.* Nairobi: Kenya Anti-Corruption Commission.

Kenya, Republic of. (2003). *The Public Officer Ethics Act 2003.* Nairobi: Government Press.

_ (2006). *Code of Regulations.* Nairobi: Ministry of Public Service

_ (2007). *Kenya Vision 2030.* Nairobi: Ministry of Planning, National Development and Vision 2030.

_(2008). *Kenya Vision 2030:* First Medium Term Plan, 2008-2012. Nairobi: Ministry of Planning, National Development and Vision 2030.

Kidombo, P. K. (2006). *Targeting Corruption: The Booming Business. Nairobi:* Sino Printers and Publishers.

Kibwana, K., S. Wanjala, and O. Owiti. (1996). *The Anatomy of Corruption in Kenya:* Legal, Political and Socio-Economic Perspectives. Nairobi: Claripress.

Katumanga, M and M. Omosa. (2007). *Leadership and Governance in Kenya.* In: Wanyande, P., Omosa, M & C. Ludeki (Eds). *Governance and Transition Politics in Kenya. Nairobi:* University of Nairobi Press, 55-80.

Mwenzwa, E. M and & J. K. Bunei. (2012). *The National Land Policy: Its Provisions and Implications on Food Production in Kenya.* In: International Journal of Professional Practice, 3(1&2): 5-12.

Mwenzwa, E. M. (2013). *Corruption in the Utilization of Constituencies Development Fund:* Implications and Remedies. In: Ontita, E. G., Mwenzwa, E. M. & Misati, J. A. (Eds).*Themes in Contemporary Community Development in Africa: A Multi-Disciplinary Perspective.* Pau: Delizon & Elvee Academic Book Publishers, 214-230.

Orwell, G. (1945). *Animal Farm. Essex:* Pearson Education Limited.

Sembuya, C. C. (2009). Amin Dada: *The Other Side. Kampala:* Sest Holdings Limited.

Transparency International. (2012). *Corruption Perception Index 2011.* Berlin: Transparency International.

Wanyande, P., M. Omosa, and C. Ludeki. (2007). *Governance Issues in Kenya: An Overview.* In: Wanyande, P., Omosa, M & C. Ludeki (Eds). *Governance and Transition Politics in Kenya.* Nairobi: University of Nairobi Press, 1-20.

Wrong, M. (2009). *It's Our Time to Eat: The Story of a Kenyan Whistle-Blower.* London: 4th Estate.

CHAPTER NINE

Devolution and Inclusive Development in Kenya: Prospects, Challenges and the Way Forward
Tom Wanyama and Hannah Kinyanjui

Introduction

In Kenya today one concept that could be on the lips of virtually everyone irrespective of age is devolution. This is not to say that devolution is a new innovation. It has been around and practiced in various parts of the world with mixed outcomes. For some authors devolution is a radical departure from centralism in which some supreme central power lords over an inferior political entity (Vernon, 2001). Through devolution therefore, mainly, political authority is transferred from the superior central entity to inferior subunits empowering them to make and implement laws and executive decisions. Blakemore and Warwick-Booth (2013) simply consider it to mean a transfer of government powers to make laws and policy of course from a higher central level to lower decentralized units.

In Kenya devolution is regarded as the transfer of political, administrative and financial authority from the central government to constitutional subunits (Counties). The devolution handbook by the International Commission of Jurists Kenya Section (2013) defines devolution as simply the transfer of decision-making and implementation powers, functions, responsibilities and resources to legally constituted, and popularly elected local governments. In this case it is important to indicate that the context in which the term local government is used refers to counties rather than the traditional local authorities that existed prior to the 2013 general elections that ushered in county governments.

The purpose of devolution as outlined in the Kenya Constitution 2010 is to:

1. Promote democratic and accountable exercise of power;
2. Foster national unity by recognizing diversity;
3. Give powers of self-governance to the people and enhance the participation of the people in the exercise of the powers of state and making decisions affecting them;
4. Recognize the right of communities to manage their own affairs and to further their development;

5. Protect and promote the interests and rights of minorities and marginalized communities;

6. Promote social and economic development and the provision of proximate, easily accessible services throughout the country;

7. Ensure equitable sharing of national and local resources across the country;

8. Facilitate decentralization of state organs, their functions and services; and

9. Enhance checks and balances and the separation of power.

From the objectives, devolution can be essentially seen as being more about expanding space for citizens and ensuring that none is left out of the national agenda whether political, social or economic.

The Concept of Inclusive Development

Before tackling inclusive development it is imperative that we pick it up by first looking at what inclusion is all about. Among the authors who have rendered their opinion on the concept is Mwenzwa (2013) who contends that inclusion is about encompassing of the entire population in the performances of individual functions in a society. He expounds on the definition by stating that it concerns access to specific benefits as well as dependence of individual modes of living on the individuals. Ganesh and Ravi (2010) have defined 'inclusive' as referring to distribution of well-being measured based on varied indices. Going by this definition, the manifestation of inclusiveness will not only be in terms of social and economic categories of individuals in society but regional diversity as well.

Inclusive development is therefore about development that addresses the needs of all peoples irrespective of their social economic background. It is development that addresses all forms of diversity and is premised on the principle of equity. It is development that banishes the language of minority and the marginalized from discourses about the welfare of citizens. According to OECD (2013), inclusive development requires some consideration to be given to different types of income and is also about equal opportunities where gender gaps are reduced, the poor are given access to information and knowledge and there is promotion of decent work. Ideally, inclusive development exists where all social groups are positively touched, geographical variations are eliminated and all components of life are sustainably managed.

Pre-Devolution Efforts

The desire to achieve inclusive development can be traced back to the period immediately after independence. This was inspired by the failings of the colonial era approach to development. The colonial powers had no deliberate intentions of pursuing a development agenda that would result in prosperity for all. Policies and programmes were largely skewed in favor of the white minorities while the African population was consigned to abject poverty and squalor. By the time Kenya was attaining independence there was an urgent need to overhaul the conceptualization of development and the framework that informed it. Regional imbalances required redressing and the gaps among social groupings needed bridging.

To attend to these development sore-toes, the first post-independence government targeted policy and institutional reforms in order to create an environment that would foster access to and inclusivity by all. Sessional Paper No. 10 of 1965 on African Socialism and its application to Planning in Kenya was thus prepared to guide development planning and indeed implementation. From the titling of the policy document it is evident that the writers were nostalgic about the pre-colonial African approach to social and economic development and were eager to infuse the principles and values from this era into the modern day planning practices. Deductively, the African approach revolved around collectivism and the care for one another. The spirit of 'brother's keeper' reverberated in every sphere of life making it nearly impossible to pursue an agenda that could condemn any segment of the community to any form of deprivation.

It is this spirit of socialism that Sessional paper No.10 of 1965 was to mainstream into development approach and planning in the young Nation. Assaulted by poverty, ignorance and disease, all of them exacerbated among African populations by discriminative policies of the colonial regime, the Nation was in dire need of a framework that could leverage on social collectivism across the country and the willingness to work towards the welfare of one another, to promote countrywide inclusive development. Harambee philosophy became the driver for the development agenda envisioned in the Sessional paper. Considered as a call to pull together, harambee became a near effective strategy for whipping citizens together to support government and community development projects. Many successes were realized through this model with many learning institutions, health facilities, infrastructure, and social amenities being developed across the country. This helped narrow the regional gap and promoted access to services by different groups in the society irrespective of their social standing.

Local Government System

Local Authorities were established across the country as a strategy to decentralize service delivery, harness local resources for development and promote local participation. The creation of local authorities was premised on the belief that the entities would have a close understanding of local needs and challenges, available resources and local dynamics that affected development. Spread across the country, local authorities were expected to forge tailor-made and best-fitted development strategies. Also referred to as Local Governments, the entities were seen as strategic institutions for the provision of basic socio-economic and environment services. Their strategic position made them valuable and viable vehicles for providing effective and efficient services required by the community (Mboga, 2009). The Omamo (1995) report outlined the key Local Government objectives as to:

1. Establish local representative government institutions through which appropriate services and development activities can be made more responsive to the wishes and initiatives of the local community.

2. Provide opportunities for local communities to exercise their democratic right to self-governance and determination at the local levels of society, and to encourage and develop initiatives and leadership potential.

3. Mobilize human and material resources through the involvement of members of the public in their local development.

4. Provide a two way channel of communication between the local communities and the central government.

However, Oyugi (1983) described local authorities as a weak form of devolution because the central government continued to exercise overwhelming political and administrative authority over the units. The situation was worsened by the weak financial position of most of the local authorities who were compelled to rely on the central government for support. Such a state of dependence could only mean one thing, inability of local authorities to fulfill their mandate of bringing about development and providing services in their area of jurisdiction. And since the weaknesses were not uniform, the scenario that emerged was that of uneven development across the country with low potential regions bearing the brunt. Corruption, inept leadership and gross mismanagement of the resources complicated the situation, hence spelling doom to particularly rural development.

District Focus Strategy for Rural Development

Another pre-devolution model that Kenya embraced to bring about inclusive development was the District Focus Strategy for Rural Development. The strategy was initiated in the early 1980s making districts the centres of development planning and execution. District Development Committees were created that brought together government operatives representing different sectors and mandated to coordinated development. A team put together by the President under the chairmanship of Philip Ndegwa avidly recommended that:

The district team under the leadership of the District Commissioner and with the guidance of the District Development Committee should be established as a major force and vehicle for the management and implementation of rural development. (Republic of Kenya, 1982)

This recommendation was adopted by the government, making districts the epicentre of rural development. The objective of the strategy was the broadening of the base of rural development efforts by shoring up local initiatives to complement government efforts and ensuring efficiency, effectiveness and boosting productivity of development projects and programmes (Oyugi, 1991).

The strategy remained active till the introduction of county governance after the 2013 general elections. Its challenges, which inevitably gnawed away at the noble intentions, included the weak and unguaranteed local community involvement. The principal players and drivers were government operatives, most of them incomers to the region and who worked at the behest of city based authorities. Their lack of understanding of the local needs and attachment to the community, and the likely pressure to serve external interests made these players unsuitable agents of inclusive development. As Oyugi (1991) put it, strong District Development Committees simply made districts the new unit of decentralization.

Prospects under the County Model

County Governments represent the latest approach to devolution in Kenya. Their configuration includes a constitutional structure comprising of the executive and the legislature. The governments are mandated to exercise financial, political and administrative authority in their areas of jurisdiction in an inclusive and participatory manner. Like the National Government, County Governments are by law required to uphold the national values and principles, whose aim is to promote among other things balanced and inclusive development. The values and principles as stated in the Constitution of Kenya 2010 article 10 include: patriotism, national unity, sharing and devolution of power, the rule of law, democracy and participation of the people; human dignity, equity, social justice, inclusiveness, equality, human rights, non-discrimination and protection of the marginalized; good governance, integrity, transparency and accountability; and sustainable development.

From the stated values and principles, inclusivity and non-discrimination are overt and a matter of constitutional requirement. Indeed the law giving effect to Chapter 11 of the Constitution on devolution, the County Governments Act No. 17 of 2012 requires that the County Assembly receives and considers annual reports from the executive on the extent of the County Government's compliance with Article 10. Where inclusive development is not evidenced then compliance can be rightly considered as lacking. We can also not talk of sustainable development in situations where certain segments of society are not on board or certain aspects of development are lacking. What provisions exist under devolution for enhancing inclusivity is a critical question for this paper to attempt to answer.

Participation and Devolution

Inclusivity acquires remoteness where popular participation is neither pronounced nor guaranteed. Bwalya (1985) considers increased quality and relevance of decisions, increased chances of success and of mobilization and a sense of self-reliance and wider and more efficient use of local resources as the benefits that accrue from popular participation. According to Oakley (1995) popular participation is a political process which affords previously excluded groups in the society an opportunity for involvement, to have a voice in and generally gain access to the benefits of economic and social development. In 1979, the World Conference on Agrarian Reform and Rural Development (WCARRD) guided that:

Participation by the people in the institutions and systems which govern their lives is a basic human right and also essential for realignment of political power in favor of disadvantaged groups and for social and economic development. Rural development strategies can realise their full potential only through the motivation, active involvement and organization at the grass-roots level of people, with special emphasis on the least advantaged, in the conceptualization and designing policies and programmes and in creating administrative, social and economic institutions.

Participation must thus be a deliberate and structured process through which people are not only beneficiaries of project and programme proceeds but have strong influence on the direction and execution of development (Paul 1987). Legislation providing for devolution in Kenya has given fundamental frameworks to guard against cosmeticism in popular participation. The County Governments Act provides for principles of citizen participation in counties and outlines them as:

1. Timely access to information, data, documents, and other information relevant or related to policy formulation and implementation;

2. Reasonable access to the process of formulating and implementing policies, laws, and regulations, including the approval of development proposals, projects and budgets, the granting of permits and the establishment of specific performance standards;

3. Protection and promotion of the interest and rights of minorities, marginalized groups and communities and their access to relevant information;

4. Legal standing to interested or affected persons, organizations, and where pertinent, communities, to appeal from or, review decisions, or redress grievances, with particular emphasis on persons and traditionally marginalized communities, including women, the youth, and disadvantaged communities;

5. Reasonable balance in the roles and obligations of county governments and non-state actors in decision-making processes to promote shared responsibility and partnership, and to provide complementary authority and oversight;

6. Promotion of public-private partnerships, such as joint committees, technical teams, and citizen commissions, to encourage direct dialogue and concerted action on sustainable development; and

7. Recognition and promotion of the reciprocal roles of non-state actors' participation and governmental facilitation and oversight.

The law further directs County Governments to facilitate citizen participation through specific modalities and platforms which include:

1. Information communication technology based platforms;
2. Town hall meetings;
3. Budget preparation and validation fora;
4. Notice boards: announcing jobs, appointments, procurement, awards and other important announcements of public interest;
5. Development project sites;
6. Avenues for the participation of peoples' representatives including but not limited to members of the National Assembly and Senate; or
7. Establishment of citizen fora at county and decentralized units.

It should further be noted that it is a legal requirement that county governors submit to the county assembly annual reports giving details of the extent of citizen participation. Such an oversight role should give sufficient impetus to county governments to make deliberate efforts ensuring that robust measures exist to lock-in citizen participation frameworks in county policies, programmes and projects.

Integration of minorities and marginalized groups

In developing countries the minority and the marginalized tend to form the bulk of groups that are usually peripheralized in development. Such groups always rank high among the poor, illiterate, less represented and unemployed, and will always be found resident in the most vulnerable of the environments characterized by acute deprivation, including poor infrastructure and social amenities.

Inclusion and integration of the minority and marginalized is therefore one of the boldest steps that Kenya has attempted through devolution. Its anchorage in law has ensured that implementers of devolution do not subject the matter to discretion but treat it as a statutory requirement. The principles of inclusion and integration of the marginalized as stated in the County Governments Act bind the county governments, public and private organizations and individuals to ensure:

1. Protection of marginalized and minority groups from discrimination and from treatment of distinction of any kind, including language, religion, culture, national or social origin, sex, caste, birth, descent or other status;

2. Non-discrimination and equality of treatment in all areas of economic, educational, social, religious, political and cultural life of the marginalized and minority groups;

3. Special protection to vulnerable persons who may be subject to threats or acts of discrimination, hostility, violence and abuse as a result of their ethnic, cultural, linguistic, religious or other identity;

4. Special measures of affirmative action for marginalized and minority groups to ensure their enjoyment of equal rights with the rest of the population;

5. Respect and promotion of the identity and characteristics of minorities;

6. Promotion of diversity and intercultural education; and

7. Promotion of effective participation of marginalized and minority groups in public and political life.

Essentially the law envisages a governance and development process that is pro-all and one in which no form of background serves as a basis or justification for non-inclusion. Where there are glaring cases of exclusion affirmative action is suggested as a short term intervention, as fundamental strategies are developed and implemented to naturalize inclusion.

Generally, lack of legislation requiring deliberate efforts to mainstream inclusion in development in the country made it possible for successive regimes since independence to pursue a development agenda that has resulted in uneven distribution of the benefits of socio-economic growth and prosperity. By legislating inclusion therefore the country has illegalized exclusion and increased the prospects of inclusive development under the devolved government system.

Prospects through Communication and Civic Education

Communication plays a very important role in empowering and enhancing involvement of community members in development. It is a pillar in development based on the fact that it serves the purpose of ensuring critical information is shared among key stakeholders. Such information includes details on existing development efforts and the diversity of their effect on the target population. Revelation is made of the effectiveness of existing interventions and those areas requiring improvement.

Rogers (1976) premises that communication research, theory and technologies can be applied to bring about both social and material advancement among community members as well as greater equality, freedom and other valued qualities for the majority of people through their gaining greater control of their environment. There is also general consensus that planned use of communication techniques, activities and media gives people powerful tools both to experience change and guide it, besides motivating enhanced involvement in a course they consider common to them (Fraser and Villet, 1994).

According to Adedokun et al (2010), adequate communication serves as a tool for effective collaborative efforts in issues of development and helps citizens engage in development. They insist that communication is important as a driver of social change among the marginalized and vulnerable population groups and fosters participation in development. Since community members are usually at the centre of any development initiative, communication boosts people's participation, decision making and action, confidence building, sharing knowledge and changing attitudes and behaviour (FAO 2006).

Comprehensive development therefore requires well planned and systematic use of communication through interpersonal channels, ICTs, audio-visuals and mass media. Information should be collected and exchanged among those concerned in planning development initiatives with the aim of understanding the needs of the people, how to address them and mobilizing people for development action (Adedokun et al, 2010).

The devolution law in Kenya has appreciated the significance of communication as a driver of development and provided for public communication and access to information. The County Governments Act requires that communication shall be integrated in all forms of development activities and that County Governments shall use the media to:

1. Create awareness on devolution and governance;
2. Promote citizens' understanding for purposes of peace and national cohesion;
3. Undertake advocacy on core development issues such as agriculture, education, health, security, economics, sustainable environment among others; and
4. Promote the freedom of the media.

The communication framework proposed by the legislation is one with the widest reach. The mechanisms favored and which each County Government is encouraged to implement include:

1. Television stations;
2. Information communication technology centres;
3. Websites;
4. Community radio stations;
5. Public meetings; and
6. Traditional media.

To galvanize the importance of communication as a driver of sustainable and inclusive development, devolution legislation confers a requirement for civic education that is intended to promote:

1. Empowerment and enlightenment of citizens and government;
2. Continual and systemic engagement of citizens and government; and
3. Values and principles of devolution in the Constitution.

Through civic education the law basically envisages an informed citizenry that actively participates in governance affairs of the society on the basis of enhanced knowledge, understanding and ownership. The specific objectives of civic education have been outlined as:

1. Sustained citizens' engagement in the implementation of the Constitution;
2. Improved understanding, appreciation and engagement in the operationalization of the county system of government;
3. Institutionalizing a culture of constitutionalism;
4. Knowledge of Kenya's transformed political system, context and implications;
5. Enhanced knowledge and understanding of electoral system and procedures;
6. Enhanced awareness and mainstreaming of the Bill of Rights and National values;
7. Heightened demand by citizens for service delivery by institutions of governance at the county level;
8. Ownership and knowledge on the principal economic, social and political issues facing county administrations and their form, structures and procedures; and
9. Appreciation for the diversity of Kenya's communities as building blocks for national cohesion and integration.

We wish to argue here that fidelity to the provisions of the devolution law regarding communication and civic education should fundamentally alter the development landscape across the country as the counties witness unprecedented popular participation in development and general success in addressing development needs of all segments of society in the context of sustainable development. Implementation of the provisions of the law by all counties should essentially translate into a countrywide coverage and phenomenal empowerment of citizens in all regions of the country to effectively participate in inclusive development.

Inclusivity through Development Planning

Development planning usually serves varied important purposes, among them ensuring disciplined channeling and utilization of resources, getting priorities right, firming up a framework within which a project should be implemented and generally making sure that development satisfies the expectations of stakeholders. The nature of and the manner in which development planning is undertaken can make the resultant development initiatives either inclusive or exclusive.

Develop¬ment planning is an instrument for achieving sustain¬able economic growth and social justice (Ohno and Shimamura, 2007). Inclusivity through planning is achieved where a variety of stakeholders is involved in generating development plans. It is about democratization of planning that in the end achieves a mutual and shared vision toward inclusive growth among stakeholders and citizens (Sakamoto, 2013). This type of planning is associated with the success of the Asian tigers (African Development Bank, 2012).

The East Asian countries used their bitter experiences of defeat in war, imperialism and colonialism to mobilize society for development in the aftermath of these traumatic experiences. These periods of oppression and war bred a kind of 'revolutionary nationalism' in these countries, which was translated into communism with a 'nationalist' slant in China and North Korea and 'nationalist' mixed capitalist developmental states in Japan, South Korea and Taiwan. (Woo-Cumings, 1999:7)

In Indonesia in particular, the situation reportedly changed dramatically after the fall of the Suharto regime. The country is said to have shifted from the top-bottom system of development planning and embraced a bottom-up approach to planning that included several levels of citizens. The country is said to have formulated The National Development Planning System Law in 2004, which enforced the development planning committee. Consequently, citizen representatives joined this committee during the plan¬ning procedure, and significantly influenced the stakeholders' perspectives (Sakamoto, 2013). By establishing the Development Planning Committee, coordination between stakeholders became institu¬tionalized, creating a consensus, which consequently allowed the voices of citizens to be reflected in poli¬cies (Iijima, 2005).

Through planning we are therefore able to address critical aspects of sustainable development. We are also able to incorporate necessary affirmative measures aimed at bridging the gap between regions and various groups in the society. In the 1970s Kenya identified the districts as the main planning units in the country. Districts were therefore strengthened to serve as units for planning and plan implementation. The assumption was that district plans would reflect more closely the actual needs of the local communities (Oyugi, 1991). A District Development Officer (DDO) was appointed who had training in development planning to offer expert support to the District Development Committee (DDC). It has however been held that though bearing the semblance of decentralization, district planning was still strongly influenced from the centre and was more about what the national office wanted done rather than what was crucial to the local communities. The extent of local community involvement remains debatable because DDCs mainly comprised of representatives of government ministries and departments.

Under the devolution arrangement, the desire to achieve inclusivity through planning is expressed firstly by the principles that govern planning and development facilitation in the counties. The County Governments Act specifically requires that planning and development facilitation in the counties shall:

1. Integrate national values in all processes and concepts;
2. Protect the right to self-fulfillment within the county communities and with responsibility to future generations;
3. Protect and integrate rights and interest of minorities and marginalized groups and communities;
4. Protect and develop natural resources in a manner that aligns national and county governments policies;
5. Align county financial and institutional resources to agreed policy objectives and programmes;
6. Engender effective resource mobilization for sustainable development;
7. Promote the pursuit of equity in resource allocation within the county;
8. Provide a platform for unifying planning, budgeting, financing, programme implementation and performance review; and
9. Serve as a basis for engagement between county government and the citizenry, other stakeholders and interest groups.

Since principles basically set the mood in the domain they apply to, and considering the implicit spirit of inclusivity in the presented principles, county planning could fit the bidding as a democratic process, drawing on the inputs of different shades of participants. Indeed county planning objectives clearly demonstrate intention and a resolve to foster an approach to development that "sees all feels all and touches all." The specific county planning objectives include:

1. Ensuring harmony between national, county and sub-county spatial planning requirements;

2. Facilitating the development of a well-balanced system of settlements and ensure productive use of scarce land, water and other resources for economic, social, ecological and other functions across a county;

3. Maintaining a viable system of green and open spaces for a functioning eco-system;

4. Harmonizing the development of county communication system, infrastructure and related services;

5. Developing urban and rural areas as integrated areas of economic and social activity;

6. Providing the preconditions for integrating under-developed and marginalized areas to bring them to the level generally enjoyed by the rest of the county;

7. Protecting the historical and cultural heritage, artefacts and sites within the county; and

8. Making reservations for public security and other critical national infrastructure and other utilities and services;

9. Working towards the achievement and maintenance of a tree cover of at least ten per cent of the land area of Kenya as provided in Article 69 of the Constitution; and

10. Developing the human resource capacity of the county.

The law basically makes citizen participation in county planning mandatory and directs that this should be facilitated through:

1. Information communication technology based platforms;

2. Town hall meetings;

3. Budget preparation and validation fora;

4. Notice boards: announcing jobs, appointments, procurement, awards and other important announcements of public interest;

5. Development project sites;

6. Avenues for the participation of peoples' representatives including but not limited to members of the National Assembly and Senate; or

7. Establishment of citizen fora at county and decentralized units.

It further requires provision to the public of clear and unambiguous information on any matter under consideration in the planning process, including:

1. Clear strategic environmental assessments;
2. Clear environmental impact assessment reports;
3. Expected development outcomes; and
4. Development options and their cost implications.

Strengthened involvement of the county citizens in the planning process is certainly with anticipation that it would translate into development initiatives that are both aligned to the needs and aspirations of the people as well as a possibility of addressing key components of inclusive development. Legislation must however be matched with illustrious actions capable of turning legal aspirations into tangible gains. At age six, empirical evidence of inclusive development as an offshoot of devolution may be too early to call. Prospects however remain high on the premise of commitment to the law.

Resourcing for Inclusivity

Resource distribution rather than availability is believed to have played a significant role in determining and shaping the nature of development currently characterizing the country's landscape. Historical injustices have been alluded to in discourses around unequal distribution of resources across the country, creating conditions that have eventually morphed into asymmetrical development. The constitutional requirement is however that revenue raised nationally shall be shared equitably between the national and county governments and that expenditure shall promote the equitable development of the country including making special provision for marginalized groups and areas. It further directs that the benefits of resource utilization be equitably distributed between the current and future generation.

Economic disparities within and among counties, the need to remedy them and the need for affirmative action in respect of disadvantaged areas and groups are part of the criteria upon which resources are to be distributed. The constitution further establishes an equalization fund and directs the National government to use the fund to exclusively provide basic services such as water, roads, health facilities and electricity to marginalized areas in an effort to shore-up the quality of such services to the level enjoyed by other regions. The creation of the Commission for Revenue Allocation as a constitutional commission mandated to advise on the sharing of revenue between the National and county governments and among county governments themselves offers an institutional framework within which inclusivity through resource sharing can legally be achieved.

Green Development

Inclusive green growth is inclusive development that ensures that sustainable and equitable use of natural resources is done within ecological limits (Banda and Bass, 2014). Many authors who have attempted to discuss inclusive development have however tended to grossly disregard environmental appropriateness as an attribute of inclusivity. The criticality of green development is phenomenal considering the potential that imprudence in terms of natural resource exploitation has on the livelihoods of particularly the already vulnerable segments of the society.

Countries are supposed to develop and implement green growth policies that will provide a framework for balanced inclusive development. Inclusive development is deemed within the ambit of a 'safe earth for all'. The International Institute of Educational Development has outlined attributes of inclusive green development as including:

1. Human wellbeing: decent jobs, health, livelihoods, freedoms, culture, as well as income.
2. Minimizing waste, pollution and damage to environmental assets: reducing carbon levels; and operating within the eight other planetary boundaries (biodiversity, nitrogen cycles, etc.).
3. Equity: inclusion of stakeholders in process, economic activity, and benefit-sharing – especially those dependent on natural resources and vulnerable to environmental risks.
4. Economic growth: in those sectors and areas where it is most needed to support wellbeing.
5. Sustainable natural resource management: improving natural resource efficiency and productivity per person to achieve economic growth.
6. Enhancing resilience of livelihoods and economic sectors: adaptation to climate change, environmental and socioeconomic risk management, and diversification.

Wanjiru (2011) sees a green economy as one able to help achieve sustainable development by alleviating environmental threats, contribute to the creation of dynamic new industries and income growth, and create quality jobs that can improve workers' economic standing and thus their ability to better support their families. (Wanjiru, 2011:8)

While commenting on gender variances in terms of environmental experiences, Wanjiru (ibid) advances a position that a truly sustainable 'green economy' is one that ably promotes gender-friendly, green collar employment and entrepreneurship opportunities and social equity and equally creates green pathways out of poverty for both genders.

At both the constitutional and national legislation level Kenya has strongly expressed a desire to promote environmentally friendly development. The Constitution particularly binds citizens through a preamble declaration to respect the environment, and introduces environmental rights as part of the bill of rights. This way, every activity carried out in the country is expected to be ecologically admissible and guarantee the citizens unfettered enjoyment of environmental rights. The rights are that every citizen should have unalienable access to a clean and healthy environment as well as the right to have the environment protected for the benefit of the present and future generations.

The state is equally constitutionally committed to ensuring sustainable exploitation, utilization, management and conservation of the environment and natural resources, and ensuring the equitable sharing of the accruing benefits. It is further expected to work to achieve and maintain a tree cover of at least ten per cent of the land area of Kenya besides encouraging public participation in the management, protection and conservation of the environment.

The country is also duty bound to create systems to facilitate environmental impact assessment, environmental audit and monitoring of the environment for the purpose of eliminating processes and activities that are likely to endanger the environment. Utilization of the environment and natural resources is generally intended for the benefit of the people of Kenya, and every person is legally expected to cooperate with State organs and other persons to protect and conserve the environment and ensure ecologically sustainable development and use of natural resources.

Inclusive green development is thus anticipated constitutionally and through other legislative and policy frameworks. As devolved units drive development across the country, inclusivity is expected in terms of fidelity to constitutional green aspirations. Policy and institutional framework will have to be developed by county governments to give effect to Article 42 and 69 of the constitution.

Challenges of Devolution

Common discourse has described them as teething problems. However, apparent poor coordination in county governments, weak institutions, low revenues, corruption, unfavorable expenditure ratio, weak over-sighting and poor plan implementation could pass for the greatest challenges of devolution that pose a danger to the realization of inclusive development.

Poor Coordination: About six years since devolution was launched through the Constitution of Kenya, 2010, functions within county governments remain largely ill coordinated. Intergovernmental forums have not been activated despite their crucial role of harmonization of services rendered in the county; coordination of development activities in the county; coordination of intergovernmental functions; and such other functions as may be provided for by or under any law. The forums are supposed to be chaired by County Governors and their membership includes County Executive Committee members or their appointees and all heads of National Government departments working in the county. Continued lack of a coordinating framework is a weakness with the potential of impeding inclusive development. County Governments ought to hasten operationalization of the forums.

Weak Institutions: Counties are yet to put in place strong institutions that can serve as catalysts for rapid and inclusive development. The problem can be partly associated with delays in domestication-necessary legislation within the counties in order to provide direction. National institutions, given the distinctive nature of the relationship between county and national governments, have no direct role in guiding county development. It is therefore urgent for counties to put in place institutional frameworks that will form the foundation for county development.

Low Revenue: Counties are expected to generate revenue to supplement allocation from the National Government. However the prevailing situation in majority of counties is that they are unable to realize their annual revenue targets. This means that the pace of development will be slow and the temptation to ignore important aspects of inclusive development will be high. Counties must therefore establish county revenue authorities which in partnership with the Kenya Revenue Authority can drive revenue collection. This should be pursued in tandem with robust economic investment and innovation.

Corruption: This remains perhaps the greatest challenge in development terms in Kenya. Overwhelming evidence indicates that both national and county governments continue to reel under the weight of corruption, which has not only resulted in loss of billions of revenue but also diversion of funds allocated for development. As a consequence of theft of public funds, many development projects have either not taken off as planned or have stalled. It is imperative that the institutions charged with supervising public expenditure ensure due diligence in their work. Strengthening such offices is a prerequisite.

Unfavorable Expenditure Ratio: Development index, which is the ratio between recurrent expenditure and development expenditure, is strongly unfavorable at both the national and county governments. Both levels of government continue to spend disproportionately with much of allocated funds going to recurrent items such as personal emoluments and travels leaving little funds for development. It may be necessary that a legislated ratio of expenditure in favor of development is established to guide spending of public funds.

Weak Oversighting: Besides national oversight institutions, the Senate and County Assemblies are supposed to provide oversight to county executives. County Assemblies are particularly supposed to approve county plans, budgets and expenditure proposals. However, due to systemic weaknesses in most county assemblies orchestrated by lack of necessary competencies to provide quality oversight, county development faces the danger of falling below constitutional expectations. Civic education is particularly necessary to empower citizens to not only provide oversight but also ensure through election that the right people enter county assemblies as members.

Poor Plan Implementation: Development planning has over the years been regarded as one of the strengths that Kenya has. However plan implementers have been accused of never delivering development outcomes as planned. Why momentum is always lost at plan implementation has never been convincingly explained, with some suspicion being about lack of good will and commitment among the various stakeholders. It is necessary for development partners at particularly county level to be availed forums where their interest in development projects and good-will will be sustained.

Conclusion

Inclusive development remains a possibility even as the world acknowledges that the current situation is far from what is desirable. From a casual look based on physical and some socio-economic indicators of development, many parts of the world may claim to have attained acceptable forms of development. However, a closer examination would certainly reveal cases of societal groups and regions that are either completely left out or are lagging behind in terms of access to the benefits of development. The situation is particularly likely in Africa given weak legal, policy and institutional framework coupled with corruption, conflicts and open discrimination.

In Kenya, efforts have been made to remedy the situation with various models of development being tried with mixed results. The current model of devolution is promising particularly considering the fact that it is about transfer of financial, administrative and financial authority to counties, affording local communities widened space for participation in decision making and determination of the development agenda. The laws providing for implementation of devolution have provided reasonable direction on the manner in which development is to be executed in the counties and the extent of public involvement. Backed by the Constitution, the legal framework stands in favor of inclusive development that particularly addresses the needs of the minority and marginalized. With proper oversighting and a strong institutional framework, devolution is indeed likely to perform impressively in terms of inclusive development.

References

Adedokun, M.O. & Adeyemo, C.W. (2010). *The Impact of Communication on Community Development.* Journal of Communication, 1(2):101-105

African Development Bank. (2012). *Jobs, Justice and the Arab Spring:* Inclusive Growth in North Africa. AfDB: Tunis.

Banda, T. & Bass, S. (2014). *Inclusive Green Growth in Zambia:* Scoping the Needs and Potentials. London: IIED.

Blakemore, K. & Warwick-Both, L. (2013). *Social Policy: An Introduction. London:* Open University Press.

Bwalya, M.C. (1985). *The Integrated Development Approach within the context of Decentralization in Zambia.* In: Kiros, F.G. (Ed.) Challenging Rural Poverty. Treton: Africa World Press.

Fraser, C. & Villet, J. (1994). *Communication: A Key to Human Development,* Rome, FAO.

Ganesh, R. & Ravi, K. (2010). *Inclusive Development: Conceptualization,* Application and the ADB perspective.

ICJ Kenya. (2013). *Devolution Handbook.* Nairobi International Commission of Jurists-Kenya Chapter.

Kenya, Republic of. (2012). *County Governments Act No. 17.* Nairobi: Government Press.

Kenya, Republic of. (2010). *Constitution of Kenya.* Nairobi: Government Press.

Kenya, Republic of. (1982). *Report and Recommendations of the Working Party on Government Expenditure.* Nairobi: Government Press.

Kenya, Republic of. (1965). *Sessional Paper No. 10 of 1965 on African Socialism and its Application to Planning in Kenya.* Nairobi: Government Press.

Iijima, S. (2005). E*nactment of Indonesian National Development Planning System Act and its signifi¬cance,* Japan Bank of International Cooperation (JBIC), Development Finance Institution Working Paper.

Mboga, H. (2009). *Understanding the Local Government System in Kenya: A Citizen's Handbook.* Nairobi: Institute of Economic Affairs.

Oakley, P. (1995). *People's Participation in Development Projects*: A Critical Review of Current Theory and Practice, INTRAC.

OECD (2013). *Innovation and Inclusive Development*: Conference Discussion Report, Cape Town, South Africa.

Ohno, I. & Shimamura, M. (2007). *Managing the Development Process and Aid*: East Asian Experience in Building Central Economic Agencies. Tokyo: GRIPS Development Forum.

Omamo, W.O. (1995). *The Commission of Inquiry on Local Authorities in Kenya*. Nairobi: Government Press.

Oyugi, W.O. (1991). *Decentralizing Development Planning and Management in Kenya*: An Assessment. In: Chitere, O. & Mutiso, R. (eds.). *Working with Rural Communities: A Participatory Research Perspective in Kenya*. Nairobi: Nairobi University Press.

Oyugi, W.O. (1983). *Local Government in Kenya: A Case of Institutional Decline*. In: P. Mawhood (Ed.) *Local Government in the Third World:* The Experience of Tropical Africa. London: John Wiley & Sons Press.

Rogers, E.M. (1976). *Communication and Development. Beverly Hills: Sage Publications*

Sakamoto, K. (2013). *Efforts to introduce Inclusive Planning in Egypt, Global Economy and Development,* Working Paper 58.

Vernon, B. (2001). *Devolution in the United Kingdom. New York*: Oxford University Press.

Wanjiru, L. (2011) *Accounting for Green Growth from the Lens of Gender Equality: Why it matters*; In Dimensions of Inclusive Development, UNDP.

Woo-Cumings, M. (1999). *Introduction: Chalmers Johnson and the Politics of Nationalism and Development*. In: Woo-Cumings, M (Ed.), *The Developmental State*. New York: Cornell University Press.

CHAPTER TEN

Performance Management amid Devolution in Kenya: Safeguarding the Gains

Hannah Kinyanjui and Tom Wanyama

Introduction

The realization of the dynamic organizational environment that requires maintenance of high levels of competitiveness and which can only be maintained by ensuring effective and efficient service delivery has necessitated the need for performance management the world over. In the context of Kenya's Public Service, the rationale for performance management is based on historical perceptions and realities of poor service delivery. Performance management system is therefore essential as an integral part of Results Based Management (RBM) within public service reforms initiative to enhance effective and efficient service delivery. The Implementation methodologies for results based management include Rapid Results Initiatives (RRI), Performance Contracting (PC) and Performance Appraisal System (PAS).

In Kenya's public service, performance management is anchored in the current national development blueprint, the Kenya Vision 2030. Emphasis on performance management for delivery of results is undoubtedly influenced by the basic assumption of performance management which lies in its professed ability to unite the attention of institution members on a common objective and galvanize them towards the attainment of this objective (Balogun, 2003). The promulgation of the Constitution of Kenya in August 2010 set the stage for major institutional reforms. Devolution of governance and public participation are critical components of these reforms. Devolution, a form of decentralization, is one of the concepts in the Constitution that has brought about a complete overhaul in Kenya's system of governance as a new system.

The need for devolution has been informed by the need to have power sharing, checks and balances in governance and the decentralization of resources in order to bring effectiveness in service delivery to the mwananchi. With the decongestion of the centre to the counties, service delivery effectiveness has been felt at the grassroots level. Even in the face of devolution, staff performance management has been taken care of by its implementation to ensure continuity, improvement and sustainability of the performance management gains in the public service of Kenya.

History of Public Service Reforms in Kenya

The Public Service inherited from the colonial government at independence had not been designed to grapple with development needs of post-independence Kenya. The colonial period administration interest was on the system maintenance. As a result, the only institutions that were well developed were those responsible for maintenance of law and order. The reforms undertaken were a continuation of activities which the government has engaged in since the colonial era. The launching of the on-going reform efforts was necessitated by the need to address the declining performance of the public service in spite of the many reforms and resources that had been invested since independence.

Although the first attempts at the reform and transformation of the public sector in Kenya began in 1965 (OPM/PSTD, 2010), it was not until the early 1990s that serious efforts were made toward their implementation and hence the transformation of the country's public service management. The implementation of systematically planned public sector reforms in Kenya can be broadly classified into two generations, the first and second generation.

First Generation Reforms

The first generation saw the introduction of civil service reforms coming soon after the structural adjustment programmes of the 1980s. The primary focus of these first generation reforms was to deal with the emerging economic challenges brought about by globalization and also the after shock waves of the structural adjustment programmes. The reforms were about dealing with issues that needed both immediate attention and solution, and reshaping the state for long term goals. These challenges were clearly stated in the introduction of the Civil Service Reform Strategy (Republic of Kenya, 1993) thus:

As the third decade of independence draws to a close, Kenyans are facing new challenges in economic management and public policy. Quality public services remain a priority, but cost considerations have become significantly more important. Not only must Kenyans needs be met, they must be met efficiently. Pervasive reform of the Civil Service is therefore required. In response to this imperative, a wide ranging review of the structure and functions of the Civil Service has been conducted, and extensive recommendations and an action plan for reform have been developed.

In 1993, the Government of the Republic of Kenya responded to these challenges by formulating and implementing the Civil Service Reform Programme (CRSP). The programme was implemented in three phases:

1. The first phase (1993-1998) focused on cost containment through staff rightsizing initiatives such as voluntary early retirement.

2. The second phase (1998-2001) focused on performance improvement through rationalization of government ministries/department/functions for effective budgetary needs.

3. The third phase focused on refinement, consolidation and sustenance of reform gains guided by Economic Recovery Policy Direction (DPM, 2004).

In the center of the three phases of reform was the need to build a public service that was capable of meeting the challenges of below optimum service delivery to Kenyans. The endeavor to improve service delivery saw a number of performance improvement initiatives being put in place. These included emphasis on the adoption of private sector business management ethos in the lines of New Public Management principles. There were high expectations from these reforms which were however not quickly forthcoming. After five years of implementing reforms, the Government of the Republic of Kenya had very little to show in terms of results. The government then through a World Bank sponsored programme hired a team of experts mostly drawn from the private sector, the Dream Team, into the public sector through short term contracts to inject the much needed private sector management behavior to improve service delivery in the public service. These were seen as lacking among public service technocrats. The Dream Team was seen as the ideal set of experts to restructure and turn around the Public Service as well as the economy.

Second Generation Reforms: Towards Performance Measurement

In December 2002, a new government was elected on a platform of reforms and, among other things, committed itself to do business differently. The new government pledged to pursue a national development strategy that would instill rapid and sustained economic growth with a promise to reduce poverty through creation of employment and wealth. This strategy was to be implemented by: creating competitive market conditions for private sector-led growth; directing resources towards wealth and employment creation; supporting both effective and efficient public sector performance and service delivery (GOK-ERS 2004). The government shifted the paradigm from a concern to do, towards a concern to ensure things are done for speedy results.

With the country facing challenges that required urgent attention, the government announced its socio-economic blueprint in 2003, the Economic Recovery Strategy for Wealth and Employment Creation (ERSWEC), 2003-2007 (Republic of Kenya, 2003). The ERSWEC also kick-started the new government's public sector reform efforts which covered the years 2003-07. This was Kenya's third wave of public sector reform and transformation. It was also in line with the government's commitment to improve performance, corporate governance and management in the public service.

Results-Based Management and Performance Contracts

Concerned with the slow pace of implementation of its reform initiatives, the Government of Kenya took a Cabinet decision in 2004 to formally prescribe results-based management (RBM) as its strategy for changing the culture and modus operandi of the public sector (OPM/PSTD, 2010). This was intended to improve service delivery as a deliberate policy to enable public service servants concentrate on results when delivering services to citizens (Republic of Kenya, 2004). The Result-Based Management (RBM) is a participatory and team based management approach designed to achieve defined results by improving planning, programming, management efficiency, effectiveness, accountability and transparency (CIDA, 2001).

The introduction and institutionalization of the RBM concept in the public service was aimed at refocusing the public servants' mind-sets on results in service delivery to citizens. RBM was therefore to help focus attention and resources on the achievement of definite objectives and the targets prescribed in the Economic Recovery Strategy (ERS). Hence, each department and ministry through its staff was expected to come up with clear objectives in line with ERS targets and define the roles of each individual staff member.

RBM strategy would refocus the operational systems in both financial and human resources arrangements with more emphasis placed on results and not mere adherence to procedures. Results orientation involves changes in current procedures, processes and practices to those that focus on attaining results (Kobia, 2006). Rapid Results Initiative (RRI), Performance Contracting (P.C.) and Performance Appraisal System (PAS) provide a structured methodology for building and practicing Results Based Management (RBM). This methodology was required for successful implementation of the Economic Recovery Strategy for Wealth Creation and Employment (ERS) by the Public Service and is still required now as we implement the Kenya Vision 2030.

The key elements of RBM are: target setting, performance planning, performance monitoring and reporting, and performance appraisals.

1. Performance target setting is the process of setting performance targets for ministries/ departments, groups or individual in carrying out specific work assignments.
2. Performance Planning is the process of establishing a shared understanding of what is to be achieved, and how it is to be achieved and managing resources to ensure successful implementation.
3. Performance Monitoring and Reporting
4. Performance appraisal is the process of evaluating organization, group or individual performance against predetermined targets.

Performance Contracting

With the public service reforms laying more and more emphasis on performance management, performance contracts were introduced. The strategic use of performance management was intended to help drive change efforts from process to results orientation in the public service.

According to Republic of Kenya (2007), a performance contract is a management tool for measuring negotiated performance targets. Performance Contracting is part of the broader Public Sector Reforms aimed at improving efficiency and effectiveness in the management of the public service It is a freely negotiated document that specifies the responsibilities, commitments and obligations of both parties to the agreement in this case the government, acting as the owner of a government agency on one hand, and the management of the agency on the other hand in order to achieve mutually agreed results. It also addresses economic/social and other tasks to be discharged for economic or other gain.

The policy decision to introduce Performance Contracts in the management of public resources was conveyed in the Economic Recovery Strategy for Wealth and Employment Creation (2003-2007). Kenya's Vision 2030 has also recognized performance contracting among the key strategies to strengthen public administration and service delivery.

Hope (2001) points out that performance contracts specify the mutual performance obligations, intentions and the responsibilities which a government requires public officials or management of public agencies or ministries to meet over a stated period of time. Performance Contract is a useful management tool for ensuring accountability for results by public officials and also creates transparency in the management of public resources. It does this by articulating clear definitions of objectives and supports innovative management, monitoring and control methods and also imparts managerial and operational autonomy to public service managers. It organizes and defines tasks so that management can perform them systematically, purposefully and with reasonable probability of achievement. An organization's purpose defines the ways in which it relates to its environment. If this purpose is fulfilled, the organization will survive and prosper (Luo and Peng, 1999).

Implementation of performance contracts will yield improved efficiency in resource utilization, institutionalization of a performance-oriented culture in the public service, measurement and evaluation of performance, linking rewards and sanctions to measurable performance; instilling accountability for results at all levels, improved service delivery, and enhancing performance (GoK, 2007). Therefore every person holding public office or managing public resources ought to be placed on a Performance Contract.

The expected outcomes of the use of performance contracts in Kenya include:

1. Improved efficiency in service delivery to the public by ensuring that holders of public office are held accountable for results;
2. Improvement in performance and efficiency in resource utilization and ensuring that public resources are focused on attainment of the key national policy priorities;
3. Institutionalization of a performance-oriented culture in the Public Service;
4. Ability to measure and evaluate performance;
5. Ability to link reward for work to measurable performance;
6. Instilling accountability for results at all levels in the government;
7. Ensuring that the culture of accountability pervades all levels of government;
8. Reduction or elimination of reliance on Exchequer funding by public agencies;
9. Ability to strategize the management of public resources; and
10. Recreating a culture of results-oriented management in the Public Service. (OPM/PCD, 2011).

Benefits of Performance Contracting

Moy (2005) in his final report to the Office of Financial Management which summarized the results of their literature search and state survey on the best practices and trends in performance contracting in a number of state and local agencies in Washington D.C., indicates that the use of performance contracts and the accompanying increase of operational autonomy had induced some developments in the internal structures of the agencies under study. The implementation of performance based contracting ranges from state-wide, agency wide, to only within specific agency divisions or programs and that its impacts in each state agency varied, but including increased accountability for service delivery and deliverables and increased partnership between the contractor community and the state agency. States agencies had defined performance as deliverables, outputs, outcomes, and effectiveness and efficiency, among others. With respect to changes in customer relations, new interfaces and instruments are installed, resulting in increased client-oriented approach. Most state corporations and government ministries in Kenya, for instance, now have functional customer care and public relations offices. These offices have acted as valuable instruments for introducing a client focus. However, the functioning of these offices is hampered, in some cases, by the insufficiency of financial and human resources (Akaranga, 2008).

The successful introduction of performance contracting is partly attributed to the political goodwill and leadership which in this case has been provided by the highest office in the land, the presidency. The enthusiasm and commitment of the Permanent Secretary, Secretary to the Cabinet and Head of the Public Service has also significantly contributed to this success (Obongo, 2009).

Bologun (2013) concludes that, the independent ad-hoc committees have brought to the process a high degree of autonomy from the management of public service, in addition to infusing credibility, objectivity and professionalism into the entire exercise. The strategy has also been implemented in an inclusive and interactive manner such that there have been very limited cases of organizations claiming unfair evaluation or being denied an opportunity for expression of opinions and ideas.

According to a study by Kobia (2006), performance contracting has reaped the following; remarkable and unprecedented improvement in profit generation for commercial state corporations, significant improvement in service delivery and operations by such ministries as immigrations and registration of Persons, Agriculture, Provincial Administration and Internal Security, Health, Finance and Water, significant improvement in operations and services by Nairobi City Council, Kisumu and Nakuru Municipalities, and unprecedented improvement in service delivery and operations by the bulk of state corporations and statutory boards, among them, KenGen, Kenya Power and Lighting Company Limited, Kenya Ports Authority, Kenya Utalii College, National Oil Corporation of Kenya, KICC etc.

Performance Appraisal System

In Kenya, Performance Appraisal System (PAS) within the Civil Service was introduced around 2006 and has over the years become a popular staff management system driven via the popular government performance contracting initiative, The system is being embraced in the Kenyan public service for tracking employees' performance in service delivery and notable improved performance in civil service productivity and employee motivation has been experienced.

The process of performance management involves the identification of common goals between the appraiser and the appraisee. These goals must correlate to the overall organizational goals. If such a process is conducted effectively, it will increase productivity and quality of output (Davis, 1995).

Performance Appraisal System (PAS) is a process of determining and communicating to an employee how he or she is performing on the job. Performance appraisal includes all formal procedures used to evaluate personalities, contributions and potentials of group members in a working organization. In performance appraisals, accuracy and fairness in measuring employee performance is very important.

According to Armstrong (2001), performance management is a control measure used to determine deviations of work tasks with a view of taking corrective action. It is also used to reflect on past performance as the organization plans ahead. Provision of feedback on the required corrective action is critical in the process.

For the appraisals to be effective, the top management must be supportive in providing information, clear performance standards must be set, the appraisals must not be used for any other purpose apart from performance management, and the evaluations must be free from any rating biases (Goff & Longenecker, 1990).

Performance Management Framework in Kenya

Performance Management in the Public Service is anchored in the National Economic Blue Prints. The current is Kenya Vision 2030 and the proceeding was known as Economic Recovery Strategy (ERS) for Wealth Creation and Employment.

Some of the key characteristics of the Kenyan performance management system include:

1. Performance contracts with specific targets.
2. 100-day targets for "rapid results initiatives," which are embedded in the performance contracts.
3. A strategic "Results for Kenyans" plan, Vision 2030, with 5-year plans to meet interim targets.
4. A performance management framework that creates alignment, and cascades to individuals.

5. Public Sector Transformation department whose focus is on: Service and transparency; cooperation, collaboration; accountability, structured stakeholder engagement.

6. Use of service charters and outcomes frameworks.

In its bid to improve performance, corporate governance and management in the public service, the Kenya government already had an institutional framework to achieve this even before devolution.

Public Sector Transformation Department

In its quest to create fundamental and sustainable change that meets the citizen's needs and aspirations, the Public Service Transformation department spearheaded The Transforming Kenya Programme. "Transforming Kenya" is set within the context of the Constitution of Kenya 2010 and is underpinned by the need to "get it right from the beginning".

This program focuses on making systematic changes and broadly embedding new management practices focused on: citizen centred outcomes across the whole Public Sector; entrenching the renewed focus on Public Service values and ethics, as well as the Bill of Rights in line with the new Constitution.

The implementation of this programme has realized the following milestones:

1. Implementation of results based initiatives to enhance citizens' satisfaction with Government Service Delivery

2. Promoting sustainable Public Sector Stakeholder Partnerships

3. Catalyzing Synergy in Government functions and operations through participating in the on-going development of an Integrated Performance Management System

4. Engendering a culture of Managing for Results engendered in all MDAs and Counties.

National Performance Management Steering Committee

In 2007, the then Minister of State for Public Service through a gazette notice established a steering committee in the public service known as the National Performance Management Steering Committee comprising of then Permanent Secretaries from various ministries and representatives of various ministries for technical support.

The Steering Committee was tasked with the following functions;

1. Advise on national target setting and consensus building in the Public Service on policy and programme priorities, within the national performance management framework;

2. Strengthen the process of open and competitive identification and recruitment of Board members and Chief Executives of State Corporations and other senior public servants and ensure that the Public Service mirrors the people of Kenya;

3. Coordinate the development of the draft Public Service Results and Performance Management Bill;

4. Provide leadership in the implementation of all capacity building programmes for change management and leadership for transforming the Public Service;

5. Provide leadership and advice in the process of inculcating a performance-based culture in the Public Service through institutionalizing results based management at, the national, provincial, district and lower levels of Government;

6. Deliberate on and make recommendations on conflicts arising from policy and implementation of Government programmes;

7. Draw lessons learnt and best practices to improve performance contracting;

8. Provide leadership in the development and implementation of a competency-based, value-driven human resource development and management strategy;

9. Co-ordinate the development and harmonization of performance management tools and instruments;

10. Advise on integrated information, education and communication strategy for the Public Service;

11. Provide overall monitoring and evaluation of institutional compliance within the performance management framework, for the achievement of results for Kenyans;

12. Advise the Government on enabling institutional framework to facilitate achievement of targeted results for Kenyans;

13. Explore opportunities for benchmarking and Government-to-Government Learning, to ensure continuous performance improvement in the Public Service; and

14. Provide leadership in the development and implementation of a comprehensive citizen-focused Public Service reform and development strategy within the framework of Vision 2030.

Concept of Devolution

Devolution is a form of decentralization. In the devolution handbook by International Commission of Jurists Kenya Section (2013), devolution is simply defined as the transference of decision-making and implementation powers, functions, responsibilities and resources to legally constituted, and popularly elected local governments.

The Constitution of Kenya 2010 establishes the system of devolved government comprising national and county level governments. The Fourth Schedule to the Constitution assigns functions and powers to the National and County Governments. Articles 186 provide for the respective functions and powers of national and county governments while Article 187 provides for the transfer of functions and powers between the two levels of government.

The two levels of government are interdependent since devolution combines self-government at the local level and shared at the national level. Interdependence is necessitated by the fact that the consumers of services rendered by the two levels of government are the same citizens of Kenya, although located in different parts of the country.

The Constitution, County Government Act and Inter-governmental Act provide mechanisms for harmonious coexistence of county governments-to-national governments, county-to-county governments and a county executive and a county assembly. The Intergovernmental Relations Act, No. 2 of 2012 provides a framework for consultation and co-operation between the national and county governments.

The citizens view the devolution process in Kenya as a prime opportunity to achieve better service delivery and to participate in the governance process, both of which are reflected in Open Governance principles.

Performance Management in the Face of Devolution

The national and county governments are under great pressure to provide results that matter to the public, and within severe resource constraints. At the same time, government officials and managers are challenged to overcome the public's lack of trust in government at all levels.

The governments must improve their focus on producing results that benefit the public, and also give the public confidence that government has produced those results. They must therefore change their approach. Public-sector management must become synonymous with performance management. There is thus the need for a performance management framework. This should be complemented with advocacy for the governments to implement performance management initiatives, tools and techniques. This should be coupled with training for the members in order to support the adoption and continuous enhancement of public-sector performance management.

Prior to the implementation of the devolved system of government in Kenya, the defunct local authorities signed performance contracts with the central government. This is not the case between the county governments and the national government. The County Governments Act (Article 47 and Article 113) however requires county governments to design performance management plans for evaluating the performance of county public service and implementation of county plans.

Continuous improvement within the ministries is emphasized, whereby ministries are required to establish a baseline measure against which a ministry will strive to achieve. As a result, ministries' ranking based on sectoral assessment has been done away with in the devolved system of governance, and assessment within the ministries encouraged. The cabinet secretaries are expected to support each other in order to achieve their collective responsibility as a cabinet (GoK, 2013).

Further, cabinet secretaries will be answerable for the performance of staff in their ministries. Staff performance management will be based on measurable targets. Individual performance will be linked to organizational performance/performance contracts and officers will be guided by the provisions of the rewards and sanctions policy. The administration of staff performance management will be undertaken through a ministerial performance management committee.

According to the Public Service Commission guidelines 2014 to the cabinet secretary on the human resource functions, the cabinet secretary is tasked with the appointment of the Ministerial Performance Management Committee members. The functions of the committee include;

1. Undertake quarterly review of the implementation of Strategic Plans and Performance Contracts.

2. Ensure linkage between Institutional Performance Contract and Performance Appraisal.

3. Ensure that the overall assessment of employee performance is within the context of institutional performance as evaluated through staff performance appraisal system.

4. Ensure that the performance appraisal of all officers is evaluated and feedback on performance is relayed in writing at the end of the year.

5. Hold quarterly performance review meetings.

6. Consider performance reports from various departments within the ministry and make recommendations for improvement.

7. Review cases of appeals on appraisal ratings between supervisors and appraises.

8. Make recommendations to the Cabinet Secretary on the application of rewards and sanctions

9. Develop and implement the internal monitoring and evaluation and reporting system.

10. Ensure that the integrity and credibility of the overall process of rewards and sanction system is safeguarded and maintained at all times.

Conclusion

Performance measurement can be the first step toward improving the performance of public sector institutions, and, when backed by an appropriate incentive system, it can also help shift organizational focus from inputs to outputs and outcomes and, consequently, improve efficiency and effectiveness (Schiavo-Campo and Sundaram, 2001). Introducing a stronger performance orientation in Kenya's public sector is very important for improving the performance of the country's public sector institutions.

The foregoing discussion is evident of the country's quest for effectiveness and efficiency in the service delivery. It has been a long gradual journey which has borne fruit. The country may not yet be where it envisioned being, but much has been achieved, evidenced by the improved service delivery in the public sector.

Devolution intended to decentralize decision-making and implementation powers, functions, responsibilities and resources from the national government hence bringing more effectiveness and efficiency. Devolution could actually be essentially taken as a performance management strategy. With devolution, efforts were made to ensure that what performance management gains already achieved were not in vain, hence the various performance management plans.

In a Commission for the Implementation of the Constitution (CIC) report of 2014, commendable progress has been realized in the operationalization of the system of devolved governance. To a great extent, the key institutional structures and systems in the County Executives and County Assemblies have been established to enhance service delivery.

It is however not clear yet regarding the implementation of structures and systems of performance management. This is among the challenges which, if not addressed, will severely compromise the success of the system of devolved government in Kenya.

In his articles on performance management self-evaluation, Much.J (2011) concludes, while governments should continually evaluate and look for opportunities to improve their services, the same can be done with their overall performance management approach. More and more becomes possible as staff, managers, and elected officials continue to gain experience using performance data, and their competencies grow. With improvements come greater returns that allow governments to become even more efficient, effective, and responsive to changing external conditions and public expectation.

Sustenance of performance management gains

Performance management initiatives cannot achieve optimum success without sustained support from an organization's top leaders. Leaders need to articulate a vision for performance management that tells stakeholders how they will benefit and encourages involvement.

Leadership must also make clear that performance management is not an experiment and is in fact how business will be conducted. Elected officials may need to be convinced of the value of implementing and sustaining performance management since some officials are concerned that instituting a process driven by high-level outcomes and numerical targets may interfere with their authority to set goals and make decisions. Elected officials need to be involved in their role as policy makers, in the planning stages where goals are set, and also in later stages, where their oversight responsibilities should be exercised.

Further, public sector leaders at all levels, both elected and appointed, will be required not only to set high expectations for performance but also to make a commitment to improving performance. Leaders must instill a sense of urgency about improving performance in their government build, performance-based organizational cultures and management structures, continuously communicate the necessity of listening to the public, and provide resources to assure that a performance-based culture and related practices are initiated and sustained.

There is also the need for a good definition of outputs and solid performance measures which will be able to promote organization internal performance through a customer-oriented ability of employees to further promote the organization external performance. This requires a well-defined training program for the public servants to support implementation of performance contracting.

There is need to study both the public servants' perceptions on the role of performance contracting in improving service delivery to the end users and also the impact of the performance contracting on service delivery to the populace. This will confirm whether the objectives of implementing performance contracting are being achieved in the public sector.

Stability and availability of resources is vital for the success of performance contracting and therefore the top leadership must ensure that necessary resources are available at all time. For the success of performance contracting, the political top leadership must respect the operational autonomy of the contracted organizations/ ministries; knowledge of strategic planning, its development and monitoring capacities.

Contract management should be accompanied by performance-oriented change in the public service structure and management culture. A culture that empowers staff to embrace and manage change is necessary. A solid legal framework, which sets out the basic premises and the status of the contract, may avoid ad hoc and fragmented solutions. When resources are not available or are availed late, the staff involved get frustrated. Stability of resources enhances the motivating effect of the contract.

Enhanced teamwork will also be vital for the achievement of the expected results by the governments. The Cabinet secretaries for instance, will need to sharpen each other for the cabinet to achieve its collective responsibility. A reward system for performers should be developed that is motivating and well understandable by all.

The governments are also obligated to be accountable to their owners, the citizenry. Performance management principles and practices give governments the ability to provide easily understood and timely information to the public so citizens can assess the results their government is producing and fulfill their role as collective owners of their governments.

References

Akaranga, E. M. (2008). *The Process and Effects of Performance Contracting in Kenyan Public Sector*. MBA Project; United States International University (USIU), Nairobi.

Armstrong, M. & Baron, A. (2004). *Managing performance: performance management in action.*McGraw Hill Education.

Armstrong, M. (2001). *Human resource management practice (8th ed.)*. London: Kogan Page Publishers.

Armstrong, M, & Baron, A. (2005). *Managing performance*: Performance management in action. London.

Balogun, M. J. (2003) *Performance Management and Agency Governance for Africa Development:* The search for common cause on Excellence in the Public Service. Addis Ababa: UNCEA.

CIDA (2001) *Results Based Management in CIDA*: An Introductory Guide to Concepts and Principles.

County Government Act (2012), *Kenyan on a trip change Paradigm, Public Service Reform and Development Secretariat*. Creation Government Press

Davis, R. (1995). *Choosing performance management: A holistic approach journal*. New Delhi, CUPA Publication.

GOK, (2007). *Ministry of Human Resources Development Strategy*. Government Printers: Nairobi.

GOK, (2013). *Results for Kenyans: Capacity Building Programme for Transforming the Public Service*. Public Service Reform and Development Secretariat.

Government of Kenya (2003) *Economic Recovery Strategy for Wealth and Employment*.

Hope, K. R. (2001). *The New Public Management: Context and Practice in Africa*. International Public Management Journal, Vol. 4. No. 2.

ICJ Kenya (2013). *Devolution Handbook.* Nairobi, Kenya.

Kobia, M. and Mohammed, N. (2006). *The Kenyan Experience with Performance Contracting.* Discussion Paper, 28th AAPAM Annual Roundtable Conference, Arusha, Tanzania.

Longenecker, C. O. & Goff, S. J. (1992). *Performance appraisal effectiveness*: A matter of perspective. Advanced Management Journal, 57 (2) 18-23.

Luo, Y. &Peng M (1999). *Learning to compete in a transitional economy: experience.*

Moy, R. (2005). *Educational Research: Competence for Analysis and Application. (4th ed.).* New York: Macmillan Publishers.

Opiyo, H. (2006), *Civil Service Reform Policy in Kenya: A review of the Retrenchment Strategy.* Discussion Paper Series: Institute of Policy Analysis and Research.

OPM/PCD (2011) *Report on Evaluation of the Performance of Public Agencies for the Financial Year 2009/2010.* Nairobi: OPM/PCD.

Schiavo-Campo, S. and Sundaram, P. S. A. (2001). *To Serve and to Preserve: Improving Public Administration in a Competitive World.* Manila: Asian Development Bank.

World Bank. (2001). Implementation Completion Report on a Credit in the Amount of SDRs 17.2 Million to the Government of the Republic of Kenya for an Institutional Development and Civil Service Reform Project. Washington, DC: World Bank.

CHAPTER ELEVEN

Change of Attitude for Wealth Creation in the Counties

Mercy Thuranira and Simon Thuranira

Introduction

Attitudes are evaluations of people, events and ideas which are acquired with time through experience, either directly or by observation. Attitudes can be explicit and implicit. Explicit attitudes are those that we are consciously aware of and that clearly influence our behaviors and beliefs. Implicit attitudes are unconscious, but still have an effect on our beliefs and behaviors (Kendra, 2013). Attitudes have three components, cognitive (thinking), affective (feeling), and behavioral (acting). The influence of attitude on subsequent behaviour comes up through mediating cognitive processes involving the individual's perceptions of and cognitions about the attitude object in the immediate situation in which the attitudinal object is encountered. (Fazio, 2006).Therefore individual behaviour is largely a function of his/her perceptions in the immediate situation. Attitudes determine what the individual will see, hear, think and do.

For wealth creation in a county the overt behaviour of the citizens is of great significance, due to the fact that work must be done for the wealth to be created. The determination and the intensity of the work to be done will depend on the evaluation of the objects that are key in the wealth creation process. When the attitude towards a given object is favourable it prompts positive qualities of the object. This selective perception produces perceptions of the object that are consistent with attitude which in turn gives a definition to the object.

The definition of the attitudinal object determines the direction and nature of the behaviour that follows. The model below elaborates this process.

Attitude
Activation

Selective
Perception

Immediate
Perceptions of the
Attitudinal Object

Definition of
the Situation

Behaviour

Creation of Wealth

Source: Fazio, 2006.

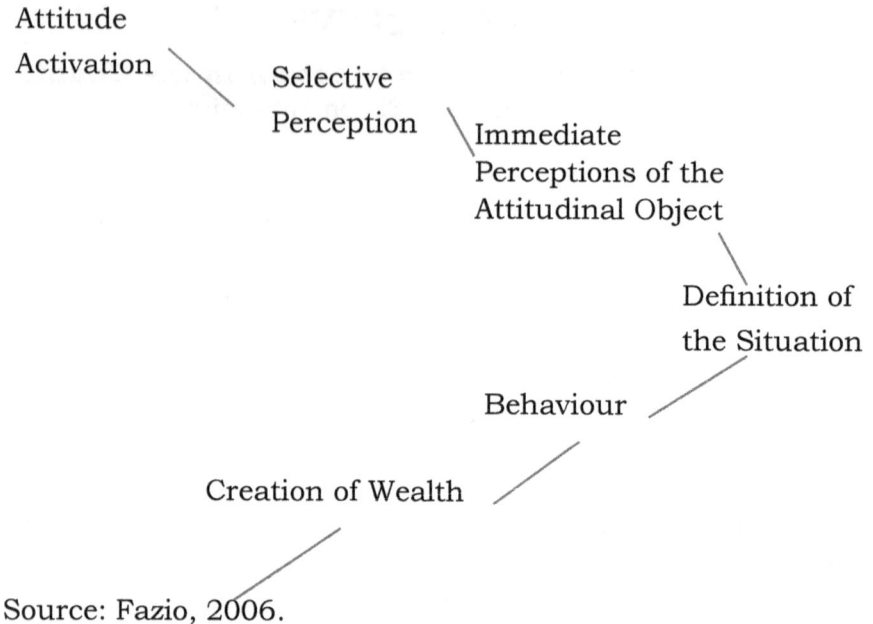

In the wealth creation process the citizens must have a favorable attitude towards attitudinal objects that form a base to behaviors that can lead to wealth creation. This paper highlights the concept of devolution, human resource, natural resource and education as major attitudinal objects that citizens need to have a favorable attitude towards for wealth to be created.

Devolution

Devolution is decentralization of power from the central government to sub-national authorities, in this case the counties. The county government is the centre of dispersing political power and economic resources to the citizens at the grassroots with the governor taking the senior most responsibility (Republic of Kenya, 2010). With the power vested in the governor and the local government the individuals holding these positions will be influenced by their perception of this position on the next move. For example if the leaders interpret this as a chance to get the resources for their individual benefit then the chances are that the disposal of the resources will be self-centered, reaching out to a few individuals.

Leaders who perceive their position as an opportunity to benefit the county on the other hand will utilize the least available resource to create wealth for the county. This includes investments for the county rather than self. Further the idea of devolution can be viewed positively or negatively which can have a great impact on the running of the county. If the citizens and especially the leaders perceive devolution as worthwhile compared to the centralized government, this motivates them to take the initiative to work and produce more for their county. Negative attitude blocks the citizens from seeing the opportunities created by devolution, leading to a state of helplessness. At the individual level helplessness makes one always depend on others and lose hope in their own ability (Kenyon, 2009). This can happen to the county such that it relies on the central government, unaware of its potential.

Human Resource

Each county is endowed with people of different capabilities. People are most crucial in production (Declan, 2011) and specifically if placed in the right positions according to their potential and job requirement. The attitude of the leaders towards people will determine how the human resource will be managed in the county, which is critical in wealth creation. The people can be viewed as a liability or an asset by the leaders (I.N. E. R. D., 2012). That means they are consumers of the little that there is or they can produce more. A positive attitude towards people enables one to notice the great potential they have in wealth creation thus planning widely on where the talents can be applied. Consequently, the attitude individuals have towards each other impacts directly on the level of teamwork displayed (Spreen, 2012). Citizens need to perceive one another as complementary in the mission of wealth creation. Negative attitude towards each other results in unhealthy competition and if not checked can cause war.

Natural Resources

Natural resources are useful raw materials that occur naturally from the earth and the air that can be used to benefit human beings. These include land, water, plants, animals, air, minerals and sunshine (Swafford, 2013). The distribution of the natural resources differs in quality and quantity from county to county depending on the geographical location. Natural resources provide raw materials essential for the creation of wealth but not without the human input. The effort human beings put on the natural resources to create wealth will be a result of their attitude towards the resource. For example, water available in a given county may be perceived to be too little for any agricultural use while in the real sense the same amount of water can irrigate a large piece of land.

Negative attitude would prompt a perceptual emphasis on the negative qualities of an object (Fazio, 2006) thus eliciting a negative response (Ajzen & Fishbein, 2005). Therefore the level of exploitation of the natural resources will be determined by the attitudes the citizens harbor towards the available resources. Kenya being an agricultural country, fertile land is perceived as the most important resource overshadowing all other resources, thus counties with less fertile land may fail to notice or do anything with other resources at their disposal. Due to the fact that attitudes guide information processing (Ajzen & Fishbein, 2005) people with negative attitudes towards available resources may not have any insight on how to utilize them and vice versa.

Attitude Change

Since the response towards various objects is instigated by the attitudes attached to them, the citizens must have positive attitudes towards the objects that form bases for wealth creation- some of which are discussed above. However they need to establish their attitudes first and then identify the ones that need to be changed. The following theories can be applied in realising an attitude change.

•   Learning Theory of Attitude Change: Classical conditioning, operant conditioning and observational learning can be used to bring about attitude change (Kendra, 2013). Citizens can be exposed to various uses of resources in creation of wealth, and through conditioning they can associate them with wealth. Classical conditioning can be used to create positive emotional reactions to an object, person or event by associating positive feelings with the target object. Operant conditioning can be used to strengthen desirable attitudes and weaken undesirable ones. Observing other people work and create wealth in similar conditions makes people change their attitudes, consequently changing their behaviour.

•   Persuasion Theory of Attitude Change: People can be persuaded to change their attitude, by arguing one's position (Feist & Rosernberg, 2010; Meyers, 2013). First, they can be motivated to listen and think about the message, thus leading to an attitude shift. Or, they might be influenced by characteristics of the speaker, leading to a temporary or surface shift in attitude. Messages that are thought-provoking and that appeal to logic are more likely to lead to permanent changes in attitudes (Kendra, 2013). The success of the persuasion depends on how trustworthy, prestigious and likable the persuader is, as well as the method of persuasion. (Feist & Rosernberg, 2010). County leaders are in an appropriate position to persuade people to change their attitudes regarding key aspects of wealth creation, especially if they are good models. Further, people in authority can influence the attitude of others through direct or indirect instruction. When the policies made by authorities yield positive results the people will automatically have positive attitudes towards the given events through that experience.

• Dissonance Theory of Attitude Change (Festinger, 1957): People can also change their attitudes when they have conflicting beliefs about a topic, that is the individuals' cognitions are dissonant or inconsistent, causing some tension.(Fernald & Fernald, (2007). In order to reduce the tension created by these incompatible beliefs, the person is motivated to dispel this state by shifting their attitudes. People need to recognize the attitudes that do not coincide with their actions and align them. For example one could have a negative attitude towards another person yet they must work together to succeed in their work.

Conclusion

Attitudes are precursors of behaviour with the behaviour intensifying when one is consciously aware of the attitude. People persist in overt behaviour that they have favourable attitudes towards. For wealth to be created in the counties the citizens must engage in activities that produce wealth. However the choice and the vigor of activities they engage in depends on their evaluation of the objects, events and ideas forming the base for wealth creation, including ideas of devolution, human and natural resources, education among others. Purposeful evaluation of attitudes held is essential to implement the acquisition of attitudes that are in line with activities that enhance the creation of wealth. Attitudes can change through conditioning, observation or direct/indirect instruction with great success achieved if individuals purpose the change and leaders act as models.

References

Aizen, I & Fishbein, M. (2005). *The Influence of Attitudes on Behaviour.*

Retrieved from Apollo.psico.unimib.it/shared/psycho.scope/site/ AF- Chap.2005.pdf. On 2/2/2017

Declan, D. (2011). *People are the most Important Human Resource.* Retrieved http://www.candidatemanager.net/news/2011/04/ human resource.asp. On 2/3/2016

Fazio, H. R. (2006). *Handbook of Motivation and Cognition: Foundations of Social Behaviour.* New York: The Guilford Press.

Feist, G.J. & Rosernberg, E.L. (2010). *Psychology Making Corrections.* New York: Mcgraw-Hill Higher Education Companies Inc.

Fernald, L.D. & Fernald, P.S. (2007). *Introduction to Psychology.5th Ed.* New Delhi: A.I.T.B.S. Publishers & Distributors.

Government of Kenya (2010). *The Constitution of Kenya.* Nairobi; National Council for Law Reporting.

India: Natural Environment Resources and Development. Module 2 (I.N. E. R. D.). (2012). Population; Our Greatest Resource. Retrieved http://www.nois.ac.in/media/documents/sec.soc. scicour.pdf. Pp 295-319.

Kendra, C. (2013). How Attitudes Form, Change and Shape Behaviour. Retrived from http://psychology.about.com/od/ socialpsychology/a/attitudes.html. On 2/2/2017

Kenyon, P. (2009). *Learned Helplessness and Depression.* Retrieved from http://www.flyshingdevon.co.uk./salmon/year2/ psy221depression/psy221depression.html. On 2/2/2017

Meyers, D.G. (2013). *Psychology 10th Ed.* New York: Worth Publishers.

Spreen, V. (2012). *The Art of Team Work.* Retrieved from http:// www.theartofteamwork.wordpress.com/tag/positive.attitude/. On 2/2/2017

CHAPTER TWELVE

Effects of Land Use Change on Airport and Flight Safety: A Study of Wilson Airport, Kenya

Paul Muthee Kanyi, P. K. Kamau and Caleb Mireri

Introduction

An aviation incident can occur at any time - day or night- under any weather condition, and in varying degrees of magnitude; it can occur instantaneously or develop slowly; it can last only a few minutes or go on for days (United States Department of Transport, 2009). This can be natural, such as a hurricane or earthquake, or it can be "man-made", such as a hazardous materials spill, civil unrest, terrorism, fire, or power outage. Moreover, emergencies of the same type can differ widely in severity, depending on factors such as degree of warning, duration, and scope of impact (United States Department of Transport, 2009).

Globally, there is growing concern over the increasing number of aviation-related disasters, most of which occur at a time when aviation and related business around airports are also increasing thus posing enormous risks to airports and adjoining areas. While aviation disasters have occurred in virtually all parts of the world, there has been a special concern for aviation disasters happening in Africa (Kwiatkowski, 2001). The potential for disaster exists everywhere, and the cost in suffering, life, and property can be devastatingly high. Since emergencies are perceived as low probability events and because preparedness requires cost in time and finances, the importance of such planning can often be overlooked. However, airports and communities that experience such disasters can pay a high price if they are not prepared. In addition to health and safety issues, social disruption, lawsuits, negative publicity, and psychological after-effects may result. While every contingency cannot be anticipated and prepared for, a strong emergency preparedness program can assist in limiting the negative impact of these events, including liability and other post-emergency issues.

In the last two decades, Kenya has witnessed a number of fatal aviation disasters including the Busia, Marsabit, Narok and Ngong plane disasters in which prominent Kenyan political and administration personalities lost their lives (Mutugi and Maingi,

2011). Reports on inquiries into these disasters have pointed to operation in poor aviation environments and non-compliance with international aviation standards and regulations (Mokaya and Nyaga, 2009). Separately, a report by the Aviation Safety Networks (ASN, 2010) provides data of several aviation accidents that have occurred in Kenya between 2006 and 2009. The report observes that 50% of the air accidents occurred during take-offs, 28.6% during landing and 21.4% during cruise. Take-offs and landings accounted for 78.6% of the accidents and thus most air accidents occur during take-off and landing. This is despite, as Mokaya and Nyaga (2009) report, Kenya being a signatory to the International Civil Aviation Convention (ICAC) that sets the standards and regulations to which airports and aerodromes must conform.

The Kenya Association of Air Operators (KAAO) has constantly warned that airports such as Wilson pose real danger to aviation security and safety especially due to encroachment into airport space through residential and commercial buildings, making flight paths invisible to pilots for smooth take-off and landing (KCAA, 2007). Wilson Airport is currently facing an acute challenge of encroachment and exponential real estate developments on its flight path. Considering an airport with approximately 120 000 landings and take-offs annually as reported by the Kenya Civil Aviation Authority (KCAA, 2007), these rapid encroachments pose a real risk to safety.

In light of the increase in real imminent threats to aviation safety challenges in Kenya, the KCCA, in response to the national developmental goals envisioned in the Kenya Vision 2030, has set out to institute measures aimed at ensuring that air operations in Kenya achieve international safety and security requirements. This will require building the capacity of the Authority to deliver quality regulatory oversight services and compliance of the industry with the civil aviation regulations (Republic of Kenya, 2007). This study is one such effort to examine effects of land use changes on airport and flight safety in Wilson Airport.

Wilson Airport is used mostly by general aviation traffic and caters for both international and domestic traffic. The facility is mainly used by tourism, agriculture and health sectors of the economy. Wilson Airport handles about 120,000 landings and take-offs every year, most of it local and regional traffic. As a result of faster check-in times and fewer flight delays, as compared to Jomo Kenyatta

International Airport (JKIA), Wilson Airport is commonly used by business executive aircraft for both domestic and International travel. Common domestic destinations from Wilson Airport include Kisumu Airport, Moi International Airport, Mombasa and Eldoret International Airport.

Despite the existence of comprehensive policies on aviation safety in Kenya, critical aviation safety challenges continue to emerge in the existing airports. Over the past decade, Wilson Airport has faced different challenges ranging from constrained spaces and aviation related accidents. Among the many security and safety concerns raised have been encroachment into airport space with claims that illegal structures and numerous other high-risk business developments within and around the airport have significantly affected flight safety in the airport. All these increasing infrastructural developments pose a threat to aviation activities at the airport.

Different studies have been done in airports in Kenya. Mukaria (2013) did a study on knowledge, awareness and conformity to International Airport emergency preparedness standards, with a focus on Wilson Airport. The study found that dissemination of information among stakeholders was average resulting in low cooperation in the cases of emergency at the Wilson Airport. Obwaya (2010) did a study on disaster risk reduction strategies and preparedness at JKIA and found that the airport plans, facilities and personnel cannot handle a large-scale disaster. No study has been done on the effects on land use changes on airport safety in Kenya and this study therefore seeks to fill such knowledge lacunae.

Land use Changes and Airport Flight Safety

Airports have grown continually since the mid-1960s, a growth which has been accompanied by a negative community reaction (Van Praag, 2005). In addition to the Federal Aviation Administration's (FAA) plan to modernize the National Airspace System through 2025, many airports in the United States are seeking to increase their capacity. A major concern related to the creation and expansion of airports is incompatible land use, in and around noise-sensitive (such as hospitals and educational institutions) and residential communities. For instance, an earlier study acknowledged that resident populations tended to move towards airports, which ultimately led to complaints by community members and a negative public perception of the airport (Kelly, 1997).

Basically, an airport-incompatible land use is any type of land development which jeopardizes the safe operation of aircraft near an airport. These uses include developments such as residential buildings, schools and libraries, nursing homes and hospitals, wetlands and open water, landfills and sewerage treatment facilities, generators of light emissions and others. According to Stephanie et al. (2010), airport-compatible land uses are defined as uses that can coexist with a nearby airport without either constraining the safe and efficient operation of the airport or exposing people living and working nearby to unacceptable levels of noise or hazards. Determining the level of compatibility of land uses around an airport is affected by the type of use and associated concerns.

According to the FAA guidelines on land use planning, incompatible land use and noise are a growing concern in the United States. Published work related to land use can be traced back to the early 1900s, however, the FAA guidelines attempting to ensure compatible land use with respect to airports and surrounding communities were compiled and published only up until recent times (FAA, 1998). In recent years, it became increasingly apparent that, "allowing incompatible real-estate development around airport signals the first step toward closing the airport" (Esler, 2006). According to the U.S. Department of Transportation, an average of 60 public-use landing facilities were shut down between 1993 and 1998 and, in almost every case, incompatible land use was a major contributor. In the case of Stapleton Airport near Denver, the airport was overwhelmed by noise complaints and eventually forced to discontinue operations due to a lawsuit by local citizens.

Guiding compatible land use has been difficult, as most airports' boundaries have had pre-existing development for years. The additional problem stems from the fact that controlling compatible land use does not preclude minimized noise impact on the community. In fact, much of the opposition from communities is generated outside compatible land use jurisdiction. In planning an airport's noise mitigation program, the economic impact of an airport cannot be overlooked. Airports are an economic engine that are vitally important to a community's ability to expand, attract industry, and improve quality of life (Arata, 1970). All of this is linked, however, to the public's perception of the airport. If individual citizens do not support their local airport, it is likely to manifest as negative economic effects for the entire region.

Impacts of Settlement around Airports

Community opposition to growth in airport operations and expansion of airport capacity arises because people are exposed to the adverse environmental impacts of aviation. Of these, aircraft noise is the leading cause of community opposition, and local air quality effects are increasingly gaining attention (GAO, 2007). In addition to being exposed to adverse environmental effects, people who live in areas around an airport face greater risk of exposure to aviation accidents than those who live far away.

While more stringent noise standards and advances in technology have made aircraft quieter, aviation noise will remain a concern when communities allow incompatible land uses, such as residences, schools and hospitals to be built near airports. Incompatible land uses expose people to aircraft noise (GAO, 2007). Exposure to aircraft noise is the leading cause of community opposition to airport expansion (GAO, 2008). People find noise annoying, so that, if exposed to it they generally prefer to reduce the loudness of noise, avoid it, or leave the noisy area, if they can. Noise can disrupt sleep, conversation, and certain leisure activities. A World Health Organization (WHO, 1993) report, found that noise also gives rise to a number of health problems, ranging from insomnia, stress and mental disorders to heart and blood circulation problems.

Despite this negative community reaction, the aviation industry continues to develop new services to meet the demands of our dynamic economy. Airports create employment opportunities, thereby making areas around airports major industrial compounds that increase the local rate of employment. Businesses that rely upon the aviation industry are established in the vicinity of airports to reduce the cost of transporting goods and supplies. A study by McMillan (2004) suggests that better employment opportunities attract people toward airports. A large number of people want to live as close as possible to their place of employment, thus minimizing the time and money they use travelling to work. This leads to more residents near the airport and, in turn, the construction of schools, hospitals, shopping centers, churches, and other community amenities.

Proximity to an airport benefits people in some way. People are drawn to live near airports to have easy access to travel and employment opportunities (Nelson 2004, Lipscomb 2003). Residential development, in turn, benefits local jurisdictions by expanding the local tax base. Often there is prime land located near the airport attracting real estate developers, resulting in higher development of those areas. However, the increased population also results in increased air traffic. It becomes absolutely essential to ensure compatible land use around airports. Airport land-use planning and noise management are challenges faced by airports around the world.

Enhancing Land Use Compatibility around Airports

Much can be done by airports to build and improve relationships with surrounding communities. In fact, over the past few decades, the number of people exposed to airport noise has decreased, which, combined with improved airport/community dialogue, can have a very positive impact (Thomas, 2004). Tedrick (1983) recommends that airports avoid using a 'cookiecutter' approach to compatible land use, but instead focus on the unique issues of their airport's environment, while maintaining a wider view of the national airspace system. Wisconsin, Oregon, California, and Florida, among others, have established guidelines or handbooks for communities near airports to help ensure that new developments near airports are compatible

According to FAA (2007), the following are proactive approaches that can be used by local governmental authorities to prevent, or discourage, near airport incompatible land uses before they occur: overlay or, conventional zoning and control of planned unit developments with certain density of clear zone requirements attached; subdivision regulations requiring open space, restrictions on development in stipulated zones, and other constraints; building code restrictions or conditions to insure sound proofing; agreement with land owners for navigation easements granting over-flight rights even if such an agreement carries a price tag.

However, some airports have expressed the desire that the federal government play a much stronger role in ensuring land use compatibility. The compatible land use guide entitled "Land Use Compatibility and Airports (1998)" was developed for airport managers, local land use planners, and public officials, with the purpose of providing information on FAA programs, and to promote an understanding of land use compatibility around airports. When local land use and airport planners evaluate new development around the airport, the FAA guidelines stipulate that (1) the local comprehensive land use plans are incorporated with the airport master plan; and (2) a comprehensive review is required for the types of future land uses.

According to the compatible land use guidelines, several regulations related to planning have been enacted over the years and are summarized as: Federal Airport Act, 1946 - Established a federal airport grants-in-aid system known as the Federal Aid to Airports Program (FAAP). It was replaced by the Airport and Airway Development Act (AADA) in 1970. This Act obligated the airport owner to operate, maintain and comply with several standards and assurances.

Many articles exist that provide a survey of federal noise legislation, and their effectiveness. Wesler (1981), Hartman, (1986), and Foster (1977) all give an account of these regulations and provide a review of how they are executed in the aviation industry. The land use compatibility guide also includes a list of preventive measures against the introduction of additional noise sensitive land areas within the existing, as well as future noise contours. These measures, also called land use controls, are as follows: zoning changes, residential density, large-lot, and multi-family zoning; noise overlay zoning, areas; transfer of development; environmental and subdivision regulation changes among others. All in all, comprehensive planning policies supporting land use compatibility can involve specific land use plans and policies to guide rezoning, variances, conditional uses, public projects and capital improvement programming to enhance land use compatibility.

Methodology

This study was carried out at Wilson airport located in Nairobi West. The airport is strategically located only about 5 kilometres from Nairobi City centre. The descriptive design was applied in this study to analyze and describe the effects of land use changes on airport and flight safety. A total of 162 respondents were targeted by the study (including 96 members of the community, 30 aviation regulators, 30 air operators and 6 service providers) out of which (including 90 members of the community, 28 aviation regulators, 29 air operators and 6 service providers) there was a response rate of 94%. This population has been targeted due to its significant role in either determining issues of preparedness for disaster and risk or being potential causes of disasters and risks at Wilson Airport.

This study collected primary and secondary data. Primary data was collected by use of questionnaires, interview guide and Focused Group Discussions, which was supplemented by secondary data. Quantitative data was analysed by use of descriptive statistics such as frequencies and percentages while qualitative data was analysed using content analysis.

Findings of the Study

Land Use Changes and Flight Safety at Wilson Airport

This section presents findings on the effect of land use changes on the airport's safety. According to the Kenya National Bureau of Statistics (Republic of Kenya, 2014), there were few buildings around Wilson airport in 1989, when the population of Lang'ata division was 23,320. By 1999, there was development of infrastructure around Wilson Airport, during which the population had increased to 26,080, an increase of about 12% from 1989. By the year 2002, structures had started to develop around the Airport. For example, Mitumba slums had started to develop, while other structures were also initiated along Lang'ata Road and hence behind the flight path. These land use changes are perceived to affect the safety of Wilson Airport and the resident communities around the airport.

Picture 1 shows Mitumba slums adjacent to Wilson Airport.

Picture 1: Mitumba Slums adjacent to Wilson Airport in 2004
Source: Google Earth (2014)

Picture 1 shows that by 2004, Mitumba slums had fully developed. As can be seen from the picture, the slum is a threat to the security of the airport as it spreads to its fence. By the year 2002, there was a clear change in land usage around the airport. Many structures had developed signifying increase in the activities around the airport as shown in Picture 2, which poses a threat to the airport and flight safety.

Picture 2: Estates and Recreational facilities around Wilson Airport, 2004 Source: Google Earth (2014)

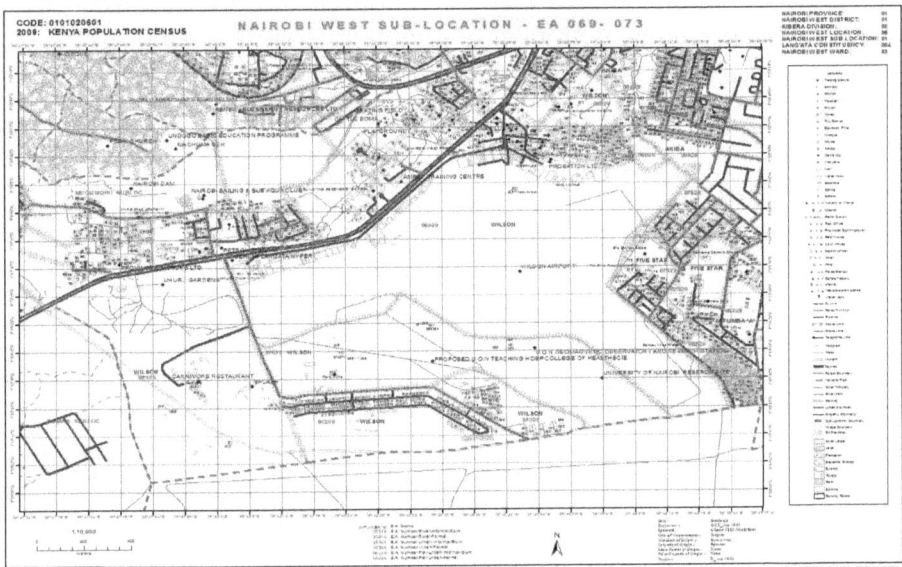

Map of Wilson Airport in 2009
Source: Kenya National Bureau of Statistics (2014)

By the year 2009, there was significant increase in the activities around the airport. The population of the division according to the population census of 2009 was 33,377. This signified an increase by 7,297 (28%) of the population within a span of 10 years. This has resulted in an increase of activities around the airport where supermarkets, schools and petrol stations have been constructed near the airport. These land use activities are a threat to the security and safety of the airport.

Effect of Land Use Changes on Flight Safety

Aviation regulators and air operators were asked to indicate whether the land use changes have affected flight safety. It was found that 42 (74%) the respondents indicated that land use changes have an effect on flight safety, while 15 (26%) of the respondents indicated that land use changes did not have any effect on flight safety.

In an interview with the service providers on the land use problems facing Wilson Airport, they mentioned the following: its close proximity to the city centre; its location in a predominantly residential area; its adjacency to major infrastructure: Lang'ata Road and the Southern By-pass; and its close proximity to key national/park landscapes: Nairobi National Park, Uhuru Gardens, and Nairobi Dam; these are habitats to various wildlife but also serve as natural structural edges that constrain growth. According to Esler (2006), in recent years, it became increasingly apparent that, allowing incompatible real-estate development around airports signals the first step toward closing the airport. In the case of Stapleton Airport near Denver in the United States, the airport was overwhelmed by noise complaints and eventually forced to discontinue operations due to a lawsuit by local citizens (Esler, 2006). Thus, the encroachment of businesses and residential buildings around Wilson Airport can be considered a major threat to the airport. According to the National Airports System Plan report (2010), the Nairobi National Park and Uhuru Gardens are adjacent to the airport and directly constrain the latter's growth.

In an interview with the airport manager, it was revealed that Lang'ata road is a major threat to the security and safety of Wilson airport. He explained that people converge by Lang'ata road to view take offs and landing by planes through the fence of the airport. In an interview with service providers on the land use practices posing a threat to Wilson Airport, the following were mentioned: the emergence of major shopping malls around the airport, proximity of Uhuru Gardens to the airport, adjacency of Nairobi National Park, Mitumba slums, upcoming high-rise development and existence of motor garages next to the airport.

Plate 1 presents the situation.

Plate 1: A major shopping mall in the flight path, Source: KAA

The plate above shows a shopping mall on the flight path, which poses danger to the airport and flight safety. It is probable that criminals can use the mall to launch attacks on an airplane while taking off or landing, with devastating consequences. Such was the concern of close to three quarters of those interviewed in this study.

Plate 2 below show residential houses constructed on the flight path of Wilson Airport, Nairobi

Plate 2: Air accident next to residential houses that have been constructed on the airport flight path

Source: KAA

It is instructive to mention that this poses danger not only to air passengers and the airport in general, but also the residents who reside proximate to the airport such as those in Mitumba slums, as shown in plate 3 below.

Plate 3: Mitumba slums along the flight path

Source: KAA

In addition, Uhuru Gardens, which is next to the airport makes some functions that are normally held in the garden including weddings, a threat to the airport. In an interview with one of the pilots at Wilson Airport, the garden was mentioned as a major threat to the safety of the airport. This was seen as such by the fact that the functions and picnics which are normally held at the garden is an attraction to birds. During the functions, it is common for birds to gather around to eat the food remains and this normally interferes with plane take-offs and landings. In urban as well as in rural areas, there are many food sources that usually attract birds, especially gulls, pigeons and starlings. A single bird having found food can attract others quickly. It may act as a decoy to other birds or attract con-specifics by food calls (Kuyk, 1981). Rodents and insects are other examples of potential food sources, for instance attracting birds of prey or flocks of passerines (Klaver, 1999). If the attracted bird species is hazardous, control of the prey population is a possible solution. In many cases, however, food attractants are the result of human activities.

Examples of food attractants are: open water, trash bins, trash containers storage areas (especially when improperly handled), worms on runways during rain, fishing vessels (these may occur on an island at sea). Other examples are fish or meat industries, landfills, sewer treatment plants or lagoons, birds being fed in parks, grain storage and agricultural activities. Awareness of such food sources at and around the airport is very important. Proper cleaning up, handling of trash, supplemental bird control measures and adjustment of land use are vital methods to prevent attraction of birds (Godsey, 1997).

Plate 4 below is evidence of frequent hitting of birds by planes at Wilson airport.

"The particular one is Marabou stock is the most dangerous bird. At least five pilots have perished because of Marabou bird strike. The bird is very heavy, as such, it may see the aircraft but because it does not have the speed, they definitely collide with the plane. Whenever these birds hit the wind screen of the aircrafts, it smashes because of its weight"
A 50 year old captain from Wilson Airport

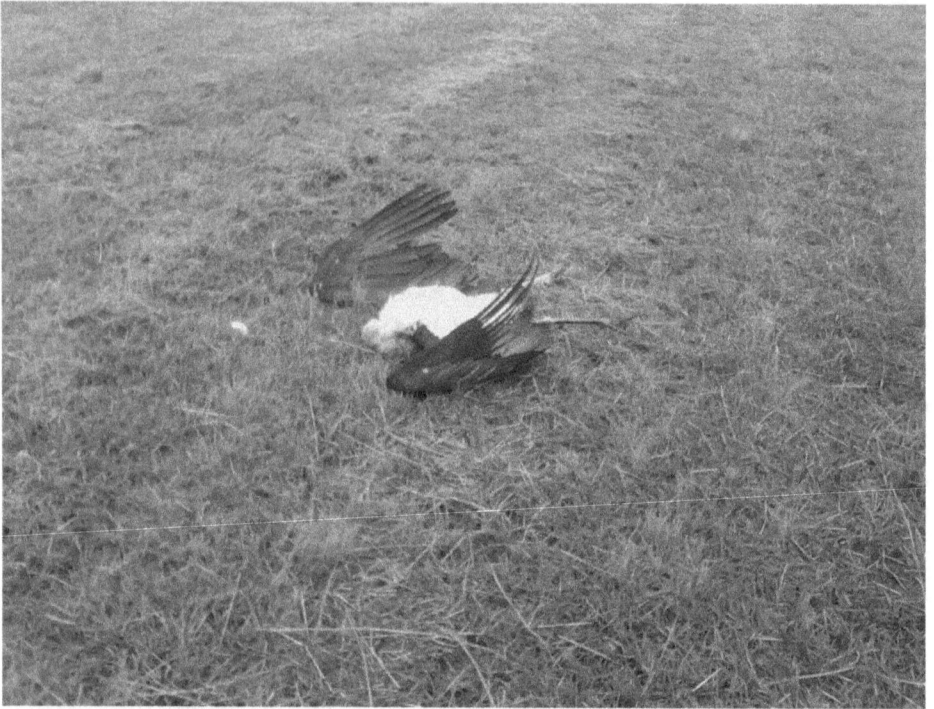

Plate 4: Bird hit by plane at Wilson Airport
Source: KAA

Plate 4 shows a bird hit by a plane during its landing or take-off at Wilson Airport. According to Devine (2009), bird hazard is one of the notable airport hazards across the world and therefore a possible risk to airport safety. The consequences of a bird hitting a plane are shown in plate 5.

Plate 5: Windscreen of an aircraft after hitting a bird
Source: http://www.birdstrikenews.com.

Plate 5 depicts what usually happens when birds are hit by airplanes during their take-off or landing. Earlier on, the method used to scare these birds was the police. This method was highly inefficient in that the police would shoot at the birds and the bullets could end up in planes. Currently, the airport authority has recruited some bird scouts to scare the birds away. The scouts have adopted better methods including recording the sound of predators such as eagles which are then released where the birds are, thus chasing them away.

Extent of Land Use changes and threat to Airport Safety and Security

Regarding the effect of land use changes on airport safety and security, the study found that 42 (73.7%) of the respondents indicated that the construction of tall buildings on the approach and take off path is a threat to aircraft safety to a very large extent. It was also found that 40 (70.2%) of aviation regulators and air operators indicated that the encroachment of non-aviation activities around the port was a threat to the security and safety of Wilson Airport to a very large extent, while 36 (63.2%) of the respondents indicated that the location of dumping sites around the airport which attract birds are a hazard to aircraft engines and thus airport safety to a very large extent. The results are as presented in Table 4.

Table 4: Extent to which Land use changes are a threat to Airport safety

The encroachment of non-aviation activities around the port is a threat to the security and safety of Wilson airport	The location of dumping sites around the airport which attract birds is a threat to visibility and thus airport safety	The construction of tall buildings on the approach and take off path is a threat to aircraft safety		Statement
40	42	36	f	**Very Large Extent**
70.2	73.7	63.2	%	**Large Extent**
15	10	17	f	**Neutral**
26.3	17.5	29.8	%	**Small extent**
2	5	4	f	**No extent at all**
3.5	8.8	7	%	**Total (%)**
0	0	0	f	
0	0	0	%	
0	0	0	f	
0	0	0	%	
57	57	57	f	
100	100	100	%	

In an interview with the service providers on how land use changes have affected airport security and safety, it was revealed that the encroachment of tall buildings around the airport was a threat to visibility during landing and take-off. Indeed, there were plenty of activities that go on around the airport which pose a security risk around the airport, including the development of slums. Defining the airport compatibility land uses, Stephanie et al. (2010) refer to it as uses that can coexist with a nearby airport without either constraining the safe and efficient operation of the airport or exposing people living and working nearby to unacceptable levels of noise or hazards. From the findings of the study, it can be said that one of the major challenges facing the safety of Wilson Airport is the encroachment of incompatible land uses around the airport.

There are also new and upcoming developments on the southern edge of the airport, that include the 5-star hotel, housing estate and the Kenya Police quarters that can be classified as high-rise, hence significant obstacles to aviation activities. There are also proposed residential developments on the parcels of land bordering the southern edge of the airport boundary, whose location is not compatible with airport activities due to noise and related safety matters.

On the Eastern side lies the middle income residential area of South C, West Madaraka, and Nairobi West that have recently been undergoing densification in some areas to include apartment blocks that could increase the obstacle risk to low-flying aircraft using runway 07-25. Carton city, another informal settlement, is also located in this area; the settlement's proximity to the airport poses a safety and security threat to airport operations. Without a proper solid waste management strategy, indiscriminately strewn litter attracts birds which are a threat to aircraft safety.

There is also the risk of spontaneous fires from such settlements and the adjacent open air motor garages that hardly observe safety standards. Such fires could spread very fast especially due to the construction materials used and the fact that fire and rescue becomes difficult because of the congested nature of the settlement. Moi Educational Centre is a school located close to the airport. This is a facility that is sensitive to noise and also could be classified as that which accommodates "captive population". Figure 1 shows the incompatible developments around the Wilson Airport

Figure 1: Land Use Practice around Wilson Airport

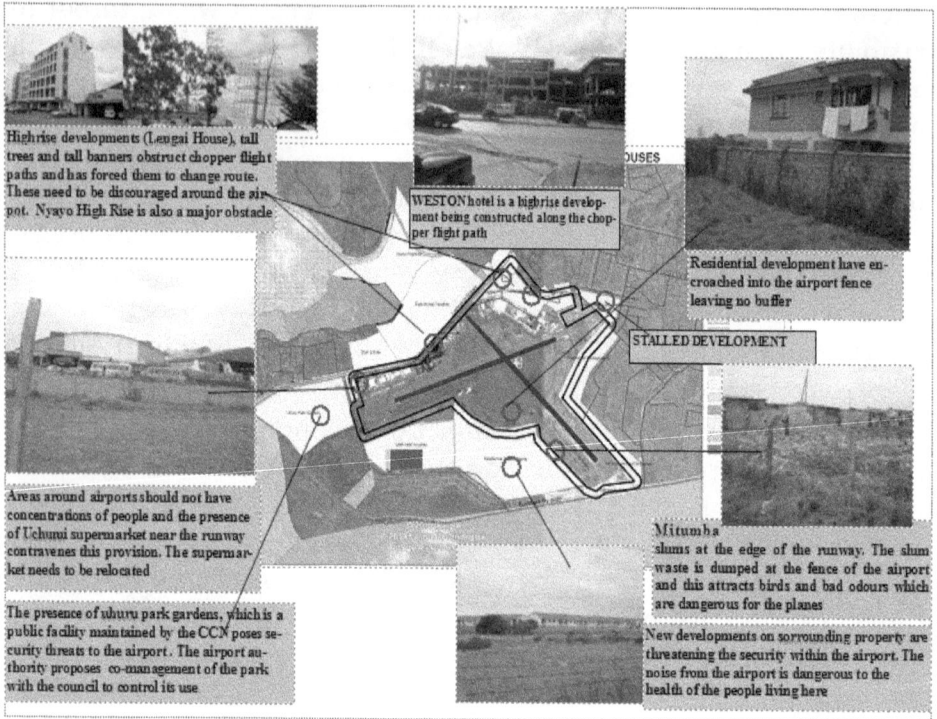

Source: National Airports System Plan Report (2010).

In a focus group discussion with the members of the community on the reason behind their occupancy of the residential houses around the airport, the following were the responses: that the house rents are affordable, that people had already settled in the area over a long period and the proximity of workplaces around the airport. In support of these findings, studies have proved that airports create employment opportunities, thereby making areas around airports major industrial compounds that increase the local rate of employment. Businesses that rely upon the aviation industry are established in the vicinity of airports to reduce the cost of transporting goods and supplies. A study by McMillan (2004) suggests that better employment opportunities attract people toward airports. A large number of people want to live as close as possible to their place of employment, thus minimizing their time commuting to work. This leads to more residents near the airport and, in turn, the construction of schools, hospitals, shopping centers, churches, and other community facilities.

In an interview with one of the pilots on the danger of the national park to the airport, he explained that the park in itself is a savior in cases of mechanical problem during take-off.

> "The busiest runway by the name "runway 07" which is in the direction of south B and south C estates which are very heavily built up. We have had several disasters on that runway. In cases of danger to an aircraft on runway 07, there is no escape but to smash buildings. What currently helps is the discretion of pilots who prefer to use runway 14 which empties into the National park. Every year we have at least 3 to 4 airplanes taking off in runway 14 but they end up landing in the National park.
> A 60 year old pilot at Wilson Airport.

The pilots mentioned that the major threats are the dogs which get in through the fence especially from Mitumba slums. During the rainy season there are a lot of pools of water which attract a lot of birds. The same case applies to the dump bins around the supermarkets near the airport. According to MacKinnon (1997), sewage lagoons or treatment plants and on-base landfills should be situated as far from the runways as possible and situated in such a way that flocks of birds attracted by dumped foods do not cross the runways. A small working surface, overnight waste dumping and immediate covering, combined with exclusion and repellent techniques are advisable. Tall trees around landfills, the presence of dumping bins and continued existence of landfills have encouraged gulls and other species of birds to congregate around the airport, thus posing danger.

Summary of Findings

On the effect of land use changes on flight safety at Wilson Airport, the study found that 74% of the respondents indicated that it had negative effects on flight safety, while 26% of the respondents indicated that land use changes did not have effect on flight safety. The land use changes included: emergence of shopping malls, proximity of Uhuru Gardens, and adjacency of Nairobi National Park, Mitumba slums, upcoming high-rise development, hotels and existence of motor garages next to the airport. The study further found that 73.7% of the respondents were of the opinion that the construction of tall buildings on the approach and take off path is a threat to aircraft safety to a very large extent. In addition, 70.2% of aviation regulators and air operators indicated that the encroachment of non-aviation activities around the airport was a threat to the security and safety of Wilson Airport, while 63.2% of the respondents indicated that the location of dumping sites around the airport which attract birds was and continues to be a threat to visibility and thus airport safety.

The reasons for the occupancy of residential houses near the airport included their affordability and the fact that people had already settled in the area thus other prompting others to join them. The results from correlation analysis showed that disaster preparedness is positively related with land use changes with a Pearson's Correlation Coefficient of r = 0.509 and that at a level of significance of 0.000 meaning that it is statistically significant as p value is less than 0.05.

Conclusion and Recommendations

From the findings of the study, it can be concluded that land use changes are a major threat to safety and security at Wilson Airport. This is evidenced by the setting up of major shopping malls near the airport, proximity of Uhuru Gardens to the airport, adjacency of Nairobi National Park, Mitumba slums, upcoming high-rise development, hotels and existence of motor garages next to the airport.

The study recommends that the government should do an urgent operation on land encroachment as this is perceived to be a disaster in waiting. This will help in clearing the surrounding areas especially along the flight path, approach and take off routes. The foregoing is expected to prevent possible disasters including terrorist attacks and at the same time save civilians who may be caught up in case of aviation disasters. This will not only forestall possible loss of human lives but also property and infrastructure.

References

Birger, H. & Jeppe, N. (2005). *The epistemological lifeboat*. Retrieved from http://www.db.dk/ (18/11/2016).

Devine, J. (2009). *Causes of airplane accident*. Retrieved from http://ezinearticles.com (26/10/2016).

FAA (2009). *Draft Advisory Circular AC 150/5200-31B*, Airport Emergency Plan.

Godsey, O.L., (1997). *Bird Aircraft Strike Hazard (BASH) Management* Techniques.

KCAA. (2007). Rules of the air and air traffic control regulations. Kenya Civil aviation Authority.

Kelly, T. C., M. J. A. O'Callaghan, and R. (Bolger. 2001). *The avoidance behaviour shown by the rook (Corvus frugilegus) to commercial aircraft. in H. J. Pelz*, D. P. Cowan, and C. J. Feare (Editors), Advances in vertebrate pest management II, pp.291-299. Filander Verlag.

Kenya, Republic of. (2007). *Kenya Vision 2030*. Nairobi: Ministry of Planning, National Development and Vision 2030.

Klaver, A., (1999). *Faunabeheerplan Amsterdam Airport Schiphol 2000 t/m 2005*.

Kwiatkowski, K U, (2001). *Expeditionary Air Operations in Africa*: Challenges and Solutions, Fairchild Paper .Alabama: Air University Press.

MacKinnon, B., (1997). B*eyond Airport Boundaries. Airport Wildlife Management Bulletin*, Transport Canada. Meeuwen in Nederland.

McMillan, J. H. & Schumacher, S. (2006). *Research in education: Evidence-based inquiry*. pp. 233-240.

Ming, K.L, Gary, E.; Laffitte, J. and McDaniel, D. (2007). *Land Use Management and Airport Controls*. Trends and indicators of incompatible land use. Report No. 1, Partner - COE – 2008. Cambridge.

Mokaya, S Chocho, T.A and Kosgey,D, (2009). *The Performance of Aviation Regulatory System in Kenya*. Paper Presented at the Moi University International Management and Entrepreneurship Conference, August 2009.

Mukaria, S.M (2013). *Knowledge, awareness and conformity to International Airport emergency preparedness standards*: the case of Wilson Airport in Nairobi, Kenya. Published Thesis. University of Nairobi.

Mutugi, M.W and Maingi, S.G. (2011). *Disasters in Kenya. A major public health Concern.* Journal of Public Health and Epidemiology, Vol. 3(1), pp.38-42, January 2011.

Senge, P., Kleiner, A., Roberts, C., Ross, R. and Smith, B. (1994). *The Fifth Discipline Fieldbook: Strategies and Tools For Building a Learning Organization. London*: Nicholas Brealey Publishing.

CHAPTER THIRTEEN

Towards Social Rehabilitation and Transformation in Kenya: Borrowing From Bandura and Rogers

Josephine Wambua

Introduction

Sociologists looks at a society as a group of people with a common territorial boundary, interaction; they get into contact with one another and share a common culture, language, beliefs, values, behavior and material objects that constitute their way of life. Kenya is a society in its own right, it has a territorial boundary, has people though from different ethnic groups, who interact and share a lot including language and other artifacts-a common culture. For any society to function well, it has some way of life that guides it, the normative system. The Kenyan normative system presents the country with the ideals and values in the form of institutions and associations that are inter-related according to the norms. An example of such a normative system is the Constitution of Kenya, the supreme law of the land that forms the genesis and guideline for human behaviour.

The normative system functions by statuses which define the roles and obligations of individuals and their institutions. The desires, aspirations and expectations of the individuals that are varied and multiple, can only be fulfilled sufficiently if the members of the society are assigned different roles according to their capacities and capabilities. For the social structure to remain well coordinated there must be conformity to social norms and to enforce the social norms, an effective sanction system must be in place. In order for a successful working of social structure, individuals in a society must play their roles and invest effort in fulfilling their duties to the society. For example, Kenya as a country has the Constitution as a normative system, which clearly outlines the duties and roles of institutions and individuals manning the institutions. It also outlines sanctions that come into effect if there are deviations from the provisions of the normative social system.

The challenges that the country faces, such as corruption, misallocation of resources including talents, poor political governance and negative ethnicity all point out to a loophole in

Kenya's social structure. As an abstract, the social structure is dynamic and constantly changing. It is difficult therefore to say that a particular individual or institution is responsible for the change in the structure. Rather, it would be more practical to note the changing patterns within a particular institution in the society. We could say that a pattern of corruption has evolved in a particular system in the society. Through various processes that culminate in the bigger picture, this chapter looks at the challenges in Kenya as a pattern, and seeks to bring theoretical perspectives to broadly understand the origin of the patterns and how these theories could be used to try to re-socialize the society into the ideal norms that make a successful social system. The theories that will be adapted are the Social Learning theory by Albert Bandura and the Client Centered theory by Carl Rogers. These two theories look at the patterns in individual thought and behaviour, which in turn affect the environment of the individual, and the society as a whole.

The Socialization Process

Every society has a way in which the young are prepared to function well and responsibly in that given society, this is the socialization process. Different cultures in the society have their own methods of socialization, and most of the teachings in these socialization processes are similar, for example, what is morally right or wrong and the social distance to keep with respect to various individuals bearing in mind their particular relationship to you. Socialization therefore prepares one for future roles; such as gender roles in adulthood, including parenthood. It also helps one cultivate sources of meaning, for example what is valued or important, such as the family—integrity as well helping one control their impulses and develop a conscience towards what is right and wrong— ethics. At a minimum, socialization makes us social animals, enabling us not to react out of our impulses, but from complicated mental process that involve weighing each action as to its rightness and wrongness and in line with societal expectations on us.

Primary socialization occurs in the early years of one's life as a child or an adolescent, while secondary socialization occurs throughout one's life even as an adult. Therefore, socialization is a process that goes on until one dies and as a social process, it takes place as one interacts with people or groups. The socialization agents including parents, siblings, school, church, friends and any other people one may meet. Socialization is intended to bring out individualism, self-expression and independence, as well as obedience and conformity. One is expected to be independent to make their own decisions and take care of themselves as well as others, while obeying and conforming to the social systems and structures in which he or she lives and happens to be a member. Socialization therefore refers to the idea that the society shapes its members towards compliance and cooperation to its requirements.

In this process, appropriate norms, attitudes, self-images, values and role behaviors develop as a result of cognitive evaluations of costs and benefits in different situations. 'The self' is seen to develop, and the individual becomes independent and an active negotiator in groups and the roles they play in society. Socialization in summary can be termed as a learning process that takes place in the social context. It would be right to say hereafter, that one can be socialized into high ideals of the society, thereby shaping an individual into a responsible citizen. In the same breath, an individual could be socialized in a harsh, indisciplined environment, thereby being shaped into an irresponsible citizen with difficulty conforming to the social norms.

The latter individuals then end up facing the sanction systems laid out in the society including the rehabilitation system, prisons, mob justice, isolation and others in order to re-socialize them into conformity and compliance with the society's norms. Young children are usually socialized into negativity by what they learn from the adults around them. For example, a child who hears the parents commenting negatively about a particular member of an ethnic group will form a negative image about that ethnic group even before they come into contact with a member of the ethnic group that the parents talk negatively about. A cognitive frame has already been formed in the child's mind.

The Learning Process

Psychologists define learning as a relatively permanent change in behavior gained over time consequent of experience. Several theories of learning such as classical conditioning, operant conditioning, both of which relied on a stimulus-response kind of learning, were used to explain the acquisition of behavior through learning. Albert Bandura (1963) argued that these theories discounted the influence of social interaction in an individual's learning experience.

He began to conduct studies about the acquisition of behaviors through observation learning. One of his insightful successes was the experimentation with the Bobo dolls; where children were exposed to a video of adults treating a doll violently, and another group exposed to adults treating the doll well. The group that was exposed to the adults treating the Bobo doll violently treated the doll violently when they were put in the same environment with the Bobo doll. Contrary, the group exposed to the adults treating the Bobo doll well, had the opposite reaction to the Bobo doll. This differentiation was brought about because the children had learned how to treat the Bobo doll purely from observations of adults' interactions with the Bobo doll.

To account for the varied learning experiences in the real world, the observational learning theory integrated cognitive and behavioral theories to explain learning. Bandura and Walters (1977) described the basic tenets of the observational learning theory as follows:

1. That learning does not purely depend on stimulus-response processes; rather, it is a cognitive process that takes place within a social context.

2. Learning can occur by observing another person's behavior and the consequences of that behavior; which they called vicarious reinforcement.

3. For learning to occur, one must observe, extract information from the observations made, and make a decision about the performance of the behavior, which could involve modeling. Therefore, learning can occur without an observable change in behavior.

4. Reinforcement is not entirely responsible for learning, though it plays a role in the learning process.

5. Cognition, environment and behavior all influence each other in a process called reciprocal determinism, in which case the learner is not a passive recipient of information.

The foregoing is in line with the socialization process, where one develops 'the 'self' through acquisition of appropriate norms, attitudes, values and role behaviors. Hence, one must make cognitive evaluations of what is beneficial to him/her, from the internalized cognitive frame of reference for interpersonal relations, which the individual learns to use in various levels of organization of society, in which case, modeling is key in the Social Learning Theory. Bandura outlined three types of modeling stimuli:

1. A live model in which an individual demonstrates the desired behavior.
2. Verbal instruction in which the desired behavior is described in detail and the participant is instructed on how to engage in the behavior.
3. Symbolic models, which are found in movies, television, internet, literature and radio.

The information captured by the observer is influenced by the type of model and a series of cognitive and behavioral processes, which include:

1. Attention-the observer must attend to the modeled behavior, which is impacted by characteristics of the observer, which include perceptual and cognitive abilities, the level of arousal and past performance. It is also impacted by the relevance and functional value of the behaviour or event.
2. Retention-to reproduce an observed behavior, one must be able to remember features of the behavior.
3. Reproduction- the observer must organize responses in accordance with the model.
4. Motivation-the decision by the observer to reproduce or refrain from reproducing the observed behavior. This is influenced by anticipated consequences and internal standards of the individual.

The concept of reciprocal determinism; an important factor in the Social learning theory states that just as the environment influences an individual's behavior, the environment is also influenced by the individual's behavior. That is to say, a person's behavior, the environment and personal qualities all reciprocally influence each other. It is with this concept that this chapter sets its base in seeking answers to the social challenges faced in Kenya today. A child's behavior is therefore influenced by the learning experiences from childhood to adulthood. Socialization through live, verbal and symbolic models all form the basis on which the individual forms their cognitive frames. It is these frames that help the individual make decisions on whether to engage in a given behavior or not. Below is a diagrammatical expression of learning through observation.

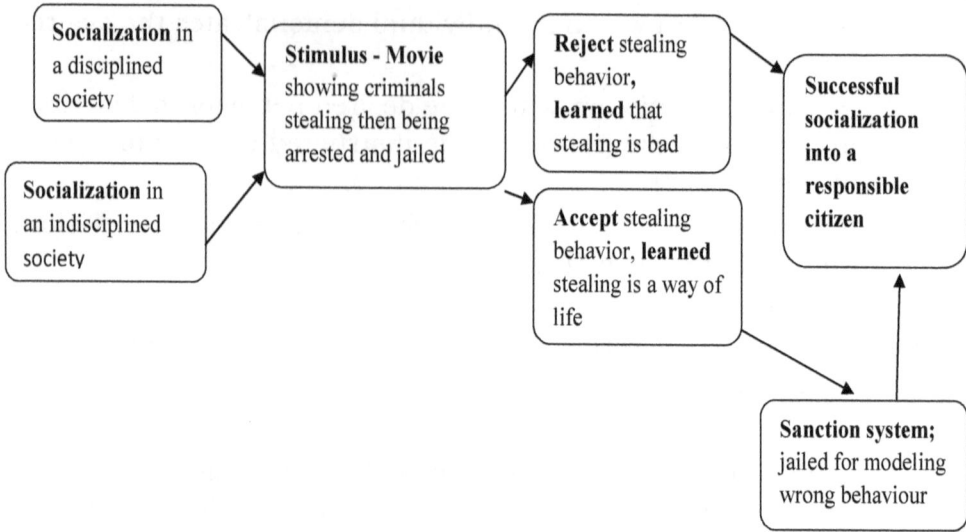

Figure. 1: The learning process through socialization

In figure 1, two individuals were socialized differently, one in an ideal society that upholds discipline, and the other in a society that is undisciplined, are exposed to a stimuli; a movie depicting some criminals stealing, then being arrested and taken to jail. These two individuals who were watching clearly have different inferences from the stimulus they were exposed to; the one from the disciplined socialization interprets the stealing behavior from the movie as bad. This is in agreement with the socialization that he/she was exposed to, and rejects the behavior, which then translates into responsible behavior conforming to social norms. The other individual socialized in a harsh indisciplined environment, reacts differently. He/she identifies with the behavior depicted in the movie, because the environment in which he/she has been brought up in is similar. The same behavior is displayed and sometimes goes unpunished or the wrongdoers are punished, jailed and let back into the society after rehabilitation. This pattern of behavior does not seem peculiar to this individual, and it is interpreted as acceptable behavior. The individual at one point then, models the inappropriate behavior and is incarcerated and rehabilitated to the right norm.

Juxtaposing Social Learning in the Kenyan Society

The foregoing is exactly what is happening in Kenya today, whereby young people who are socialized into the society by parents, relatives and institutions of learning are exposed to a myriad of learning experiences. Some of these experiences conflict with their early childhood socialization, while others are in line with their socialization. When the 'self' has fully developed, these young people refer to the cognitive frames that were modeled to them as they grew up. As such, corruption, negative ethnicity and many ills in the Kenyan society are also learning experiences that could be modeled by the young citizens. Cases like the Anglo-Leasing, Goldenberg and the Eurobond, Chicken Gate and National Youth Service financial scandals, land grabbing, ethnic violence, whistle blowing and moral fidelity witnessed in Kenya are all forms of experiences which the young people can learn to either reject or accept as a way of life.

Reciprocal determinism comes into play here. A social ill like corruption causes many ripple effects that reach far beyond the immediate environment of the perpetrator. This causes unemployment in cases of nepotism, which is one of the biggest challenges facing the country today. Many young scholars graduate from colleges and universities optimistic of getting employed, which is not always the case. The few who are connected to influential people then get lucky, and the rest remain without employment. When these young people then get into these influential positions, they replicate the behavior they observed, and because the behavior was not sanctioned, they were positively reinforced to learn that it is acceptable behavior, which is wrong.

The sanction systems in any country including Kenya are enshrined in the constitution and legislation and citizens are expected to adhere to them. For example, the Ethics and Anti-Corruption Commission has been in place in Kenya for a long time, and this institution has had challenges in stamping its authority in curbing corruption in the country. As the institution bequeathed with the responsibility of arresting any form of corruption including the sensitive cases, it should model the pattern of upholding integrity especially in public offices. This may be done by following through the reported cases and making sure the perpetrators get their date in court. This form of pattern then forms a model of behavior that, should one be found to be corrupt or acting contrary to the law, they should be punished. This will serve as a model not only to the young people, but to the older generation as well.

Kenya has good models from whom moral and ethical behavior can be emulated. For example, the late Professor Wangari Muta

Maathai who combined science, social commitment and politics succeeded in environmental conservation as well as women empowerment. Despite many challenges she faced in this endeavor, she succeeded to the level of winning the 2004 Nobel Peace Prize. Such is the ideal socialization full of learning opportunities that despite many challenges one can succeed in standing for what is right, fidelity to one's country and society.

The Expectancy Value theory according to Vroom (1964), states that behavior is a function of the expectancies one has and the value of the goal toward which one is working. When more than one behavior is possible, the chosen behavior will be the one with the largest combination of expected success and value. The behaviors people perform are in response to their beliefs and values and are undertaken to achieve some end. According to the Expectancy Value theory, if one is socialized to value integrity and loyalty to moral uprightness, then they are more likely to choose behavior that upholds moral integrity. On the contrary, if one learns that need for power and influence over others is valuable, then they will always choose the behavior that will gratify this belief, be it wrong or right. It is important therefore, to inculcate and model moral values to the young and reinforce the behavior by rewards and recognition in order to bring out the desired behaviour.

In the Social Learning theory, the balance of reinforcement may act as a motivation to go against the norm even when one's socialization is contrary. Hence the individual may act in the contrary when the reinforcement balance and the balance of one's own definitions are in the same deviant direction. The social learning process is reciprocal and sequential. Imitation, which occurs after the direct or indirect observation of similar behavior by others, is more important in the initial acquisition and performance of novel behavior than in the maintenance and cessation of behavioral patterns once established. If an individual observes a kind act, where that kindness is reciprocated with a reward, then the likelihood of the behavior being imitated is high. When a pattern of reinforcement after the kind behavior has been established, then imitation remains in the background as the behavior has already been learned and cognitively framed, indeed institutionalized. In this, we see the importance of modeling the right behavior in the initial stages of socialization given that it forms the basis for learning what is right.

The Process of Re-Socialization

Moral character is appropriately viewed as a combination of social integrity and personal integrity. A person with moral character is predisposed to show kindness and compassion with empathic understanding, acquire a wide range of abilities that enables them to resolve problems and analyze situations independently. This is especially where principles may be in conflict and adapt to change in a way that is personally and socially constructive. One also shows courage to be honest and principled irrespective of circumstances and display a high level of commitment in line with the group norms, goals and standards.

According to Dewey (1998), good instructional models for character development take into consideration the need to:

1. Define for learners what is good and right, keeping the definitions simple and learnable.

2. Develop in the learners a sense of moral responsibility and commitment to the virtues taught.

3. Develop in the learners the ability to think independently about moral issues and to make autonomous judgments.

4. Know what children can learn and infuse and in what environment at different stages of their development.

5. Suffuse and inject moral instructions in all aspects of their lives

6. Keep all stakeholders on board with the learning experiences being exposed to the children.

7. Operate on what is respectful to all religious beliefs of parents and children.

8. Bring together all interested and affected participants into the planning of the model so that a unique combination of design could be brought out.

Personal integrity includes the virtues of kindness, courage, ability and effort. Social integrity includes the virtues of friendship, teamwork and citizenship. From the foregoing definition, do we have personal and social integrity in our socialization processes at home and in school? Do we foster a sense of moral responsibility and commitment to virtues, empowering the young to think independently and make autonomous judgments? It is the view here that social integrity could be lacking in our socialization processes while courage and citizenship need a boost in the learning processes in order to strengthen the sense of nationalism and pride among Kenyans. Not long ago there was a slogan that was formulated to bring out a sense of pride and nationalism in our country, Proudly Kenyan. The social and personal integrity virtues seem simple and commonly sense, but are they truly practiced?

History is replete with stories of personal sacrifice, people who helped in their own way to make a difference wherever they were, and they touched the lives of many and offered in their lives a model of virtues to be upheld not only in their immediate environment, but across the globe. Examples here include Mother Teressa of Calcutta and her work with the poor in India, Nelson Mandela, who despite the challenges of apartheid united South Africa at a time when conflict was almost inevitable. Indeed, Nelson Mandela demonstrated, unlike other African leaders that power can be utilized for unity and peace as opposed to silencing opponents. Both Nelson Mandela and Mother Teresa modeled kindness, courage, ability, effort, friendship, teamwork and citizenship in their public lives.

The Mau Mau fighters in Kenya modeled courage, ability, teamwork and a great sense of citizenship, to the point of giving their lives in exchange for the independence of the country. A critical look at the foregoing instances brings out the virtues that place before us learning experiences that we can emulate to strengthen the moral fiber of the society in Kenya and instill patriotism. If a group of men and women could go through torturous challenges to bring independence to the nation, why would a responsible citizen enjoying peace engage in corruption, irresponsible leadership and negative ethnicity, in essence jeopardizing the independence that was so expensive to get? The principle of reciprocal determinism comes into play here, in thinking about what damage we cause to ourselves and others when we engage in such immorality. These processes are important, they stem from socialization, and the learning process gained from experience.

Some private schools in Kenya have started inculcating the virtues of social and personal integrity, by offering practical models of the Kenyan government in the running of their schools. Pupils in the schools get to independently hold elections in the students' body. Officials that help run the school, in conjunction with the school administration are elected. The elected posts of senators, governors and even school president are in the offing. Campaigns are run freely and fairly within a given period, and thereafter elections are held transparently in the school grounds. The process culminates in the crowning of the school president and other officials in colorful ceremonies.

The foregoing is a very important exercise for the pupils because the positions they hear about in the greater national elections are de-mystified, and they are educated about the responsibilities of holding these positions. What can we infer in the future if all the schools would educate their pupils about good governance and create an opportunity for them to model the virtues in real time in their schools? A balanced social structure with high moral ideals and with citizens with the requisite social and personal integrity to lead Kenya is likely to be the outcome. This will be reinforced if there is attendant support for what the schools are doing from parents and significant others. Indeed, the challenges of negative ethnicity, corruption and irresponsible leadership would be a thing of the past, making Kenya a good place for present as well as future generations.

The foregoing illustrations are in line with Vessels (1998), in his study about the Learning Models. He came up with an ideal situation in which pupils could learn, which he outlined as follows:

1. Pupils require a supportive environment that includes relationships with parents, teachers and generally significant others.
2. Pupils require unstructured peer group interaction and play that minimizes adult intrusion.
3. Pupils require developmentally appropriate discipline and reinforcement that treats pupils with dignity and respect.
4. Pupils need exposure to virtuous models, with which children and adolescents can identify.
5. Pupils require developmentally appropriate direct teaching about moral standards and desirable virtues.
6. Pupils require an environment in which they can participate actively-just, democratic and caring communities.

Where then do the pupils learn the virtues that have been thus outlined? From the adults and there lies the critical question: are the adults modeling the right behavior? Can they truly say that they wish their children could emulate their modeling? If so, then the society is in safe hands. However, this is not the pattern we see depicted in our society today. We can endeavor to re-socialize the adults into modeling moral behavior and virtues that the young can learn from and pass on to generations to come.

Adults, unlike children, may not necessarily need to be trained or taught about virtues. Instead, they need practical reflection that leads to transformative learning. Adults in their socialization make meaning out of experiences and events, because the self has already fully developed. The adult is able to independently make an autonomous decision about a particular issue. Re-socialization in this case will involve reflection of behavior and decisions one has made. Reflection enables one to correct distortions in beliefs and errors in problem solving. Learning here would be defined as the process of making a new, revised interpretation of an experience, which will guide subsequent understanding.

Going back to the Expectancy Value theory, we can deduce that adults are powerfully influenced by habits of expectation and these habits constitute their frame of reference, which help them interpret their experiences. Adults always have to make meaning out of what they see or do. Therefore, meaning interpretations or perspectives refer to the structure of assumptions within which new experience is assimilated and transformed by one's past experience. For example, if an adult's cognitive frame from socialization knows that stealing is bad, then when that adult is faced with a situation like bribery in their line of work, he/she will automatically refer to the frame. Because they know the consequences of stealing, the interpretation of the situation will be that bribery is a form of stealing and I should not be involved in the behavior.

Habits are structures of experience that enable one to make sense of a situation. Believing, valuing, perceiving, thinking and feeling are all affected by habits with which one interprets the meaning of objects and events (Ostrow, 1987). In this light, why not create good habits that create a platform for interpretation and perception of issues? For example, when a police officer refuses to take a bribe and makes an arrest for a traffic offence, a token of recognition, should be given to him or her. This will then trigger the particular police officer and others to do the same when faced with two conflicting situations. The token of recognition for refusing a bribe is a socialization experience that presents with it a cognitive frame of reference to refer to when faced with the situation in the future. The question is, do the old police officers train new recruits this way or do they instead induct them into the bribery culture?

Many situations that go wrong usually call for punishment of the offenders. While this is a good platform for inferring in the future, it is also good to reward the people who are conforming to the norm and make it a habit to do the right thing. Rewards are better as they have a two-fold effect, they encourage the behavior to be repeated, and they encourage other people to model the behavior. The importance of rewards lies in the consistency and timing of the reward system in order for learning to occur, the vicarious reinforcement. Adults put importance in what others communicate concerning values, ideals, feelings, moral decisions and concepts of freedom, justice, love, labor, autonomy, commitment and democracy.

It is therefore important to put this into account when coming up with a re-socialization model for any institution. The token of recognition communicates the importance of autonomy to make the right decision, commitment to one's duty, moral decisions in one's work, as well as upholding justice for the greater benefit of the society. The person who is arrested faces the law in accordance to his/her offence, thereby deterring the behavior from recurring. The action of the police officer when repeated reduces traffic offenses and socializes motorists into safe driving.

In Kenya, not long ago there were punitive policies including suspension of night travel for the public vehicles that were published for any traffic offense in order to reduce road accidents. Sometimes when a Public Service Vehicle belonging to a particular organization is involved in a traffic offence, the whole organization is punished. These punitive measures yielded some normalcy in reducing accidents on the road, and public service vehicles seemed to adhere to the traffic rules. This is also a good example of using punishment in re-socialization of the drivers and the PSV companies to reign in their members to conform to the law.

Another form of socialization could be Behaviour Change Communication (BCC), a technique that has its roots in the Rogerian Client-Centered theory (Rogers, 1951, Corey, 1986, 1991)). Carl Rogers (1951) discovered that the best vantage point for understanding how people behave was from their own internal frame of reference. He focused the self, a process of becoming one's own experiences, characterized by openness to experience, an internal locus of evaluation and the willingness to be a process in change. BCC is a communication strategy that is used in improving the health of individuals in communities. The strategy uses Education Through Listening, a facilitation technique that catalyzes a participatory and productive community dialogue resulting in behavior change. This method has worked successfully in sensitizing communities in Kenya in the use of condoms to reduce HIV transmission, and the use of mosquito nets in the prevention of malaria.

The same technique could be used to desensitize the Kenyan people in the small communities about vices like corruption and negative ethnicity. Through focus group discussions, edutainment, drama and outreach sessions, Kenyans in these communities can express their disappointments as well as get educated on some of the country's policies that can better their lives. Rogers (1972), said that people listen when they are listened to and this is proven to be the case in the Rogerian Client-Centered therapy, in which the client is given a conducive environment to express themselves. In this light, why not present opportunities for dialogue and debate to listen to the experiences of the citizens, after all, they are the very same people who engage in the behavior that we so wish to change. Forums for open dialogue have already been set in the social media, where the president and various leaders can communicate and get feedback from the citizens. This is commendable, although not many citizens can access internet services.

Conclusion

The socialization process forms a platform for inferences in the future for children and adults alike. It is a learning experience in which the society shapes individuals into conforming to its norms. Bandura (1977), found out that learning occurs in a social context, whereby the individual is an active participant and negotiator in what happens in the environment around them. Learning experiences could be positive or negative, and it is up to the individual to make a decision based on their best judgment on which behavior to model, based on the cognitive inferences one accumulates in their socialization process.

It is important therefore that children are presented with a moral environment with which the right cognitive frames are formed. Personal integrity, which involves kindness, courage, ability and effort are socialized to the young. Social integrity, which involves friendship, teamwork and citizenship are socialized to the young at a tender age and these continue to be reinforced as they grow up.

An environment of autonomy should be availed for the children to practice what they learn from their socialization. Opportunities for them to re-enact what they learn should be presented, like the government model in the schools. This gives them real experiences with which to practice their learned virtues as well as new ones. Socialization agents are important to children, and they should be of upright moral character in order to present to the young people a pattern that can be emulated.

Adults place meaning in their expectations, which like the young, are infused in their cognitive frames formed during socialization. In order to re-socialize adults into social norms, it is important to present an opportunity for reflection of behavior, by presenting an environment of democracy, justice and commitment. A consistent pattern of reward and punishment is best at work as this presents the adult with a learning experience.

The social learning theory has been used to show how modeling can influence individuals to do the right or wrong things. In a society like Kenya, good models are important in changing the patterns of corruption, negative ethnicity and irresponsible leadership. Good models should then be reinforced for doing the right thing in order to make sure the behavior is not only replicated, but also modeled by others.

Way Forward

From the foregoing exposition, it can be concluded that any society that faces consistent patterns of negative ethnicity, corruption or irresponsible leadership needs re-socialization on the social norms. Indeed, sanction systems enshrined in the constitution of a country should be strengthened to ensure norms are adhered to, while at the same time coming up with reward systems as a matter of importance to reinforce behavior that conforms to the norms of the society. These rewards should be timely and consistent to ensure appropriate behavior has been learned.

Again, virtues of personal and social integrity should be infused in the learning institutions, and opportunities to act out the virtues presented to the young in addition to models such as parents, teachers and authority figures playing a key role in the socialization processes of children. Therefore these significant others ought to model appropriate behavior that is in line with the norms that the young can model.

In addition, different institutions should have reinforcement schedules in place, so that behavior in line with the norm can be reinforced and modeled by others. This is in addition to open forums for dialogue and discussions that should be highly considered for all people to express their experiences, offering learning opportunities for all including the government. Moreover, behavior change is a process that happens over a period of time, and therefore constant probing and education can be used in the media as a way of reinforcing a process of change that has been initiated.

References

Bandura, A. (1984) *Self-Evaluative and Self-Efficacy Mechanisms Governing the Motivational Effects of Goal Systems*. Journal of Personality and Social Psychology, 45: 1017-1028.

Bandura, A & N. Adams. (1980). *Tests of Generality of Self-Efficacy Theory*. Cognitive Therapy and Research, 4: 39-66

Bandura, A & N. Adams. (1977). *Cognitive Processes Mediating Behavioral Change*. Journal of Personality and social Psychology, 35: 124-139.

Burnaska, R. F. (1976). *The Effects of Behavior Modeling Training upon Managers' Behaviors and Employees' Perceptions*. Personnel Psychology, 29, 329-335.

Corey, G (1991). *Theory and Practice of Counseling and Psychotherapy (4th Ed)*. Pacific Grove: Brooks Cole Publishing Company.

Corey, G. (1986). *Theory and Practice in Counseling and Psychotherapy. (5th Ed)*. Pacific Gove:Brooks Cole Publishing Company.

Dewey, J. (1998). *How We Think*. Chicago: Regnery.

Rogers, C.R. (1957). *The Necessary and Sufficient Conditions of Therapeutic Personality Change*. Journal of Consulting Psychology, 21: 95-103.

Rogers, C. R., (1961). *On Becoming a Person*: A Therapist's view of Psychotherapy. Boston: Houghton Mifflin.

Vroom, V. H. (1964). *Work and Motivation*. New York: McGraw Hill.

World Bank. (2003). *Causes of Corruption, Module IV*. Retrieved from:

http://info.worldbank.org/etools/docs/library/35971/mod04.pdf 23/10/2016

CHAPTER FOURTEEN

Pitfalls and Prospects of Sheltering the Urban Poor in Nairobi, Kenya

Moses Mutiso

Introduction

The term 'slum' is loose and deprecatory. It is used in Millenium Development Goals (MDGs) in a general context to describe a wide range of low-income settlements and/or poor human living conditions. These inadequate housing conditions exemplify the variety of manifestations of poverty as defined in the Programme of Action adopted at the World Summit for Social Development. 'Slum', at its simplest, is 'a heavily populated urban area characterized by substandard housing and squalor'. This definition encapsulates the essential characteristics of slums: high densities and low standards of housing (structure and services), and 'squalor'. The first two criteria are physical and spatial, while the third is social and behavioral. These associations indicate, not just the definition of slums but also our perceptions of them. Dwellings in such settlements vary from simple shacks to more permanent structures, (UN-Habitat, 2003).

Table 1: Summary of the Characteristics of Slums

Characteristics	Indicators	Definition
Access to Water	Inadequate drinking water supply (adjusted MDG Indicator 30)	A Settlement has an inadequate drinking water supply if less than 50% of households have an improved water supply. • Households connections. • Access to public stand pipes • Rainwater collection With at least 20 liters/person/day available within an acceptable distance.

Access to sanitation	Inadequate sanitation (MDG Indicator 31)	A settlement has inadequate sanitation if less than 50% of households have improved sanitation • Public sewer • Septic tanks • Pour-flush latrines • Ventilated pit latrines The excreta disposal systems is considered adequate, if it is private or shared by a maximum of two households.
Structural quality of housing	a) Location	Proportion of households residing on or near a hazardous site. The following locations should be considered: • Housing in geologically hazardous zones (landslide/ earthquakes and flood areas); • Housing on or under garbage mountains; • Housing around high-industrial pollution areas; • Housing around other unprotected high-risk zones (e.g. railroads, airports, energy transmission lines).

	b) Permanency of structure	Proportion of households living in temporary and/or dilapidated structures. The following factors should be considered when placing a housing unit in these categories: • Quality of construction (e.g. materials used for wall, floor and roof; • Compliance with local building codes, standards and bylaws.
Overcrowding	Overcrowding	Proportion of households of households with more than two persons per room. The alternative is to set a minimum standard for floor area per person (e.g. five square meters)
Security of tenure	Security of tenure (MDG Indicator 32)	• Proportion of households with formal title deed to both land and residence. • Proportion of households with formal title deeds to either one land or residence. • Proportion of households with enforceable agreements or any document as proof of a tenure arrangements.

Source: UN Habitat 2002

Urbanization and Slums in Nairobi, Kenya

Urbanization has played a major role in the development of informal settlements. After the colonial period cities in developing countries grew rapidly during the 1960s and 1970s. Rural-urban migration has greatly affected settlement patterns leading to the emergence of informal settlements (Navarro, 2008). The inability of governments to plan and provide affordable housing for low income earners in urban areas has also contributed to the emergence of informal settlements. For example Ronald Mears in his book Historical Developments of Informal Settlements in Johannesburg since 1886 clearly demonstrates the social and political intrigues that led to the emergence of Soweto, which is one of the biggest slums in the world. The author blames poor political decisions on the development of Soweto informal settlements as the government of the day segmented its citizens by class and race and hence undermined the poor (Wilson, 1998).

According to UN- Habitat (2008), Africa is urbanizing rapidly with 38.7% of its population living in cities in 2007 and is now at 50%. By the year 2030, more Africans, about 1 billion people, will be living in cities than in the rural areas. This rapid increase in urban growth stretches the demand for urban residential housing, services and livelihoods. By the year 2030, more than 60% of Kenyans will be living in cities and towns. In Kenya, the estimated current residential urban housing needs are over 150,000 units per year (Republic of Kenya, 2007). It is estimated that the current production of new residential housing in Kenyan urban areas is approximately 30,000 units annually, which is only 20% of the demand, leaving a huge shortfall (Ministry of housing, 2004; Republic of Kenya, 2007 and UN-Habitat, 2013). This situation has given rise to the mushrooming of informal settlements, construction of unauthorized extensions in existing residential estates and overcrowding (UN-Habitat, 2003). In Kenyan urban settlements, 59 % of households live in one-roomed dwelling units (World Bank, 2006).

Informal settlements in Nairobi date from the colonial period, where most Africans were barred from some of the city's designated residential areas since they were reserved for Europeans and Asians. Kenyans who came to the city in search of work had to create informal residential settlements outside the central business district and the planned residential areas which were largely ignored by the colonial government (Amnesty International, 2009).

The urban layout was therefore based on government-sanctioned population segregation with separate enclaves for Africans, Asians and Europeans (UN-Habitat, 2003). During this period, slums essentially developed because of the highly unbalanced allocation of public resources towards the housing and infrastructural needs of the separate sections.

The post-colonial period saw a relaxation of the colonial residential segregation policies, and major population shifts occurred, notably rural-to-urban migration, with little obstruction to the proliferation of urban shacks 'as long as they were not located near the central business district'. Between 1971 and 1995, the number of informal settlement villages within the Nairobi divisional boundaries rose from 50 to 134, while the estimated total population of these settlements increased from 167,000 to some 1,886,000 individuals. In terms of percentage of the total Nairobi population, the share of informal-settlement village inhabitants rose from one third to an estimated 60% (Mitullah, 2003).

Mitullah (2003) argues that the city's first development plans did not include early settlements; hence essential services to the settlements and road construction to link them to other areas of the city were not provided by the local authorities. As a result, Nairobi developed along segregated lines. The city's 1948 Master Plan and other major urban development plans continued to neglect informal settlements (Anyamba, T. J. C., undated). Nairobi, the capital city of Kenya and one of the largest in Africa, is the hub of trade and business in Eastern Africa. The city's population has grown over the years from 11,500 inhabitants in 1906 to 3.1 million people in 2009 (Republic of Kenya, 2010) with more than half the city's population living in informal settlements and slums occupying less than 1% of Nairobi's area and less than 5% in residential area (Mitullah, 2003.

The biggest slums in Kenya are in Nairobi and include, in descending order: Kibera, Mathare valley, Mukuru Kwa Njenga, Korogocho, Sinai, and Majengo (UN habitat, 2009). The informal settlements are scattered within Nairobi's nine administrative divisions. Residents in these marginalized areas live in very inhuman and desolate conditions and suffer lack of clean water supply, poor sanitation, housing, health services and solid waste management facilities (Umande Trust, 2007). Kibera is one of the largest slums in Africa (as well as the largest in Nairobi) with an average population of approximately more than nine hundred thousand people (Umande

Trust, 2010). The slum stands on an area of 2.5 square kilometers and is roughly five kilometers away from the city center. In 1912, Kibera was a settlement in a forest outside Nairobi. After the World War I, it became a resettlement area for Nubian soldiers returning from service. The colonial government then, allowed settlements to grow and opened gates to other tribes from across the country.

In 1963, the first government of the Republic of Kenya declared Kibera settlements illegal. However, the population of the slums continued to grow from as low as 6,000 people in 1965 to around one million today. Proximity to the city center provided a cheaper ground for people from rural areas who moved in while searching for and taking up employment opportunities. Lack of reliable data on population and growth parameters on Kibera slums has led to disagreements on the size of the slums as one of the largest in Africa. UN-Habitat puts the total population at between 350,000 to one million. International Housing Coalition estimates the population at more than half a million people, while experts on urban slums give an estimate of more than 800,000 people. Government statistics on the total population of Kibera slums provide a figure of 200,000 people (Republic of Kenya, 2010). Kibera is one the most densely populated places on earth, housing over 600,000 people according to situational analysis done in 2001 (Syagga, Mitullah & Gitau, 2001).

Land ownership regimes in slums and informal settlements in Nairobi, Kenya will very often reflect land ownership regimes in the country. Generally it is difficult to pin point with precision the owners of land in these settlements. This can be explained by, among other factors, the origin and growth patterns of the settlements. For example slum areas which were originally planned and put up by the Government/Councils will very likely either belong to the developer or the tenants depending on the policy applicable at the time. This is the situation applying in, for example, slums found in the eastern parts of Nairobi such as Kariokor, Shauri Moyo, Muthurwa and Makongeni. These estates belong to the city Council and the railways pension fund respectively. Others like Kibera which were put up on government land still belong to the government.

Informal settlements in Nairobi are therefore a consequence of both explicit government policy and decades of official indifference. In particular, informal settlements were excluded from city authority planning and budgeting processes. The governments in power have ignored their existence until recently when national authorities and international bodies outlined the dangers of slums to humanity. Complexities surrounding slums in the City of Nairobi have made it difficult for the government to pass workable policies which if enacted and applied in the right way could help Kenya improve conditions in the slums. Figure 1 is a typical slum in Kenya:

Figure 1: A Typical Slum Environment in Kenya

Kitui Slums, Nairobi, Kenya, 2014

Challenges Associated with Slums in Nairobi

Slums dwellers face inadequate schooling facilities, unemployment, poor access to energy, poor drainage systems, high crime rates, and poor governance including security services. This has resulted in life threatening outcomes which lead to mass poverty, contagious diseases, conflicts, and other social, ecological and economic hazards (UN-Habitat, 2007).

The incidence of crime, robbery and gang violence, as well as gender based domestic violence in informal settlements; undermine both macro and micro economic growth and productivity of a country's development, as well as social and individual well-being (Executive Director, UN-Habitat, 2007)

In addition, Kibera like other slums is heavily polluted by human refuse, garbage, soot, dust, and other wastes. The slum is contaminated with human and animal feces and all sorts of wastes which are worsened by open sewages and lack of drainage systems (Hardoy, Mitlin & Satterthwaite, 2003; Hodson & Marvin, 2009). Poverty, poor sanitation combined with poor nutrition among residents accounts for many illnesses and diseases in slums (Heynen, Kaika & Swyngedouw, 2006; Kumar, Shigeo & Harada, 2003). It is estimated that 20% of the 2.2 million Kenyans living with HIV live in Kibera slums.

Most slums dwellers have three main concerns regarding water: access, cost and quality. They complain about the limited access to water points, which are often located far from their houses, while, some landlords ration water such that it is only available on specific days of the week and at specific times (Water Sanitation Program, 2007). This is a limitation especially for people who have children and would require high amounts of water. However, for those who have access they decry the high cost of buying water in the informal settlements. This is costly especially relative to the slum residents' income levels. Some Kibera slums dwellers use sewerage water for bathing and washing. They also use boreholes, rainwater, and sometimes draw water from broken pipes. This water is highly contaminated and filthy (especially when plastic pipes burst) and can potentially cause contagious diseases.

Most of the times slums are seen as a thorn in the flesh of governing authorities because they work to the reduce land available for physical development. They are also seen as expensive to the government in case people have to be relocated from one area to another so as to ease population congestion. The distance between the inner city and the slum in most cases is high. As a result, the city boundary has to be expanded to include such settlements which will include such factors as time and cost. The County Government of Nairobi for instance, has to increase provision of water, health facilities or electricity to slum dwellers, which means increasing their budget.

For instance, the value of land depreciates once a slum crops up with attendant low investment since few people are willing to invest in such areas. In most cases the investors in slum areas are mainly the elite group within the slum dwellers. Slums also exacerbate conflict with the administration basically when the latter attempts to relocate them. Most of the houses in slum areas are located on marginal land. For instance, Mathare slums are located in a valley while other slums are located in flood areas such as river banks leading to destruction of homes, loss of lives and increased water contamination during the rainy season. Due to poor sanitary facilities in slums, people use paper bags (flying toilets) as their toilets. With no designated disposal points the used paper bags are thrown anywhere including in water sources which are then contaminated.

As slum areas increase so does income inequality. This is largely a result of economic deprivation as the occupants are taxed in various ways without being provided with social services such as education and health. This results in political violence and anti-social behavior, increasing conflicts and crime rates. Indeed, a sub-culture of violence therefore develops in slum areas. To make matters worse, disasters such as fire outbreaks have catastrophic consequences since there are inadequate water facilities to fight fire while access by the fire engines and life savers is made difficult by the small pathways in the areas. The houses are built irregularly and paths are narrow making it difficult for a vehicle and a large group of people to pass. It has also been found out that there is discomfort in living in these structures since on average one room is occupied by six people, making privacy irrelevant.

Development Planning and Urban Housing in Kenya

Housing has been a key development issue during the colonial and post-colonial eras. It is therefore necessary to understand both the housing situation and the policies that sustain it. This is done mainly with reference to the City of Nairobi, which has been the national focus as far as housing policy formulation and implementation is concerned. As indicated elsewhere in this chapter, the colonial segregation policy was responsible for the development of informal settlements in Nairobi (Parker, 1948). Post-colonial housing policies can mainly be categorized into two eras; from Independence to about 1972 and the period after.

Immediately after Independence, a UN Mission to Kenya led by Bloomberg and Abrams (1964) was commissioned to conduct a short and long term housing needs survey and make recommendations. This report reiterated the position of other colonial reports of the 1950s which showed that housing for Africans was inadequate and insufficient, hence the prevailing conditions of extreme overcrowding. In view of the pressing problems, the mission recommended the establishment of a housing authority within a new Ministry of Housing. This led to the establishment of the National Housing Corporation (NHC), replacing the colonial Central Housing Board. It was mainly charged with the development and initiation of Local Authorities housing programs. Through it, the production of large scale, low cost housing was to be ensured. Subsequently, in 1967, the Housing Finance Company of Kenya (HFCK) was established with the objective of making funds available to people wishing to acquire their own houses in the main urban centres.

The foregoing restructuring was made with the overall aim of ensuring that every family in Kenya would live in a decent home, whether privately built or state-sponsored. The expectation was that the housing units should provide at least the basic standards of health, privacy and security (Republic of Kenya, 1974). Despite this desire, the 1965 Sessional Paper on Housing remained the only policy guideline, (although it had been overtaken by events) until 1986 when the Government of Kenya made major changes on economic management. This began with a key Sessional Paper on Economic Management For Renewed Growth (Republic Of Kenya, 1986); a paper which displayed a departure from the previous practice of relying on the public sector, for provision of services and economic growth. In the area of housing, this paper acknowledged the importance of the informal sector and gives directions on sale, rental of housing, housing plots, and to the leasing of government lands in urban areas.

The foregoing sessional paper was followed by the declaration of 1987 as the year of Shelter for the Homeless which realized concerted efforts on government performance towards reviewing her policies. A policy document entitled 'National Housing Strategy for Kenya' was prepared by the Housing Department, for presentation to the UN. In this document, the government referred to its new directions which aimed at shifting its role from one of 'direct developer' of housing for low income households involving moderate subsidies to one of working with and facilitating the development of housing by private entities charging market prices. This was consistent with the aims of the Sessional Paper of 1986 and was accelerated by the preparation of a housing policy document (Republic of Kenya 1990). Besides these key documents there have also been other studies commissioned to look into the by-laws and general issues relevant for policy review. These include studies by Yahya & Associates (1981), Struyk & Nankman (1986) and Agevi (1989).

There has hardly been any specific housing policy passed through parliament, except for the Sessional Paper of 1965. Housing issues such as those relating to land and planning have been handled piecemeal whenever deemed necessary. In this respect, it is appropriate to reflect on aspects of the development plans related to housing.

The first independent Kenya Government Development Plan (1966/70) demonstrated the government's desire to provide 'decent' housing through both the public and the private sector. This plan came almost at the same time as the Sessional Paper of 1965, which enunciated the housing problems facing the country and how the government planned to deal with them. One negative aspect of this paper was that it also ratified demolition of slums, which eventually became a consistent ugly feature in the housing policy of the independent state. By this time Nairobi had several unplanned housing areas and the policy was used as a tool for demolishing unplanned settlements.

The history of the development of informal housing in Kenya between the mid-sixties and mid-seventies is therefore replete with demolition operations. Haldane (1971) notes that through demolitions, the Nairobi City Council (NCC) continued reducing the number of housing units available to city residents. Despite this, more structures came up, a clear demonstration of the housing need, but it took the authorities too long to recognize the efforts of the informal housing sector. By 1970 the rationale of the policy for demolition was being questioned. In any case it was based on the premise that the government would manage to reduce rural/urban migration by enhancing rural development and at the same time would manage to provide adequate urban housing. These desires remain unfulfilled to-date as unplanned housing expands.

Among all the Development Plans, the 1970/74 one had numerous housing policy directives. It postponed slum clearance until the housing shortage would be substantially reduced. This Plan provided the first tentative step towards what might be called a housing policy examination. However, as can be deduced from the foregoing, the policy was vague and was a nonstarter. It was to be achieved through both the NHC and the HFCK in liaison with relevant organizations.

By the time the third development Plan (1974/78) came out, the government agreed that a more realistic housing policy should be pursued. In this respect, demolition of slum/squatter settlements was not only postponed but stopped. In cases where it was unavoidable, it would not be undertaken without providing the concerned households with alternatives. The plan also outlined slum improvement as an alternative to demolition. This was a departure from the governments' housing policy of 1965, and the 1970/74 National Development Plan which backed the demolition of slums. At the same time, it recognized the futility of slum demolition, an approach which had its origins in colonial development and did not take the interest of the majority into consideration. Whereas the move to stop demolition of slums was seen as positive, it has partially resulted in speculative moves by those who have learnt to invest in such areas. This trend is not negative as such, but contributes to proliferation of unplanned areas and the escalation of rent. It has also partly played a role in the prevalence of more tenants than owner occupiers in such areas.

Both the Fourth and Fifth Development Plans (1979/83 and 1984/88), reiterated the government's commitment to increase housing stock, meet shortfall, and ensure that the produced stock benefited the low income families. However, there was no specification as to how they would benefit. In particular, the 1979/83 Plan indicated that of the existing 440,000 urban households, only about 30% have sufficient incomes to afford minimum cost of conventional housing. The 1989/93 Development Plan dedicated a very small portion to housing but gave directions relating to regulations and building codes. It pointed out that the government intended to review a number of regulations and building codes under Town Planning, Land and Housing Laws, the Public Health Act and the Local Government Adoptive By-Laws, which are obstacles to rapid housing development. These aspects have been a problem to housing development and should have been reviewed immediately after Independence. However, the government has tended to postpone their review, partly due to lack of financial resources but mainly due to lack of political and bureaucratic commitment of leaders.

Given these development plans as the basis, Kenya has attempted to implement a number of housing programmes aimed at housing urban residents. Such programmes have mainly been dominated by both the World Bank's funded sites and services and upgrading schemes and USAID's tenant purchase schemes. These programmes have been geared for low income urban households but have not ended up being occupied by them. This has mainly been due to lack of access. Accessibility is a complex matter as it is linked to affordability, income and preference of any given household.

The Government of Kenya has attempted to initiate various interventions aimed at addressing the issues raised previously, however with limited attention to low income housing. Initially local authorities put affordable housing for the low income earners in several towns and cities but with time, due to corruption and lack of effective monitoring, most of these units effectively became 'privatized' with the local authorities getting only nominal rents while the private 'landlords' got the market value rates. In the 1970s the Government, with support from the World Bank, initiated the site and services scheme that succeeded in putting up a number of housing units for low income earners in areas such as Dandora and Umoja. Once again due to improper policy and legal mechanisms, the scheme soon became a victim of the market forces.

Current initiatives include efforts by the government, local authorities, NGOs, CBOS, FBOs and development partners, all working independently of each other or in limited partnerships and hence resulting in limited levels of success and impact to the beneficiaries. It is in light of this scenario that the Government decided to develop The Kenya Slum Upgrading Program aimed at addressing the challenges of housing problems facing the majority of low income earners living in informal settlements in all urban areas in Kenya. Since 2004, through the Kenya Slum Upgrading Programme (KENSUP) and Kenya Informal Settlements Improvement Project, for example, the Government has been undertaking slum upgrading projects in several urban areas. These interventions are however hampered by the absence of a comprehensive policy and legal framework.

The program also seeks to address the problem of infrastructural services, land tenure, employment issues and the impact of HIV/ AIDS in informal settlements. It aims to eradicate poverty and achieve Millennium Development Goal 7 of improving the lives of slum dwellers. The grant agreement to finance the program was signed jointly by the Government of Kenya and the UN-Habitat/ World Bank Cities Alliance on July 2002. The KENSUP program was initiated in 2000 between the UN-Habitat and the Government of Kenya and revived in 2003. Kibera slum is a well-documented and studied informal settlement in Sub-Saharan Africa. It therefore represents a perfect example of how many African countries could go about the problem of housing as envisaged in the UN Sustainable Development Goals.

In 2012 the Government, through the Ministry of Housing, initiated the process of developing the National Slum Upgrading Programme (NSUP). This was as result of a multi-stakeholder process held under the auspices of the Multi-Stakeholder Support Group Forum (MSSG). The need for NSUP had initially been agreed upon during the MSSG held in November 2011. In July 2012 a draft concept paper was developed and the same was formally inaugurated in December 2012. Work commenced under a coordinating secretariat, steering committee and various thematic groups.

The NSUPP is being undertaken within a number of policy and legal frameworks. These include the National Housing Policy 2004, the National Land Policy 2009, the Constitution of Kenya 2010, the Draft National Urban Development Policy (NUDP) and Kenya Vision 2030. The documents explicitly provide for the need to have a slum upgrading policy. The Constitution of Kenya 2010 under Article 43 guarantees the right to accessible and adequate housing. Article 21 requires the Government to take appropriate policy and legislative measures including the setting of standards to ensure that the right is achieved. By developing the NSUPP the Government is in effect discharging its mandated constitutional obligation.

The National Land Policy Sessional No.3 of 2009 is also quite explicit on the need for a slum upgrading Policy. It recommends the development of a Slum and Resettlement Programme and the need to put in place measures to prevent further slum development. From the international and regional perspective, Kenya is signatory to a number of declarations and treaties such as the Universal Declaration on Human Rights (UDHR), the African Charter on Human and Peoples Rights and Millennium Development Goals that recognize the right to adequate housing, whose realization cannot be attained without addressing the issue of slums. The Policy is therefore properly anchored on clear factual, policy and legal basis.

Conclusion

The growth of the City of Nairobi has largely been without a forward-looking plan for services and as such existing infrastructure has been overburdened by the hyper growth of the city in both formal and informal directions. Policy interventions meant to guide development present mixed results in terms of success and failure. There are overwhelming problems city dwellers in Nairobi face, particularly shortage of social amenities in Nairobi slums including acute deficit in clean water supply, improved sanitation, and solid waste management. These remain a serious challenge especially to social and environmental urban development. Indeed, housing and associated infrastructure remain wanting fifty years into self-rule and it would seem that urban dwellers must brace themselves for these and other problems several years into the future.

Way Forward

First, there is need to legally recognize informal settlements as legal parts of the city and support comprehensive development programmes and projects in slums. In addition, it is important to support and foresee that implementation of the slum upgrading programme complies with the government's obligations in relation to the right to adequate housing. This would ensure that the slum upgrading programme and policies address immediate needs in relation to social services.

Second, there should be all-inclusive stakeholder collaborative programmes and projects and effecting of adequate budgetary allocation for all programs relating to slum upgrading and prevention. This should be accompanied by clear frameworks for the participation of all stakeholders including the vulnerable groups in all stages of slum upgrading processes. There is also need to strengthen the capacity of urban community groups to enable them meaningfully participate in upgrading processes. There is also the need to enact a comprehensive slum upgrading legislation and policy to deal with all the key issues of slum upgrading.

References

Amnesty International. (2009). *The Unseen Majority: Nairobi's Two Million Slum-Dwellers*. Amnesty International Publications.

Anyamba, T.J.C. undated, *Nairobi's Informal Modernism*, Retrieved from http://www.kutokanet.com/issues/culture/nbinformalmodern.pdf-on 2/2/2017

Beatley T. (2000). *Green Urbanism. Washington, DC: Island. Centre on Housing Rights and Evictions*. (2008). Women, Slums and Urbanization: Examining the Causes and Consequences, p.108.

Guy S, Marvin S, Moss T. (2001). *Urban Infrastructure in Transition*. London: Earthscan.

Hardoy J. Mitlin D, Satterthwaite D. (2003). *Environmental Problems in Third World Cities.* London: Earthscan.

Heynen N, Kaika M, Swyngedouw E. (2006). *In the Nature of Cities: Urban Political Ecology and the Politics of Urban Metabolism.* London: Routledge.

Hodson M, Marvin S. (2009). U*rban Ecological Security: A New Urban Paradigm?* International Journal of Urban and Regional Research 33(1): 193–215.

Kenya National Bureau of Statistics. (2010). The 2009 Kenya Population and Housing Census.

Kumar S., Shigeo K, Harada, H. (2003). *Living Environment and Health of Urban Poor:* A Study in Mumbai. Economic and Political Weekly, August 23.

Mitullah, W. (2003), *Understanding Slums: Case Studies for the Global* Report on Human Settlements, 2003 – The Case of Nairobi, Kenya.

Mutisya, E.M. (2010). *The Sustainability of Downscaling of Microfinance in Africa: Empirical Evidence from Kenya.Germany:* VDM Verlag.

Pamoja Trust. (2009) *An Inventory of the Slums in Nairobi.* Matrix Consultants, 1998.

Satterthwaite D. (2001). *Sustainable Cities.* London: Earthscan.

Smith, L., Hanson, S. (2003). *Access to Water for the Urban Poor in Cape Town: where Equity   meets Cost Recovery.* Urban Studies 40(8): 1517–1548.

UN-Habitat (2003): *The Challenge of Slums* - Global Report on Human Settlements.

UNDP. (2007). *Fighting Climate Change: Human Security in a Divided World.* New York: United Nations

United Nations. (1998). *World Population Monitoring, 1997.* New York: United Nations.

United Nations, (2006). *The Millenium Development Goals Report.* United Nations: New York.

Water Sanitation Program (2007): http://www.wsp.org. Last Accessed January 2010.

Water Sanitation Program (2008). Improving Water Utility Services through Delegated Management. Water and Sanitation Program Field Note. World Bank Water and Sanitation Program.

World Economic and Social Survey. (2008). Overcoming Economic Insecurity. United Nations, Department of Economic and Social Affairs.

List of Contributors

Caleb Mireri is a professor in the Department of Environmental Planning and Management at Kenyatta University, Nairobi, Kenya. He holds a Doctorate degree from the University of Düsseldorf, Germany where he majored in Geography and Sociology. He has had various administrative responsibilities within the university including Chairperson, Kenyatta University Regional Center of Capacity Development and a member of the university teaching, research and referral hospital project committee. He has participated in and attended various conferences in the past and his latest academic work is the Review of Environmental Governance in Kenya: Analysis of Environmental Policy and Institutional Frameworks.

Elizabeth Murray Manoah holds a Bachelors of Business Management (BBM) Degree and a Master of Philosophy in Development Studies, both from Moi University, Eldoret, Kenya. She is an Assistant Lecturer in the Department of Development Studies, School of Human Resource at Moi University, Eldoret, Kenya where she is also pursuing a doctorate degree in Development Studies in the same university. Her research interests are Green Economy and integration of green practices in upgrading of informal settlements.

Hannah Wambui Kinyanjui is a Faculty Member at Kenya School of Government (KSG)-Embu and holds a Master of Business Administration degree in Human Resource Management. She is currently pursuing a Doctor of Philosophy degree in the same field. She specializes in Human Resource Management with emphasis on Performance Management, Performance Contracting and Performance Appraisal. Her functions in the School include Training of public servants, Research and Consultancy. She leads the Performance Management Committee at KSG-Embu. She has previously taught in Pan Africa Christian University and Jomo Kenyatta University of Agriculture and Technology as an adjunct faculty.

Jamin Masinde is an Associate Professor of Sociology at Moi University, Eldoret, Kenya. He holds Bachelor of Arts and Master of Arts degrees in Sociology from the University of Nairobi, Kenya and a Doctorate in Sociology from Jawaharlal Nehru University, New Delhi, India. He has been teaching in the Department of Sociology and Psychology, Moi University since 1989. Currently, he is the Head, Department of Sociology and Psychology at Moi University. He has several publications and has been involved in several joint research projects as well as initiated numerous local and global institutional collaborations. He has successfully supervised several Doctoral and Master of Arts students. His areas of specific research interest are Gerontology, Rural Sociology and Labor Relations.

Joseph Kariuki Murithi is a Senior Lecturer and currently chairman of the Department of Environmental Studies and Community Development, Kenyatta University, Nairobi, Kenya. He studied Environmental Sociology and Human Geography at both the University of Nairobi, Kenya and the University of Bordeaux, France respectively. He has taught and conducted research at university level since 2008 specializing in the broad areas of participatory development, environmental conservation and governance, water and sanitation and community asset building, among others. He has also published scholarly articles and book chapters as well as participated in academic conferences locally and internationally.

Josephine Mbula Wambua holds a Bachelor of Arts degree in Psychology from the University of Nairobi, Nairobi, Kenya and a Master of Arts Degree in Counseling Psychology from Kenyatta University, Nairobi, Kenya. She teaches Psychology in Kenyatta University among other universities in Kenya as adjunct faculty. Her areas of specialty research, training and practice are Youth and Adolescent Counseling, Family and Couple Therapy and Trauma Counseling.

Mark Arap Kiptui is a lecturer, School of Environmental Studies at the University of Eldoret, Eldoret, Kenya. He holds Bachelor of Education (Arts) from Egerton University, Njoro, Kenya, a Master of Arts in Population Studies from the University of Nairobi, Nairobi, Kenya and a Doctorate in Environmental Human Ecology from Moi University, Eldoret, Kenya. He has special research interest in Dryland Ecology and Livelihood and Environment-Population intercourse.

Mercy Nkatha Thuranira holds a PhD in Counseling Psychology and Master of Education in Guidance and Counseling both from Egerton University, Kenya and Bachelor of Education from Kenyatta University, Kenya. She is a practicing Counseling Psychologist specializing in personal and group therapy, administering psychometric tests, career guidance and counseling, training of peer counselors, stress management and conflict resolution. She facilitates seminars on work, family and developmental issues. She has over 10 years of experience teaching at the university and she has taught at the Department of Counseling, Kenya Methodist University. She is currently a lecturer and chair of the Department of Educational Communication Technology at Meru University of Science and Technology, Meru, Kenya.

Michael Chesire is a lecturer in the Department of Sociology and Psychology at Moi University where he specializes in Community Development. He holds a Bachelor of Arts degree in Sociology from Kenyatta University, a Master of Arts degree in Environmental Planning and Management from Moi University, Eldoret, Kenya and is currently pursuing a Doctorate degree programme in Sociology at Moi University focusing on public participation in water resource development in Arid and Semi-Arid Lands. His areas of interest are rural development, group dynamics, project management, monitoring and evaluation and environmental management.

Moses Kimnyango Beru, a lecturer in the Department of Development Studies at Moi University, Eldoret, Kenya holds a Bachelor of Education and a Master of Arts in Development Studies from Moi University. He is currently pursuing a Doctorate degree in Human Ecology at the University of Eldoret, Eldoret, Kenya. His area of special research interest is Rural Development particularly Natural Resource Use and Decision-Making, on which he is undertaking research for his Doctoral thesis.

Moses Mutua Mutiso holds a Bachelors of Arts and Master of Arts degrees from Moi University, Eldoret, Kenya. He is a faculty member in the Department of Sociology and Psychology, Moi University, where he is also a doctoral student. He has particular research interests in Gerontology, Social Demography and Rural Development, on which he has carried out research assignments particularly in monitoring and evaluation of projects.

Munene Mugambi holds a Bachelor of Science degree in Biology from Bowling Green State University, Ohio, USA and he is in the process of completing a Master of Environmental Science degree at Egerton University, Njoro, Kenya. His area of particular research interest is in Environment and Natural Resource Management.

Peter Kariuki Kamau is the Dean of Studies in the School of Architecture and the Built Environment at the Kenyatta University. He holds a Doctorate in Policy and Planning Science from the University of Tsukuba, Japan. He is an award winning scholar who has scooped several awards such as the Post-Doctoral fellowship by the Japan Society for the Promotion of Science for Research on Sustainable Urban and Housing Management. He has previously worked with the Government of Kenya in the Ministry of Lands and Settlement responsible for planning, coordination, implementation and development control of urban and rural physical development.

Paul Muthee Kanyi is a Doctoral student in Disaster Management at Kenyatta University, Nairobi, Kenya. He holds a Masters degree in Sociology (Disaster Management) from the University of Nairobi. He is an aviation consultant/trainer specializing in human factors in aviation, crew resource management, aviation security and aviation safety management systems. He has managed and conducted training projects in Uganda, Tanzania, Southern Sudan and Togo. He currently trains flight attendants, pilots and aircraft engineers for Aircraft Leasing Services (ALS), Ghana Airways, Air Uganda, Fly 540, African Express, Sudan Airways, Blue Bird aviation, 748 Air Services among others. He is the author of the book Airport Disaster Preparedness and Mitigation: A Case Study of Jomo Kenyatta International Airport, Nairobi.

Tom Wanyama Oundo holds a Doctor of Philosophy in Environmental Sociology from Kenyatta University, Nairobi, Kenya. He has over 19 years' working experience with the Public Service of Kenya having started as a Probation Officer before joining the Government Training Institute Embu as a Lecturer, where he taught Research Methods, Sociology, Social Policy, Environmental Management and Performance Management as his main subject areas. He has also worked as adjunct faculty in both Kenyatta University and Karatina University where he taught Rural Sociology, Sociology of Work and Industry, Environmental Sociology and Development Administration. He is currently a Director with Kenya School of Government, Kenya.

www.ingramcontent.com/pod-product-compliance
Lightning Source LLC
Chambersburg PA
CBHW021700210326
41599CB00013B/1472